LEVERAGED
CONSULTING
IN THE DIGITAL AGE

HOW TO BUILD AND GROW A SUCCESSFUL SERVICE BUSINESS
IN AN INCREASINGLY COMPETITIVE MARKETPLACE

JAY ALLYSON

Limits of liability and disclaimer of warranty

The author and publisher shall not be liable for the outcomes of using this material or for any loss or damage caused or alleged to be caused directly or indirectly by the information contained in this book. The purpose of the book is to educate and inspire and does not guarantee that anyone following these strategies, approaches and techniques will become successful. The guidance found within may not be suitable for every situation. This work is sold with the understanding that neither the author nor the publisher is held responsible for the results accrued from the advice in this book.

ISBN: 9781976974830

DEDICATION

This book is dedicated to family, close friends and colleagues who have provided a steadfastly supportive presence in my life and business endeavours; my children who in their individual and unique ways inspire and delight me every single day; and my unsung hero who encouraged me to write the book, complete the final manuscript and finally get it out into the world ☺

This support has kept me moving onward and upward towards greater clarity about my big vision mission and helped clarify my thinking. I see the book as a "taking stock" – a pitstop on a continuing journey to achieving sustainable success. It's a synthesis of principles and practices to underpin one's growth as an individual as well as growth in business terms.

For anyone who wants a life of fulfilment and freedom, implementing the strategies of *Leveraged Consulting in the Digital Age* is a choice that is totally yours - totus tuus!

First Edition: 2020

Author:

Dr Jacqueline Allyson Dempster

BSc Hons (Aston), PhD (York), PGCE (Warwick)
FHEA, CMALT, FIOEE, MABM

Working from home in the heart of rural England

Find me at:

belandaconsulting.co.uk

jayallyson.com

linkedin.com/in/aboutjay

My Free Gift to You:

Download the free digital *Companion Workbook* that includes my exclusive *iSuccess Leverage Test* self-evaluation and activity checklists.

Available with your book purchase receipt at:

jayallyson.com/leveragedconsulting/workbook

Any questions?

If you have specific questions that haven't been addressed in the book, or just want to connect, you can get in touch with me via:

facebook.com/groups/TheLeveragedLivingClub/

Did this book help you in some way?

If so, I'd love to hear about it. You don't need to finish the last page to hop over to Amazon http://mybook.to/lcitda and leave me a quick review. Honest reviews help readers find the right book for their needs. Thank you, much appreciated ☺

CONTENTS

CHAPTER INDEX

PREFACE

Leveraged Living

Leveraged Consulting in the Digital Age – *How to Build and Grow a Successful Service Business in an Increasingly Competitive Marketplace* – offers both a strategic compass and practical playbook for independent professional experts looking to start, survive and thrive with their own business and who want a plan that balances meaningful work with living a life of true freedom.

Leveraged Consulting is your secret weapon and competitive advantage in the digital age in which we all now operate. We face many challenges in finding clients, keeping clients and sustaining growth. Some are age-old challenges for professional services and some are brand new for all businesses in what is an increasingly connected and competitive arena.

Achieving success with a service business, in both personal and financial terms, will require you to step outside your comfort zone (and indeed your failure zone) in order to take your business to a higher level. The book offers leveraged strategies for solo professionals and small consulting firms, which take on board the service-oriented values of your profession, the now inescapable commoditisation embedded in the industry, and the new opportunities open to you in today's digital world.

In a career spanning professional development, educational development and business development, I've been teaching, consulting, coaching, marketing and innovating in technology enhanced practices for over two decades - in the trenches, learning the lessons, sifting out the hype and cutting to the chase.

And I believe in the value of passing on that expertise, because I think "leveraged living" is something we all seek as independent professionals. But how do we build that into our business architecture?

Being leveraged in business means putting in the same effort but getting a much bigger result. For consultants and other professionals, this equates to utilising your unique expertise and your time, to maximum advantage in terms of the influence and impact you can have and the income you can generate.

Leveraging your value and how you work with clients is easier today than ever before. In the digital age, you can save time, work more efficiently, impact more people and share your expertise in multiple and flexible ways. This is as true for your service delivery as it is for your marketing. When you integrate a clear message about what you do and what you offer with an efficient distribution and/or delivery system, you create a scalable way to influence and impact an unlimited and global audience.

Although digital has the power to transform your business, it's not all about technology. And although both the consulting and coaching industries are still growing, globally, culturally, things have shifted. Firstly, our clientele is looking for outcomes that are more tangible; and secondly, competition in the industry is rife. Nowadays, that means you need to stand out with a clear message and compelling high-value offer or risk being just another commodity service provider left to compete on price in the marketplace. The aim is to be sufficiently unique as to make your competition irrelevant.

I wrote the book as a resource for the consultant, coach and professional services provider who is adept at performing in their area of expertise but struggling to achieve either the income, impact or work-life balance they desire. It's for those of you who are overwhelmed and confused by the glut of marketing tools and growth tactics "out there" today, and who want a simple step-by-step approach to true success.

I'm using the terms "consultant" and "client" to designate the type of work we do and the type of *consumer* of our services. In your particular field, "consultant" may be more aptly termed service provider, expert, trainer, adviser, coach, mentor, designer, therapist, stylist, nutritionist, retail specialist and so on and so forth.

And rather than "client", you may prefer to switch these out with terms like customer, participant, patient or student. Depending on your specific sector or audience, you may find pros and cons in how each term is used and received by your target market. You're the best judge of what works in your industry and for your audience (including how they see themselves).

My aim has been to create an empowering guide for consulting professionals who want to lock in place an effective strategy for consistently bringing in good, high-end clients and scaling their business. By "high-end", I mean clients you work with in a systematic way to produce a tangible outcome they desperately want and are willing to pay fees in the order of £5-10k to achieve.

Terminology aside, whether you're currently failing to engage your ideal audience, win clients or gain a more consistent income, this book is for you. If you're feeling stuck in a low-end "trading time for money" business model, undercharging on your value and working all hours, this book holds answers. It will help you understand where, when and how to use leverage, and show you a roadmap for implementing tangible solutions that create a workable model that's right for you. We draw on the opportunities that digital platforms offer to position and promote yourself, as well as to systematise and scale both your marketing activity and your service delivery.

The book is a kind of sense and sensibility for the solo professional or small firm with a big vision of success as an independent business. It provides solid thinking ground for those new to business planning as well as practical marketing guidance for people who have been in the game for a while yet are not achieving the growth they want.

Everyone needs a strategic reset from time to time in order to take things to the next level.

When I think about my approach to business building and the kinds of books, courses and support I have invested in over the years to help me, one thing always jumps out. I notice there's quite a gap between (what some might construe as) the soft "touchy-feely" coaching industry and the hard "mechanical" consulting world. Rarely have I found resources that integrate the different dimensions of business success.

This is reflected in the way each is marketed too. Coaching type support appears heavily aimed at intuitive "heart-centred" entrepreneurs (often female), and business consulting and training is aimed at business owners who think in more deductive technical terms (often male). I know that sounds like generalising or stereotyping, but there's plenty of evidence out there in the marketplace to back this up.

Admittedly, there is coaching that has technical elements and there is business training that covers personal development. But there is a definite skew. By its own definition, coaching is typically non-directive while consulting tends to be more directive in nature. Since I see coaching as a subset of consulting, I run my business across both dimensions.

Like most of my own clients, I need help with both the mental and mechanical sides of running a business – and not always at the same time. I need help to carve out an accurate picture of my business ethos as well as to evaluate end-to-end operational processes, to identify blockages and bottlenecks and help me see clearly what are the most pressing barriers and should be resolved first. I'm sure it's the same for your own clients, it's hard to see solutions if they're in your blind spots.

Some people are convinced they have a marketing problem when at the heart of it they actually have a mindset or money model problem.

With this book, I wanted to show you a cross-dimensional picture and let us work at the interfaces to find the right blend as a solution for you. The book offers you a strategic framework for looking at things across multiple dimensions – things about you, your purpose and positioning, and things about your business, its design and its operating system. At the intersection is where your strongest brand message and service model will emerge.

I see far too many consultants and coaches drained from the intensity of constantly chasing after clients and going to uncomfortable sales meetings. If you hate prospecting, pitching and selling, wouldn't you prefer to be the hunted not the hunter?

And those of you that have a good flow of clients are exhaustively working personally with them day in and day out, tailoring and customising every project to each one. If you want the freedom that working for yourself should provide, wouldn't it be less stressful and more rewarding to be the best at doing one thing really well and charging what you're worth?

To beat the cycle of unpredictable client flow and income, you need to commit to making changes in how you think about marketing, selling and business growth. If you can do that, then this book will help you greatly. *Leveraged Consulting in the Digital Age* shows you how to strike a perfect balance between your purpose, profits and preference (for how you wish to work). I believe this is what business success is really all about.

Of course, each stage in your business growth trajectory has its own set of challenges and constraints, so your strategic roadmap must take account of where you are now, what is the vision you have for your business and what success means to you in terms of your desired destination.

Writing this book, I appreciate I'm going against the grain of how consulting firms conventionally market and deliver services; and indeed how "success" is measured in the corporate world. Many firms have yet to understand the subtle yet profound benefits of moving from a cost-based, sales-focused business development strategy to one that is value-driven and client-centric.

In an industry where consulting and coaching are increasingly seen as indistinguishable commodities, you need to stand out to gain competitive advantage. You need to have a clear and compelling message. You need to demonstrate value and credibility. And you need to build authentic connections.

A digital strategy driven by high-quality educational content can achieve this because it helps increase your reach and revenue. Importantly, sharing valuable content on the front-end helps build a trusted relationship with a potential client that leads more gracefully to a "sale" and seamlessly to continuing to add value in how you help and serve them as a client.

First in teaching and learning, and latterly in business and marketing, I've spent most of my career helping people to use technology to improve performance by doing something familiar differently. With this book, I wanted to offer new "rules" – perspectives, strategies and best practices - for what is possible in the digital age for the professional service provider who wants to maximise their reach and revenue.

I could argue that the book's life actually began back in 2004 when I started out on my solo voyage into entrepreneur territory – new to business, new to sales and new to internet marketing. Whilst working in a full-time career managing educational development and e-learning at a leading UK university, I hopped on board a "work from home" direct sales opportunity as a fun, little side-line.

I had quite low expectations of "making it big" with my new business, despite having a more serious intent of building a plan B in case my young daughter's epilepsy and disabilities meant eventually I couldn't hold down a 9-5 job. When I did eventually leave my job three years later, I earned way more from the consulting business I set up than from my networking marketing business. In fact, I earned almost twice the "salary" working half the hours of my university job. ☺

My mindset may well have had something to do with this – you tend to put less into something that's not working and more into something that is! But frankly, I think it was because networking and sales were never things that came naturally to me, so back in those days, I ducked it. It's surprising to people who know me as a bubbly and energetic person that I'm actually rather a social introvert – happy to be at the party but rarely the life and soul of it. (Given 95% of people never make more than they spend in network marketing, I don't think I'm alone in this!)

Network marketing seems a very different endeavour to networking in professional situations so this never affected the consulting or coaching side of my business. Doing presentations or teaching in front of huge audiences - no problem; small group seminars or webinars - love them; one-to-one coaching – in my element; writing and developing courses - totally my zone. But selling - uncomfortable as hell ☹

For this reason, I turned that first "direct sales" business into an online, coaching-based retail business and other education-focused internet marketing ventures swiftly followed. And yes, for a while I actually matched my consulting income and was "living the dream". To say it's been an adventure in enterprise would be over-glamorising it, although I had some amazing trips to exotic locations and met some pretty incredible people along the way!

My journey is far from a straight path to success. Right through my first ten years in business, while I was busy, making good money and doing all kinds of interesting work, I never felt I was working in my genius zone or following my true calling. I wanted my work to impact more people, and in more meaningful ways. Deep down, I always believed I could do bigger, better things if I could just focus in on the "one thing" that makes a difference to people. I reached the point when I said enough is enough and changed my game plan in order to drive forward the bigger vision. That meant making cognisant choices about my business model, taking a leap of faith to reinvent my professional brand and rebuild my digital platforms.

All of us are on a journey: in life, in our careers and with our business, there are twists and turns. In fact, it's been a bit like that game "snakes and ladders", a rather convoluted path of ups and downs. Still, this is what shapes us.

Your unique story is what sets you apart from everyone else in your industry. As well as influencing a whole new side to my business, for me, my journey to date has culminated in the writing of this book and the insights contained within for what's working in the digital arena, even for those who services are largely face-to-face.

The ideas and approaches I share stem from both study and practice, and are deliberately intertwined with my personal learning experiences. This is not to bore you with every avenue of my ups and down or career development, but to emphasise that for you too, there will be common themes as well as plot twists in your story that you may notice only through structured reflection. Put another way: what drives us in one or other direction is not always obvious at the time.

In your career, perhaps you have a similar story to me, one of chasing dreams and a little voice that has been nagging away at you saying you're worth more than you're earning. Do any of the following resonate for you?

* You have a bigger vision for your success than your current consulting or coaching work is delivering for you.

* You know that something isn't right with your strategy for how you're marketing yourself or to whom.

* You need more clarity in your professional identity, brand messaging and/or business plan.

* You're overwhelmed with being busy building your business and want to learn ways to work smarter not harder.

* You want to repackage what you offer, and learn how to do digital marketing that actually generates good clients, consistently.

❖ You know that today's digital and global audience offers an opportunity to leverage your time and expertise, and you're looking for ideas and guidance.

❖ You want to make a bigger impact and earn what you're worth.

If any of the above applies to you, then the book will provide you with vital insights and exercises to help steer your thinking and planning in the right direction. Over the hundreds of business reviews that I've undertaken - whether in the private or non-profit sector - similar frustrations and problems come to light that have reasonably straightforward remedies with the right strategy, systems and support in place.

My mentoring work has focused on helping consultants, coaches and other service-orientated businesses to surface the root causes of these common frustrations and problems. We dive into aspects of their business design or revenue model that are potentially limiting their momentum or growth. In some cases, the weak link was a lack of clarity around what they do (even people in business for years who feel the market has shifted because it's harder to get clients). For others, the bottleneck was a poor sales process or inflexible service delivery model.

To support this work and systematise what I was doing with each client, a while back I created a 7-dimensional diagnostic framework – called *iSuccess*. After years of writing articles and running workshops around the *iSuccess* principles and practices, I finally moved everything into a membership-based online education platform – which accordingly I named the *iSuccess Business Academy*.

I never thought I would find myself writing an actual book. I originally created a 40-page workbook to go alongside a course I was developing. As an education and e-learning specialist by background, it seemed a natural way to add value to my consulting work.

Next thing I knew that 40-page document had mushroomed into a 400-page book. After much soul searching, expanding, tinkering, tweaking and polishing – perfectionists are terrible procrastinators – I eventually finalised the compilation of insights and leverage strategies you have in front of your eyes right now.

Leveraged Consulting in the Digital Age was written to provide guidance to professionals like myself who want more from the expertise and capability they have built over their career. The book offers a self-directed roadmap not a prescriptive model. It acts as a compass to help you review your current business (or business plan), establish where you want to go in terms of lifestyle goals, and guide you towards the right path in terms of what you need to do to get you there.

There are many paths one can take along the journey to business success, and what we need is a compass we can use to create our own best roadmap.

The book represents the culmination of an evolving body of thinking, study, lessons learned that I've acquired in building my own high-end client business. The leveraged consulting model has enabled me to grow a successful – purposeful, profitable, sustainable and fulfilling – business and to stay competitive in the marketplace.

My business is now very different to what it was a decade ago or even three years ago. For me, business success is not about mansions, yachts, fancy holidays, or crazy expensive cars - it's about the little things. Leveraged consulting means I get to do meaningful professional work in a way that fits my personal lifestyle preferences. More importantly for me, is I can now work when I want, with whom I want, and where I want. Yes, I like to drive a nice car, but I can live pretty much anywhere and be happy.

I'm grateful every day for the freedom to choose: to take time off when I want, go for a walk in the middle of the day, not be forced to shop evenings or weekends, spend time with family when they need me.

If you don't wish to remain on the rollercoaster of unpredictable income and unleveraged growth and are committed to making changes in how you market and deliver your consulting services, this book is for you. It will help you to implement a leveraged business plan that frees you to scale and grow, or just take more time off. It's about deciding on what's the right balance for you, personally and financially, between your purpose, your preferences and your profitability.

A key outcome of writing a book is that it builds your brand and helps you connect with people you can help. If I'd learned sooner how being a published author gives you a massive leg up on your competition, I'd have got my act together faster!

From reading the book, I want three outcomes to transpire for you:

1) To think differently about how you market and deliver your professional expertise – with regards to your brand message, business model, packaging, and revenue streams – so you can see the opportunities for a more leveraged consulting practice.

2) To identify the critical elements that are most likely holding back your business growth - in terms of aligning, targeting, positioning, branding, pricing, systematising and scaling - so you can break through current barriers.

3) To create an action plan for transforming your marketing and business growth towards an approach that is steadfast and scalable so you can achieve the work-life freedom you desire.

The downloadable companion workbook is a resource to help you be proactive with implementing the ideas you get from the book. Print out the workbook and put pen to paper or just edit your ideas and action plans into the digital document. Either way I urge you to make sure that, as you go through the book, you are actively reflecting and recording the actions you will take.

Everyone's starting point and skill set is different, and success means different things to us as individuals. My aims are that the book enlightens you on the possibilities for more leverage in your business and supports you to implement *your* vision of leveraged living.

> ※
>
> "The only person you are destined to become is the person you decide to be."
> - Ralph Waldo Emerson

ACKNOWLEDGEMENTS

This book has been years in the making, partly because the body of knowledge is growing and pace of technology continues unabated. But partly, it's a case of "mea culpa" for not pulling the trigger for fear it wasn't good or perfect enough!

Nonetheless, I now undoubtedly see it is the better for the extra time pondering in terms of producing a stronger structure and set of cohering ideas. Self-editing has its positives, but you can feel so close to your own material that you can't see the wood for the trees. Thus, I'm super grateful to my editor and my beta readers for their great input. (At the final stage, we had some "fun" sifting through UK versus US spellings for quite a few words, such as "enrol" and "enrolment" – for my readers in the US and Canada these are not errors!)

The approaches in the book represent the full, rich blend of my 15-year learning curve towards achieving the bigger vision I always had for my life and work. What I love most about the final manuscript is that it reflects a chorale of inspirational voices from across the community of peers, clients, partners and mentors I've encountered along my entrepreneurial journey. All have shaped my thinking around the ideas and client-centric philosophies behind leveraged consulting and digital strategies for business growth.

Throughout the book, I'm thrilled to acknowledge the wisdom of people from whom I've derived much inspiration and stewardship. I share their ideas with pride and passion because these teachings continue to this day to permeate my personal philosophy, drive and persistence to succeed.

Since I first started on the tumultuous journey of business building back in 2004, my engagement with thought leaders has been paramount. Many are quoted throughout the book. The list that follows is a mere selection of the key experts who have influenced and impacted my thinking, marketing and business building strategies over the years.

Russell Brunson   DotComSecrets, Expert Secrets

Dorie Clark	Stand Out, Entrepreneurial You
Andy Cope	Shine, The Art of Being Brilliant
Robert Craven	Grow Your Service Business
Ryan Deiss	Digital Marketer
Denise Duffield Thomas	Get Rich Lucky Bitch
Ray Edwards	How to Write Copy That Sells
Seth Godin	SethGodin.com, The Purple Cow
Tai Goodwin	Will It Sell
Carrie Green	Female Entrepreneurs Association
Andy Harrington	Passion into Profit
Rachel Henke	The Niche Expert, Living Fearlessly
Danny Iny	Engagement from Scratch, The Audience Revolution, Teach & Grow Rich
Dan Kennedy	No B.S. Direct Marketing
Frank Kern	Consultative Sales, The Next Million
Mike Klingler	Renegade Professional
John Lavenia	Integrity is Everything
Jason Leister	Incomparable Expert
Grace Lever	The Doers Guide to Automation
Nathalie Lussier	AccessAlly
Lee McIntyre	Get More Momentum
Stu McLaren	Tribe, The Recurring Revolution
David Meerman Scott	The New Rules of Marketing & PR
Christian Mickelsen	Free Sessions That Sell
Marisa Murgatroyd	Live Your Message
Derek Murphy	Guerilla Publishing
Anna Parker-Naples	Get Visible
Michael Port	Book Yourself Solid
Jim Rohn	7 Strategies to Wealth & Happiness
Lisa Sasevich	The Live Sassy Formula, Speak to Sell
Rich Schefren	Strategic Profits, The Maven Matrix
Max Simon & Jeffrey Van Dyk	Big Vision Business
Simon Sinek	Start With Why
Karen Skidmore	True Profit Business
Kendall Summerhawk	Soulful Business & Money Coaching
Brian Tracy	Goals, Maximum Achievement
Dennis Waitley	The Psychology of Winning
Taylor Welch & Chris Evans	Traffic & Funnels, ClientKit
Alan Weiss	Million Dollar Consulting

ABOUT THE AUTHOR

My full name is Dr Jacqueline Allyson Dempster ("Jay") and I'm a biomedical scientist turned e-learning specialist, professional services provider, entrepreneur, business strategist, and marketing enthusiast.

I exist in two worlds – education and business. My consulting work in the education world is supporting universities and colleges (but also charities, housing and health services and some other non-profit sectors) with strategic planning, marketing and operational improvement in particular.

With over 25 years' experience in the education sector, I've held some quite senior roles managing strategy and operations in support services and delivering innovation projects. I'm a nationally recognised e-learning and evaluation specialist, and hold membership and accreditation with various internally-recognised professional bodies.

In 2007, I successfully established my own consulting practice, building on a solid reputation gained over the years from all of the above. My main "bread and butter" has been high-end consulting projects, but over the period, I've also set up several businesses in direct sales and internet marketing - some successful, some not, as is the nature of those industries.

In the business world, my consulting work focuses on support for start-ups, operational improvement, marketing and regional growth programmes. I also work in association with RSM UK, a leading provider of audit and consulting services to the middle market - the seventh largest business advisory firm in the United Kingdom, and I think about the sixth largest globally. I continue to do occasional projects for education sector clients even now, because it gives me great insights into organisational development and continues to build partnerships.

It's interesting how the worlds of education and business have increasingly collided over the past ten years. Universities and colleges are striving to become more business-like and businesses which find ways of educating their customers are thriving more than those that just focus on selling.

What this has meant for my business is that I've moved with the market. Being able to re-blend my different skills and experience - business, marketing, education – into my consulting offers enables me to bring in high-end clients across public, private and third sectors. I've done work as varied as national project evaluations, teaching a communications course at a top University, managing a certification programme, setting up a training initiative, supporting SMEs on regional business growth programmes and undertaking advisory audits.

My mission is two-fold: to do work I love and to help others thrive. Over time, deepening my expertise in key areas of need in the marketplace has enabled me to charge higher fees than my counterpart education and business consultants. I say this not to brag but as a prelude to the varying ways that leverage can be applied to consulting.

Most of us believe our driving force to work is money, and we may cling to a career for security reasons long after the joy has gone out of it. But, at a deeper level – whether philosophical or spiritual – we may have a yearning for change and seek "more" – more purpose, more challenge, more satisfaction, not just more money.

The road less travelled leads to the greatest treasures.

I believe one's personal collection of experience, lessons learned and wisdom continuously feeds into what you uniquely offer as a consultant, coach or expert service provider. My expertise is certainly the culmination of a long and varied career and a wide range of work. But we don't always know how to get clear on it, package it and promote it to the right audience.

If you're like me, you always need to feel you're moving forward not standing still – that you're growing, discovering and reinventing yourself. Looking back, I know most of my career, I'd always been wrestling with that big question of "what am I meant to be doing".

Some talk about this being your calling, your genius zone, your true north. It's simply a metier for where you're doing work you love and that you're great at. How well you do it is based on your unique set of special gifts and specific talents.

Most consultants are typically a "jack-of-all-trades" able to turn their hand to a range of challenging needs or problems. It's not at all a straight arrow to work out what you can (or could or should) be the "master" of, and consequently where to focus your efforts in building a business.

With this book, sharing the power of leverage using digital technologies to grow your business, I believe I found my special gift. I trust in reading it, your own path may become clearer.

Nowadays, you'll find me focusing mainly on strategies for business growth. It's an interesting area given we're living in an age of fast technological and economic change and pressing digital disruption. I homed in on leveraged consulting, because it brings together the elements of business planning, digital transformation, process improvement and strategic marketing that draw on my specific areas of expertise. I believe strongly that these are key areas that underpin success in building and growing a high-end service business and engaging customers effectively in today's competitive arena.

While my different spheres of expertise have caused considerable confusion in the past, it seems the intersection of everything provides a rather distinctive position in the marketplace. I can still keep some degree of diversity across a common theme of supporting business growth and success, which has led to some really interesting and enjoyable work.

Since my goal has always been driven by a desire for a more leveraged business than consulting work affords - to be entrepreneurial not just self-employed - for truly leveraged living, I've also made the move to leverage my rightly earned expertise by developing online education.

Throughout the book, I've interjected a little of my own story out of which the online education part of my business - the *iSuccess Business Academy* - emerged as the realisation of my own bigger business vision and a digital success roadmap to guide you through from strategic planning to implementation.

Here's a visual representation of where I'm at with my plan based around the leveraged strategies we'll explore across each chapter. It's not a prescription - mine is just one example of what's possible for building and growing a service business in the digital age.

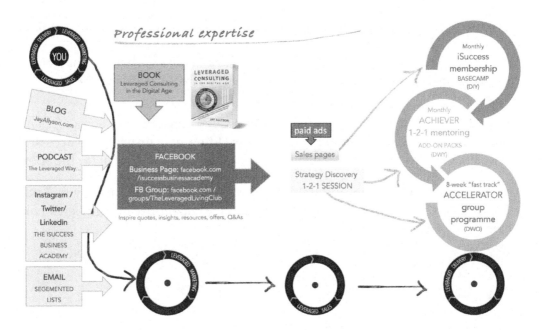

Sharing my professional expertise by writing a book and creating courses, I'm in a stronger position to help others build a leveraged business, and to unleash themselves from the trading time for money treadmill. I get a huge satisfaction from helping other consultants and coaches see the opportunities for creating a sustainable and scalable business using the power of digital platforms and education as a tool for business growth.

As digital technology advances what's possible and because people's expectations and behaviours are continually shifting, a business that can adapt and innovate has the best chance of surviving and thriving. This has been clearly apparent in the aftermath of 2020's global lockdown; some struggled as client work dried up while others thrived on the sudden burst in online consumerism and remote working.

Abraham Lincoln famously said if he had six hours to chop down a tree, he'd spend the first four sharpening the axe. Personally, I've shifted my core audience and rebranded my business several times and with each iteration, I've had to sharpen my axe to achieve success.

Sharpening the axe for business growth in an ever-changing and challenging marketplace is all about strategy. I continue to observe, learn, pivot and transform. In the context of leveraged consulting, this means:

- Becoming crystal clear about what you uniquely offer as an expert - this sharpens your business brand;

- Understanding the marketplace in which you can develop offers - this sharpens your business plan;

- Productising your expertise - this sharpens your reach and revenue capability;

- Putting meaningful metrics in place to measure success – whatever that means to you, financially and personally – this sharpens your performance.

If I can use my own individual pursuit of leveraged consulting to empower and enable you to take an enlightened path to building and growing a successful service business, then I will have achieved my "pay-it-forward" goal for the book.

And if you find the insights and guidance I've shared of value, I trust you'll pay it forward too and leave me a great review on Amazon because reviews help others find the book and benefit.

Now, let the journey begin!

INTRODUCTION

The End of Consulting As We Know It?

———————————————〜———————————————

THE TIMES THEY ARE A-CHANGIN'

Come gather 'round people
Wherever you roam
And admit that the waters
Around you have grown
And accept it that soon
You'll be drenched to the bone
If your time to you is worth savin'
Then you better start swimmin' or you'll sink like a stone
For the times they are a-changin'

– BOB DYLAN

"We rise to great heights

by a winding staircase."

Francis Bacon

KEY POINTS

❖ In today's digital society, the pursuit of solutions creates an engaged and responsive audience who know what help they are looking for.

❖ High-end consultants help clients solve big complex problems - we work at the top of the tree.

❖ Armed with an irresistible offer in the marketplace, you will vastly increase your relevance, reach and revenue.

❖ When you "supply" consulting type services in different ways, you can enter into the lucrative educational market and participate in more entrepreneurial pursuits.

❖ You don't need a magic bullet or new tactic. You need a *strategy* and you need a *system*. But first and foremost, you need *clarity* about your identity, your audience and your message.

❖ Breaking through the profit ceiling of trading time for money is the best leverage for scaling up a service business. Breaking through your limiting mindset to do things differently is a prerequisite.

❖ Wanting to reach and impact more people, as well as generate higher levels of income, is the sign of a true entrepreneur – what you need to succeed is leverage.

❖ The world is changing rapidly and how you harness technology to communicate and build relationships is vastly different today than even just a few years ago.

❖ Taking a strategic approach to business helps you achieve a workable operation and a consistent, reliable income that can end the "feast and famine" cycle that many consultants and coaches experience.

❖ At another level, it can mean confidently knowing you are living your purpose, reaching your true potential and making a bigger impact in the world.

❖ In the digital age, leveraged consulting is easier and more profitable than ever before.

❖ For success to manifest, you need to develop a clear vision of what you want the business to become, what's the ultimate goal of your business and what success will look like for you.

CHANGING TIMES, SHIFTING TIDES

The times are indeed a-changing for the professional services industry and for business in general. Whether you're a solo practitioner, a small practice or a big corporate firm, you'll have noticed the rising challenges to secure new business and the necessity to stand out in a marketplace not to mention the recent scurry of traditional businesses to transition to more online services. Competition is rife.

At the time of writing, I hadn't reckoned with a global pandemic so this paragraph has been added right at the point of publication. Lockdown and social distancing have created a boom in online alternatives in many industries - from groceries to video - so no surprise it's also boosted the desire and demand for online learning and all things digital. Economists predict the transitions will stick in the longer term. Competition will remain rife both offline and online.

However, a crowded market is not necessarily a bad thing. I see it as an opportunity. Firstly, a crowded market shows there's a high demand for products/services in that niche. Indeed, in the consulting and coaching space, recent years have witnessed massive growth in the number and size of businesses, which means increased competition in the marketplace, regionally, nationally and globally.

At the same time, tides are shifting with regards to the market views on the *value* a consulting or coaching outlay delivers to the client, which gives rise to opportunities in how well we differentiate and communicate with our target market. If you're finding it difficult to get clients because the market is crowded, it may be time to redefine who your customers are and create a micro-niche.

Secondly, and related to the first, technological change is rapidly shaping today's approaches to business engagement, communications and commerce. The digital opportunity enables massive leverage in how we engage with our target market, as well as how we deliver services.

Continuing growth trends in online marketing, publishing, learning, sales and distribution are outmanoeuvring many long-standing "brick and mortar" and "suit and briefcase" consulting modes. Now, digital platforms and tools are universally available "off the shelf", enabling both large and small players to influence and impact more people and generate income more easily than ever before.

Winning high-end consulting clients in an increasingly crowded marketplace is both harder and easier in the digital age. Because taken together, cultural shifts and technological innovation can transform your business substantially. But only when you build strategically, harness the power of leverage and take a structured approach to uncertainty.

As a basic definition, "leverage" means getting a big lift from a small force – using a "lever" to lift the ball up the proverbial hill. In the case of your business, it means investing resources – such as your time, money and energy – into something and getting a consistently greater return from those resources than the norm. That's leverage.

Through digital know-hows, this book teaches you how to design a leveraged business architecture to grow your reach and revenue building on what you already do as an expert professional.

In today's digital society, the pursuit of solutions creates an engaged and responsive audience who know what help they are looking for.

Consultants, coaches and other experts are primed to quench the increasing thirst for knowledge, learning, know-how, guidance and advice of individuals, small businesses and large corporations alike. We now live in an abundant knowledge environment where people are constantly on their computer or phone searching for information that addresses, improves or solves a problem they have.

Every day, millions of people in almost every country across the globe consume digital content: they read articles and books; they watch videos and TV programmes; they listen to podcasts and audio books; they attend workshops and masterclasses; and they sign up for courses or coaching programmes. They have a question or problem and are looking for answers. They want a solution for how to do something (or do something better) and they're usually quite specific about what that is.

Larger organisations have long promoted themselves as "solutions providers". High-end clients hire consultants and coaches to help them in some way to solve the bigger more complex problems - we work at the top of the tree. We may help them to do it, or do it for them, but ultimately, they want a result.

High-end consultants and coaches help clients to solve the bigger more complex problems - we work at the top of the tree.

When you learn how to clarify the one outcome your ideal client wants that you can deliver, it becomes more straightforward to carve out your unique offer. Rather than promote your CV, you can beat off the competition by promoting a clear brand message and producing, packaging and promoting high quality, branded educational content.

An essential technique for getting found online is to optimise your content for the search engines – known as search engine optimisation or SEO. Aptly tagged keyword content draws the right people to you, so they can see if you're a good match for the help they want. When you build credibility and trust, your material becomes a magnet, consistently attracting leads for your business, pre-qualifying potential clients, and creating potential new streams of revenue.

Armed with an irresistible offer in the marketplace, you will vastly increase your relevance, reach and revenue.

There are many opportunities to increase your success in the marketplace, crowded as it seems. This book provides both a strategic guide and practical playbook for independent consultants, coaches, and other experts wanting more structure, stability and success in their business. In helping you to build a purposeful, digitally smart and scalable high-end client business, *Leveraged Consulting in the Digital Age* taps into a variety of mindset, marketing and money elements enmeshed in the solution.

The book looks first and forecast to leveraging *you* – your personal attributes, professional expertise, intellectual property and brand - and increasing both your reach and your revenue. We will then build on this with leveraged strategies to support and bolster your *marketing* and *sales*. Here you'll see how to home in on, and stand out in, your most fitting segment of the marketplace and put processes in place to draw clients into positive enrolment conversations.

The book also focuses on leveraged *delivery* - new ways of working with clients - that helps create additional streams of revenue to overcome typical income plateaus that independent consultants and small service firms experience when trying to grow and scale the business.

When you "supply" consulting type services in different ways, you can enter into the lucrative educational market and participate in more entrepreneurial pursuits.

In building a successful high-end client business myself, I've certainly chased a lot of opportunities and shiny objects in my time. In 15 years, I've seen a fair few trends come and go, and I've learned a lot of hard lessons of what works, what's hype and what's just downright exhausting. My ambitious goal in sharing these insights in this book is that it will help take many years off your learning curve but also show you a way to create your own best roadmap to growth and success.

Most consultants are high achievers who have an amazing CV yet struggle to tap into the many opportunities available to grow their business, especially in the increasingly digitally connected world we live in. Many self-employed consultants or small firms rely heavily on unleveraged marketing and unpredictable sales, mostly using paid appointments, referrals and networking to gain new clients. Or in desperation, they turn to random social media tactics and hope something works out.

The truth is you don't need a magic bullet or another new tactic. You need a strategy and you need a system. But first and foremost, you need clarity about your identity, your audience and your message.

You could put in place the best marketing, advertising and sales process in the world, but if you're not crystal clear or compelling in what you offer to whom and why it's important, no special tool is going to help you.

Any strategy needs to be a good fit for you, what you achieve and how you want to serve. One of the big cohering ideas of leveraged consulting is allying your purpose and preferred ways of working, with productivity and profits. The fastest way to prosper is in the high-end consulting profession, using your expertise to help people tackle difficult problems, do outstanding work and be paid high fees.

However, a one-to-one, face-to-face model is not the sole means to achieving this – it's essentially unleveraged consulting. If you have no leverage in how you market, sell and deliver your services, you will experience a constant uphill battle to attract, sign up and work with great clients.

If you want to unleash your consulting work from the constraints of trading time for money and create a doable, predictable and scalable income-generating system, you should definitely read this book. If you're tired of riding the revenue rollercoaster and looking for more consistency and stability, *Leveraged Consulting in the Digital Age* is your secret weapon and competitive advantage.

Leveraged consulting is firstly about matching a clear and compelling, high value offer and specific deliverable that you care about to a specific, hungry and receptive audience. Secondly, it's about implementing systems to market, sell and deliver in both one-to-one and one-to-many modes.

Surprisingly, few consulting firms manage to do this well and suffer the consequential constant struggle to grow their client base and revenue cost-effectively.

> ※
>
> "Money certainly isn't everything, but at a basic level, it's the fuel that makes your vision possible. Recognizing its importance and thinking strategically about how to bring in the revenue you need is critical to making your idea sustainable over time." – Dorie Clark

For me personally, the book sits at a significant intersection of my 25+ years' experience working in consulting services, educational development, e-learning, teaching, coaching and mentoring, business development, direct sales and digital marketing.

After an initial career in academia and e-learning, I've run a successful consulting practice since 2007 working with both small and large organisations on strategic planning, operational improvement and impact evaluation. Over that period, I also set up numerous direct sales and internet marketing businesses, supporting business growth programmes and jumped into mentoring other consultants and coaches on mindset, marketing and money aspects of building a successful business.

As demand in the education sector waned, I began to focus increasingly on working with small businesses on strategic marketing for business growth. This really became my passion and I turned more and more to working with solo professionals and small firms to grow and scale their business beyond the paradigms of how consulting and coaching is traditionally marketed and delivered.

Leveraged Consulting as a concept emerged from my own experiences of building a successful business. I'd spent 20 years working in educational development (predominantly e-learning and support services) and 10 years running my own consulting business and supporting other small businesses. There came a point when my two worlds collided. My education clients started wanting business support and my business clients started wanting educational support.

Like many consultants, I've had a long and varied career and what makes me effective in the advisory role as I can see a situation more holistically than most. But for the purposes of this book, my journey provides a uniquely blended perspective on a strategic business model that is fast becoming critical to survival and growth in the consulting, coaching and other professional services industries.

In this introduction, I lay out the big picture for how to grow your client business strategically in the digital age using the power of leverage. This way you can see the road ahead and understand the benefits before diving into the detail.

READ WITH THE END IN MIND

If you're looking to grow your consulting business and you have ambition, drive, a sense of adventure, willingness to learn and the spirit to succeed, *Leveraged Consulting in the Digital Age* provides the roadmap.

My aim with this book has been to create a powerful guide for independent consultants, coaches, and small professional services businesses who are adept at performing in their area of expertise but struggle with business strategy, marketing and sales, especially online approaches, and are looking for inspiration, encouragement and tangible solutions to grow their reach and revenue.

At the end of the day, what we all want is a doable business, dependable income and a desirable work-life balance. But your business is only as good as the business strategy behind it. This is how we build for success.

> ❋
> "You read a book from beginning to end, but you build a business from the end to the beginning." – Rich Schefren

The "best" strategy for you is determined by what it is you want from your business - professionally, personally, socially and financially. In other words, what does "success" mean to you? Once you have your business model dialled in, it's far more straightforward to pick the right methods to drive that strategy and understand the metrics for measuring success at key milestones along the way.

Despite a significant sum of value, expertise and experience you have to offer, maybe you picked up this book because you're often asking yourself why you can't get more clients and get paid what you're worth. I suspect you have one of two challenges (aka problems): ineffective marketing/sales and inefficient delivery. This book explains how these problems arise and how to fix them.

If you've ventured out on your own and started a consulting or coaching type of business, you can unquestionably consider yourself an "entrepreneur".

Whether you give yourself that label or not, you've hopefully survived the first year or so of self-employment. But it's likely you experienced some curveballs and now find yourself hitting some stumbling blocks, particularly in terms of achieving consistent income, feeling fulfilled and/or enjoying any sense of time freedom. Right now, you need help, and you need leverage.

If you feel you're made for more than the constant struggle to get clients and deliver projects, and if you're frustrated by the limitations of operating solely as a consulting practice, this book will be your guide to the strategy, setup and systems you need to take your business to a next level.

Stories about business success can give you the impression that growth is a straight path, but behind the scenes, it's a much messier journey of ups and downs, spurts and dips. Staying on the "straight and narrow" with a consulting business does not always lead you down the path to success. I know that sounds counterintuitive, but often our biggest opportunities lie in the plot twists of our journey. You may have clear goals for your career and your business, but in my experience, the path you take is much more like a game of snakes and ladders.

Often our success means taking a new path; and we have to overcome that fear of failure, to see the gift within more positively in terms of lessons learned. We need to a new idea as an opportunity to refocus and gain more momentum so that we, and our business, can grow. That's certainly been my mantra. I'm certain a lot of my journey, and the problems and solutions I'm sharing here, will resonate with you.

Throughout the book's seven chapters, you will learn how leveraged consulting works to nail down your unique offering and to overcome typical income plateaus at each stage of business growth. We'll first look at laying strong foundations for a successful high-end client business architecture and progress to developing an action plan for implementing your critical levers for change.

Whether you're new or old school in the consulting industry, whether you're feeling entrepreneurial or just looking for one or two ideas, I urge you to spend time on the groundwork – namely, strategy and clarity - before moving onto systems and tactics. There are some very practical parts to this. You'll use my *Engage-Educate-Enrol* pathway to structure your buying process to drive and automate marketing and sales. And later, I'll introduce you to my *7 Dimensions of Success* system, a diagnostic tool I use to help clients create a tangible roadmap for getting a leveraged strategy into place.

When you know how to match your knowledge, skills and expertise with the needs of the marketplace and create tangible, value-driven and digitally smart deliverables, you will discover a method for business growth that only a few in the professional services industry are currently exploiting.

The approaches advocated in *Leveraged Consulting in the Digital Age* build upon a unison of huge growth trends, global influences and digital disruption that is already electrifying our industry. Online content delivery and mass distribution channels have opened up possibilities for online education to support business marketing, new product development and flexible delivery of client services.

Without the constraints of delivering solely one-to-one services, your business can expand. When you focus on one core area in your expert arsenal that your market wants, you'll be able to create a premium offer, attract and work with "best fit" clients. When you systematise your client flow into that programme, you'll finally be able to predict your income beyond the next 1-3 months.

The book offers the rationale and a set of plausible scenarios for business growth, and achieving greater personal success. It also helps you examine the headwinds and tailwinds that may influence your consulting success into the future.

Taking a strategic approach to business building helps you achieve a more workable operation and a consistent, reliable income that can end the "feast and famine" cycle that many consultants and coaches experience. At another level, it can mean confidently knowing you are living your purpose, reaching your true potential and making a bigger impact in the world.

Leveraged consulting is not altogether a quick fix, although a lot of my clients have found a few simple tweaks have yielded some quick wins. The book is intended, however, to provide a comprehensive guide and planning tool for getting all your ducks in a row, so to speak. One objective for successful marketing is to demonstrate you can help people by actually helping them – I hope the book achieves this for both our sakes.

Take each section at your own pace and focus on the steps that have immediate appeal and benefits. The book is designed for anyone in professional services, but not everyone will be familiar with every element of a leveraged strategy or education-driven marketing.

People with experience in business development, and digital marketing in particular, may find some parts act as a useful reminder so you can refine your practice, while some parts will bring entirely new insights. Those who already have experience in delivering education or training may find themselves focusing more on the business aspects. Those trading solely on their subject or technical expertise will find the marketing aspects of particular value.

There's also plenty to reflect on in a holistic sense with regards to planning for strategic growth, building an authentic professional identity, overcoming limiting beliefs, escaping the fear of selling and creating a digital platform to promote yourself, your brand and your business.

If your destination is unclear or you think you lack the time to think about goals, then no marketing strategy or tactic will find favour. Your motivation, focus and commitment are critical success factors here too. The book is kind of sense and sensibility for the self-employed consultant or small firm. It provides solid thinking ground for those new to business building as well as practical marketing guidance for people who have been in the game for a while yet are not achieving the success they want. Everyone needs a strategic reset from time to time in order to take things to the next level.

Read the book because hopefully it's enlightening - my story is undoubtedly partly or wholly your story. Somewhere along the timeline, you are where I've been and want to be where I'm heading. Each of us is on a journey propelled by our education, experience and lessons learned. This is as true in business as it is in life and I trust you will learn from the shared insights as we journey towards a fully leveraged consulting business.

In my experience, real education is a process of exploring views and ideas that lead to learning and transformation. Being open-minded is a vital component in achieving continuous

> ※
> "The whole purpose of education is to turn mirrors into windows." – Sydney J. Harris

improvement and change. I love the Sydney J. Harris quote here that embodies this concept.

Let me briefly explain how I understand the purpose of turning mirrors into windows. When you look into a mirror, the only things you see are your reflection and a limited area behind you (representing the past) whereas when you look out of a window, the view in front of you (the future) can be almost limitless. I see mirrors here as representing the barriers we erect around our thinking based on previous understandings and experiences, and windows as providing new ways to see things differently.

Education is like a window helping to expand our horizons, while a mirror only shows us what we already know. The whole purpose of education is to take what you already know and are doing, and turn it into something better.

> ※
> "Begin challenging your own assumptions. Your assumptions are the windows on the world. Scrub them off once in a while or the light won't come in." – Alan Alda, Actor, Screenwriter & Author

However, knowing more is insufficient alone. You first need to understand what to do and why, before diving into how to do it. And you need to shrug off deep-set assumptions and break through barriers only by taking action.

That's what the book aims to teach. Once the fog is removed then mirrors can turn into windows and you can see the way forward – the best direction of travel and possible actions to achieve the success you desire.

COMPETING IN A GROWTH INDUSTRY

Competition in most every industry has never been fiercer. In the digital age, tech-savvy businesses are increasingly using direct marketing and sales approaches to enjoy extraordinary ease of entry in the marketplace. They're lacing their websites and social media compelling, customer-focused and socially-conscious brand stories.

Traditional service and retail businesses alike are struggling to differentiate themselves not only from digital-native newcomers but from their peers, in a landscape oversaturated with information, marketing messages and sales offers.

Globally, there are literally hundreds of thousands of professional services firms and service businesses, and the industry continues to expand as more people change careers and opt (out of choice or necessity) to start their own business. These enterprises are of varying sizes, the majority being independent sole traders, or small to medium size partnerships, privately owned and managed companies. The clientele may be the general public (B2C – business to customer) or other companies (B2B – business to business).

Professional services is a very big and diverse industry, one that is set to grow even bigger over the next 5-10 years. Regionally, the picture is a mirror image so don't expect competition to be any easier in your local city or town. As economic times toughen, more professionals and specialists choose (or are forced) to turn to self-employment.

Talking about UK employment, a recent *Financial Times* article remarked that "Over 50s are the new business start-up generation" fuelling the growth in self-employment since 2000. They reported 4.6 million self-employed people in the UK at the end of 2015 compared to £3.8m in 2008, according to ONS data, and 43% of those are over 50; the number 65+ has more than doubled in the past 5 years.

These "olderpreneurs" from the baby boom years approaching retirement are faced with poor job prospects but with savings or pensions to invest, and many decide to go it alone. They have all the potential to embark upon a second career doing something that they've always wanted to do.

I'd argue this is nearly as true for "youngsters" too who increasingly seek entrepreneurship over employment in order to follow their interests and lifestyle preferences. They're now more aware than ever that even people with good qualifications can't get a decent job, it's more about the value you bring to the table.

At the other end of the career continuum are professionals who have had a long-serving, probably successful career yet find themselves unexpectedly thrown out of a job through corporate downsizing, restructuring and redundancy. In any event, many people are simply tired of the rat race or their personal circumstances may have changed. They opt to "go freelance" so that they can take more control over their lifestyle and financial future and do work that makes a tangible and valuable difference to the people they serve.

Service businesses I've worked with include a vast array of industries, anything from accounting to yoga, and everything in between. While each industry would argue its uniqueness, many similarities span all service businesses, which have a bearing on how they start, market and grow in order to survive and thrive.

The basic characteristics of a service business are generally:

- The business owner has usually founded the business based on his or her passion or past career vocation and still undertakes client work directly.

- Services are delivered to clients one-to-one, project-by-project, in real-time over a contract or engagement period.

- Overheads for a small service business are typically very low and most self-employed professionals work from home, at least initially.

- Unless the business has grown beyond 15-20 staff, there are probably no functional departments such as Admin, IT, HR, Sales, Marketing, although someone may be designated to look after such matters. (If you're a sole trader with no associates, outsourcing or assistance, it's all on you!)

- Depending on your business, as a small player you will have to do shine very bright to get noticed in the ocean of similar freelancers or small service firms.

And most importantly:

- Distinct to manufacturing and/or distributing products, as a service business essentially what you sell is your *time and expertise*.

- Being able to charge premium isn't just about your fees, it also speaks to how well you connect with your target market, the quality of what you do, your professionalism, your procedures, policies, guarantees, customer support and so forth.

Let's unpack the last couple. As a service provider, you are trading your personal time, knowledge and skills for money, usually on an hourly, daily or project basis, or you're on a monthly retainer. In all cases, in order to deliver "good value" to your clients and maintain premium profitability for you, you must know how to plan, price, prioritise, package, promote, schedule and leverage your expertise for maximum efficiency.

An inability to connect with customers is a big part of the problem for businesses that find themselves lost in the undifferentiated middle of their marketplace.

Yet it's the one thing self-employed consultants or small firms rarely do (or know how to do), mainly because they are experts in what they do, not necessarily business people or marketers. Most think daily or hourly fees is the only way to go, because that's what everyone does (isn't it?)

Let's look briefly at the service business life cycle and introduce some new perspectives here about the power of education in adding value, increasing revenue and delivering tangible results and transformation, which is what your clients want.

Starting up as a service provider, you first need to gain some traction in your market: work with a few clients and demonstrate that you can deliver what you promise to deliver and that your clients are happy with the results and their experience of working with you. This gets your momentum going, gives you "proof of concept" in your business ideas, yields valuable testimonials and case studies, and typically puts you into positive cash flow.

Serving your clients' needs should be the core part of what constitutes your "life-defining work" as an individual as well as your desire to be profitable as a business owner.

Having satisfied clients is important for start-ups, but also for any business that wants to grow, especially when it comes to harnessing the power of the internet and social media to create your digital presence and establish a good reputation.

It's argued that if you have limited online presence or little positive engagement with your customers, then unfortunately you won't be in business for long!

What is common to both service and retail industries is that how your business is *positioned* and *performs* is as much down to meeting customer expectations, ensuring customer satisfaction and a positive experience (the qualitative indicators), as it is about the number of sales and your revenue (or quantitative measures).

In fact, the one supports the other – we'll look at this later in the book, with regard to customer retention and "lifetime customer value".

The world is changing rapidly and how you communicate and build relationships, how you harness technology to establish professional visibility and trust, is vastly different today than even just a few years ago.

> ※
>
> "Experts present themselves in the position of authority or knowledge; they tend to be seen as "positioners" (where they set out to adopt a specific position in the eyes of the customer) rather than "prospectors" (where they are chasing work and clients)." – Robert Craven, Grow Your Service Firm.

I believe what drives a successful service business is passion plus professionalism, not just "I want to do something I love" or "I want to make some money". Value-driven customer engagement underpins your authenticity as a service provider and should be aligned with both your integrity to serve and commitment to your client.

Let's explore some of the ways you can ignite your commitment to serve and provide value as a business.

- *Personal drivers* - Talking about where your insights and interests in your area of expertise come from highlights your authenticity, experience and authority in the industry and allows your audience to resonate with you.

- *Revenue drivers* - Knowing your market and competitors demonstrates that you understand at a deep level what your target audience's specific problems and frustrations are, which brings trust in why you can help them.

- *Promotional drivers* – Adding a distinctive benefit to what you deliver to your specific clientele means your marketing is not solely a vehicle for sales but also supports brand positioning and customer engagement.

ACHIEVING YOUR BUSINESS AMBITIONS

Your ambitions for your business should feel like there's something inside you bursting to break free – and your desire to grow and scale is an indication that you're ready and eager to build a bigger playing field for yourself and the people you serve.

Wanting to reach and impact more people, as well as generate higher levels of income, is the sign of a true entrepreneur – what you need to succeed is leverage.

But before building commences – before you jump to the practical construction work - you first need to decide on the what you want to achieve, prepare the ground and ensure foundations are deep enough to support the architecture you want to build.

For success to manifest, you need to develop a clear vision of what you want the business to become, what's the ultimate goal of your business and what success will look like for you.

This clarity will underpin creation of an authentic message and signature offer; what platforms are going to suit you; and what are realistic timescales to gain momentum, grow and scale.

If a high profit business is not your ambition then fine, this book probably isn't for you, at least not yet! If, however, your ambition is to grow your consulting or coaching services beyond what you can deliver personally in any given month and to become more strategic in enterprise building - and what I'm outlining here resonates with you - then I really do hope you read on. Because foundations are pretty critical to anything you're building!

I believe it's so important to spend time on preparing the ground to build on - the fundamentals of clarifying your business vision, setting out solid footings and creating a strategic architectural design. This is why I've devoted a large chunk of this book to these aspects – it's not just pointless waffle before you can get to the concrete parts.

My question to you at this early point is this: are you willing to open your mind, to embrace new perspectives and new opportunities in order to successfully achieve your bigger business vision?

If so, then throughout the book, I'm going to help you with a few prompts – questions, exercises, checklists and tools to identify areas for improvement and innovation in your business architecture.

In this way, you'll start to analyse strengths and limitations in your business (including in yourself and that of your competitors). I do hope you find this workbook approach helpful – use the tools, apply changes, refine your approaches and you will see results.

Regardless of how far you go down the digital route, here are some typical struggles or unknowns that solid groundwork should help you to address.

- How do I communicate more clearly what I do and for whom?
- How do I work out a specific result or benefit that I deliver for clients or customers?
- How can I use my time and expertise to increase profitability?
- How do I package my expertise so it's looks and feels right to the people I want to attract?
- How do I work out how much to charge?
- How do I get more consistency in my income?
- How do I create a good offer?
- How do I get people to see/hear my offer and take action on it?
- How do I generate an abundance of high-quality leads?
- How I automate the whole client acquisition process?
- How do I develop processes and build teams?
- How do I build /deliver online programmes of support to clients?

Before any of these questions, there's one thing you need to do that drives everything else.

Focus on the one thing you do for your clients/customers that solves (or starts to solve) their biggest problem or need and create high value, educational content around this one thing.

The first area to tackle is to clarify what you specifically *deliver* for your ideal audience, so you position yourself as an authority and trusted adviser, and can talk about a tangible output or result(s) you help your clients achieve.

The second area is to for you to see the vision of what's possible when you leverage your time and expertise, with new service developments, maximise your revenue potential and create that all-important freedom to live the life you want.

Once you see how leveraged strategies helps you to market and deliver your consulting or coaching services in more profitable and sustainable ways, you can adapt your own approaches. Pick out the online and offline tactics that fit best with your business and your personality. This may be a step-wise transition or a transformational change depending on how fast you want to innovate, adapt and grow.

FULFILLING YOUR CALL TO SERVE

Whether you call yourself a consultant, or a coach, designer, therapist, copywriter… the list is endless, no doubt, you have a gift - knowledge, skills and experience that people value - and some kind of a call to serve.

If you want to start, survive and thrive in what is an increasingly global, digital and competitive environment for consulting professionals, this book provides the roadmap. *Leveraged Consulting in the Digital Age* gives you a step-by-step methodology to build a high-end client business that is capable of fully supporting your vision, values and goals.

Leveraged consulting in the digital age provides an incredible growth opportunity for consultants who have a mission to make a difference to people's lives and in so doing improve their own!

The book focuses on building a *consulting* business; it is therefore primarily aimed at independent consultants – both solo professionals and small consulting firms. However, the approaches are equally applicable to other expert service providers, such as an adviser, a coach, therapist, designer, and in fact any service-based business that wishes to strengthen their brand, attract more clients, grow and scale.

If you offer professional services alongside a largely retail-driven business, leveraged strategies will also be enlightening and help you build out other revenue streams.

Advising, coaching, mentoring and training are often subsets of consulting, and professional practice working with a client. The common trait is that you're an expert in your field and, as an expert, you use what you know and can do to help a specific type of person in a specific market achieve a specific outcome that they want and will pay for.

But the market can be unforgiving if you're unclear on specifically what you do and why you do it. In order to fulfil your calling, live your message and leverage your expertise, you will need to be capable of clearly articulating what problem you help people resolve, and how you deliver the solution to them as clients.

If you're just starting out as a freelancer or an independent consultant and still building up your client base and income, the book will help you push through many of the typical frustrations you may be facing with professional identity and/or inconsistent client flow.

If you're looking to grow your revenue and scale your business, the book will help you focus on clarifying your brand messaging, getting more ideal clients, systematising your key business process and offering new, more leveraged ways to engage and work with more people.

As you move through each stage of leverage - from an employed professional to a self-employed independent or small firm, increasing capacity, growing and scaling, as shown below - you gain greater freedom yet more challenges.

Using digital platforms as key business tools, you can overcome most of the obstacles you're likely to encounter - attract, win and serve a far greater number of clients and generate profits far beyond the capped income of traditional consulting practices.

In the digital age, leveraged consulting is easier and more profitable than ever before.

It's not all about money, mind you. I believe a leveraged strategy works in harmony with your values as a consultant or coach and desire to serve. Nonetheless, it solves many of the frustrations faced by solo professionals and small businesses and allows you to make the leap from day-to-day surviving to year-on-year thriving. It enables you to reach, influence and impact more people in a positive way, and in so doing, earn more revenue and to impact yourself in a positive way too.

Harnessing the remarkable power of education is something that everyone can aspire to do, and actually succeed in doing. The strategies taught in this book can help business owners to attract, engage, educate and enrol clients without feeling like you're selling.

The "cool" duality to an education-fueled business strategy is that it's both a way to attract clients to you and a way to add value across a customer's entire experience with you.

Leveraged marketing enables you to attract your ideal clients (or at least not consistently), charge premium fees and automate lead generation. Leveraged sales enable you to enrol clients seamlessly and gracefully into your high-end programmes and services. And leveraged delivery enables you to build new revenue streams and increase your influence, impact and income.

As a consultant and professional services provider, leveraging your expertise to create digital content that can benefit your target audience far and wide is the natural next phase of a journey you have already begun.

What I mean by this is simply that you can drive your marketing and business growth by sharing education-rich content, which demonstrates you can help someone by actually helping them, creates tremendous goodwill and delivers a high-value end-to-end customer experience.

Digital outreach and distribution of your expertise is the epitome of leveraged consulting.

Becoming an educator is not a million miles from where you're already standing as an adviser, consultant or coach. Firstly, education is a core part of the value you provide as an expert, and you may be missing a trick if you're not using it to drive your marketing and business development.

Secondly, a key part of entrepreneurship means having a positive attitude towards new ideas for growing a business, and the determination and grit to achieve success.

As an expert in your profession, and someone who decided to buy this book, I figure this is testament, more likely than not, to you having what it takes to develop both educational material and your own entrepreneurial skills. In this case, the book will help you to turn ideas into actions, to turn challenges into strategies and innovation into advancement.

A quick slice of advice: Don't let technology become a barrier to success; you can start with a simple set-up and build out from there. Stay open-minded!

CREATING A SUCCESS MINDSET

If you want to drastically change your success in business – you need to be willing to change your strategy.

Because a new strategy or innovation is not always going to work straight out of the gate, the best way to move an idea forward is to test and validate it first. By working with a small "pilot" group, you invest time in learning what's working well or not so well, and build the final programme in partnership with your clientele.

> ※
> "Shallow men believe in luck or in circumstance. Strong men believe in cause and effect." — Ralph Waldo Emerson

If we wish to be "successful", it's time to harness powerful ways of leveraging you – not only your expertise, but also your mindset, marketing and money model so you're developing a business model that does not rest upon "luck".

> ※
> "Having a success mindset isn't as simple as reciting affirmations. It doesn't mean never doubting yourself, always being fearless, and only having positive thoughts.
>
> It does mean mastering your mind, so that you're in the best position to succeed: to produce your best work in the midst of self-doubt and limitations, and to make good decisions in the face of fear and uncertainty." – Danny Iny, Reimagining the Success Mindset

Success is not luck; it is a science made up of thinking, behaviours and actions that are driven by our (mostly subconscious) mind.

Do you ever wonder why some businesses start, grow and thrive, while others never get off the ground, struggle to survive or bloom then die?

Why do some people breakthrough what seem like insurmountable challenges, even failures, and come up trumps? Is it luck? Are some people just lucky, in the right place at the right time? To an extent, I think that is true. But it's far from the norm.

While strategy and tactics are both paramount for business success, many of our challenges to succeed lie inside ourselves. In his renowned book *"Million Dollar Consulting"*, Alan Weiss purports that success is the convergence of three criteria: market need, competency and enthusiasm.

In other words, business success is not driven solely by your ability to conceive a great idea or see a great opportunity, but also by your personal drive: for instance, your ability to develop focus and discipline, to be resilient to ups and downs, and to take action - sometimes imperfect action is better than no action at all. Those actions can turn your vision into a successful reality.

> ※
> "80% of success is mindset, 20% is mechanics." – Amy Porterfield

In fact, there's a documented phenomenon known as the 80:20 Principle, which states that only a small percentage of the things we do every day is responsible for the majority of our success. In the coaching world, I've also seen this in another guise, as a skew between mindset and mechanics.

At whatever time you decided to start a business, it's likely the notion of a better lifestyle or bigger income is at least one driving factor, even if you're what we call a "heart-centred" or "soul-based" service provider. But those who have been around the business block (and those who have not!) will tell you that running a business comes with many mental headaches – aka challenges, risks and obstacles.

At times, day-to-day struggles and worries can undoubtedly distract and divert you from your original vision. They can also demotivate and derail you if you don't understand why you're not having the "success" you crave.

Every day I see highly gifted, expert professionals and business owners who are not making the kind of money they want and feel they deserve, who are fraught with the battle to survive month to month.

Or there are those who are actually broke and heading back to a job, disillusioned with self-employment and almost ready to give up on consultancy and entrepreneurship altogether.

I've certainly found myself at very low points in my career and business: self-doubt, anxiety, stress, and tiredness can all lead to indecision and zap your mojo. In those situations, I give myself the permission and space to take time out, recharge and refocus.

It's important to take time to focus your mind and build resilience around your goals; to reconnect with why you do what you do; to consider what's working well and not so well; and to get to the root cause of any problem so as to take the right corrective action.

The route and pace for achieving success may shift, so there's no point forcing things when you're at a crossroads or feeling lost. I know from personal experience, that letting go for a while and taking the "busy" out of business – counter-intuitively perhaps – can be super productive.

I'm not the first to say this of course. I've heard countless entrepreneurs say that when you move to a place of calm and "float" for a while, you can more easily mentally engage and keep your ideas and insights flowing.

Taking time out of your business can increase productivity – counter-intuitive, I know. But doing nothing (consciously) often really helps focus the mind because it's at these times we hear our inner wisdom that help us make a key decision, gain that moment of clarity or work something out. Sometimes you only need to take a couple of hours, a day out, or half a week; but sometimes getting re-centred can take much longer.

So, I'd most definitely argue that success not about luck, unless we mean creating your own luck. It's about investing in your own education, finding and grasping opportunities and eliminating barriers. And it's also about staying in touch with your inner voice and letting solutions come naturally to you.

FINDING YOUR BEST STRATEGY

Success in any business involves an inner game and an outer game. Your strategic plan needs take account of this. Your business success is based on how well your marketing converts, but your marketing message is based on how strong you are in your belief about what you do and why you do it.

You probably get the importance of mindset in entrepreneurship, but let me put it another way just so we're clear. Even in the most numeric of consulting professions, in building a business, internally there's inevitably some personal growth work you need to do to get out of our own way before you start implementing the external practical stuff.

Breaking through the profit ceiling of trading time for money is the best leverage for scaling up a service business. Breaking through your limiting mindset to do things differently is a prerequisite.

In this book, I'll help you start with some of the necessary inner work. (Some of it is actually very practical too!) The first three chapters tackle principles and purposes of leveraged consulting so we're on the same page and you've started to think what it could mean for you. This can get deep and difficult, as there may be inner demons you need to excise about money or success, past failures and belief in yourself. If you want to take your business to the next level of growth and what's possible for you, you need to do the internal work and create solid foundations to build upon.

As well as looking at what you uniquely bring to the table in terms of your expertise, attributes and story, we'll take a little time to surface what's most important to you in terms of building a better life for yourself and your family. This might be a broad visualisation, such as speaking on stage; or something very specific, such as getting 2, 5 or 10 new clients every month.

The key thing is to illuminate what that goal means to you, why it's important – to identify your big vision of success. Your goals don't need to be totally pinned down- we're not talking SMART objectives or anything like that - you just want to clarify the desired high point for what's important to you right now.

For instance, is there a bigger game you want to play in terms of reach or revenue – what does that look like and what would it feel like if you achieve it? Or do you just want less stress and a bit more time freedom – again, what does this mean in work-life balance terms?

Turning then to the gap, this is where we need to look at the "distance to travel" from where you currently are to where you want to be. From there, we can create the implementation roadmap to plan out each step as a tangible action. This also provides you with milestones along the way so you can clearly see *how* you will reach the desired destination.

Next, we begin some of the outer work, the practical stuff. In chapters 4, 5 and 6, we'll explore what kinds of leveraged strategies might be right for you to achieve your notion of success in your business – financially, personally, emotionally. From there, we can set out an action plan to get these in place.

Business owners who have learned how to transform their services to a more leveraged model have a far greater chance of long-term survival and success. Those who invest in developing their marketing, sales and delivery to suit the modern world we live in are way more likely to prosper, and do so without resorting to pushy or manipulative tactics.

Leveraged consulting is a way to grow and scale your business in income terms, but also how you contribute to the world in terms of the influence and impact your expertise can wield. If you're happy where you are and just want a few more clients, this book may be overkill.

On the other hand, the leveraged strategies in the book should resonate very strongly if you want to develop yourself as:

✓   A thought leader not just a hired help;
✓   An educator as well as a consultant or coach;
✓   An entrepreneur not just a service provider.

If you tick all three then I'm happy to say the book will give you lots of light bulb moments. In shifting some or all aspects of your business to embrace a more leveraged consulting model, I'm confident this will transform both your personal sense of fulfilment and your business revenue.

When you open yourself up to new ideas, it's not that the world will change – it's that your perception of it will change.

A fully leveraged strategy may seem a step too far if you're just venturing out with your own consulting or coaching business or you're struggling to attract clients or sell a service - which are the problems many of my clients come to me with first. But it's all part of the continuum for growing and scaling your business.

Regardless of the final destination, the most important thing you need in place (and in the marketplace) is a crystal-clear message and offer (your product, so to speak). This needs to be purposeful, predictable and profitable to you and of value to your potential client. From there, we work on placement and promotion to attract the right audience. Remember, you have to impact the hard problems where people spend their money, not just the soft issues where they spend their thought time.

Once the dimensions of aligning, targeting and positioning are locked into place, you can work on crafting your brand image, packaging and pricing. As you do, what you'll start to notice is that you attract clients to you, rather than having to chase them down. It takes time to build a good audience, but it doesn't have to take years.

Implementing *systems* for leveraged marketing, sales and delivery, and getting them working well, is most definitely a key part of the business growth plan. But it's sensible to get your "message to market" magnetism working first before systematising and scaling anything.

One of the best ways you can build a targeted, responsive audience is by sharing expert content that is relevant to their specific needs and problems. Once you have this dialled in by testing and tweaking your message, it's a triple win: you attract the right people, demonstrate your expertise and increase their desire to enrol with you.

When you leverage your expertise to drive your marketing and sales, you won't have to go out and chase clients, because they will come to you.

When you demonstrate your understanding of your ideal clients' needs and teach them on the solution you're offering - it's 90% about improving your relationship with your audience more than it is about selling.

Education-based marketing is incredibly effective for growing your audience and driving sales, because it creates demand in your prospects and generates social currency in the marketplace – the "pass-along" effect. Demonstrating you can help someone by actually helping them is a powerful way of building trust and goodwill with your prospects.

Digital platforms provide opportunities to reach and engage with your target audience far easier and faster. The world wide web (does anyone still call it that?) has opened up the potential audiences that you can influence and impact, near and far, the different ways they can engage and work with you, and the new streams of income this can create for your business.

Moreover, when you automate aspects of your marketing and operations, it's way more hands off than traditional methods, which means you're freeing up time to spend elsewhere – i.e. building your capacity to grow and scale. You are not just exchanging one kind of "busy" with another.

You can use this book to generate ideas around high leverage models and the digital platforms that support them. From there, you will need to choose those that fits with the vision you have for your business, your preferences for how you want to work with your clients, and the level of freedom you want in your life.

For now, let me tackle upfront two key challenges in terms of what digital transformation might mean for you in practice.

Firstly, bear in mind that any innovation is going to take hard work: changing perspectives, learning new skills and taking consistent action. But hard work is a relative term; most of us are inherently lazy, we take the path of least resistance and we all would love a quick pay off.

Make sure you pick from the low hanging fruit I'm giving you too. Identify things you can implement immediately that are going to have a noticeable impact on your business. This may be making your website work for you, bringing in more leads or having an enrolment process that yields better quality clients.

Secondly, let's consider the tech side. While there is much focus in the book on online approaches, this doesn't have to be scary because it's not about the technology per se. It's far more about showing you a *strategy for growth*, that helps circumvent the chasing, pitching and often fruitless sales presentations many professionals hate to do.

What's often left out of books and courses about business success, internet marketing or creating online courses is what is actually needed to achieve a doable, dependable and desirable process. With this book, I've incorporated what I believe is needed for action taking: the foundations, the thinking, planning and doing to support your individual practice.

GROWING FROM GOOD TO GREAT

With the right vision and strategy, you have the potential to move things up a notch for yourself and your business, to go from good to great. Whether you're just starting out and building on your career to date or you're already established in a consulting practice, there are ways to increase results leveraging things you are already doing.

The strategies shared should help you to identify the effectiveness and efficiency of how you attract and serve clients without stressing about selling, pitching and prospecting; and consider ways you can deliver your expertise to help more people than is possible working within the self-limiting, traditional paradigms of face-to-face and one-to-one consulting services.

The book has a deliberate sequence for bringing about transformation and growth for your business. Each chapter enables you to take a firm step forward towards building a doable, dependable and desirable high-end client business. There's no prescription – it's a matter of setting your preferences and choices in to a personalised action plan.

Throughout the book, you'll find *Key Learning Points* at the start of each chapter to focus your attention and a prompt at the end to capture your *Action Notes*. There are some "stop and think" questions posed along the way, diagrams intended to aid understanding and quotes to inspire.

In the **digital companion workbook**, I've given you a self-evaluation exercise to help you dive deeper reviewing your business architecture. It's available **free** with your book receipt at:

http://jayallyson.com/leveragedconsulting/workbook

The first steps in *Leveraged Consulting* are all about doing that real important groundwork I talked about earlier. This supports you to get your next level growth strategy into place. To inform this, after each of the main chapters, I've prompted you to write down *Action Notes*, the ideas and insights that emerge as you think through the principles covered and what these mean for your business.

We'll start by looking at the leverage opportunities, then move to leveraged strategy, thinking about where you are now and where you want to go, identifying what might be the biggest barriers and bottlenecks for you right now in growing your business. Then we'll look at what consulting or coaching work you're currently doing and how you're promoting yourself, with a view to clarifying and strengthening your brand message and getting it "out there" in the marketplace.

The intention with this is that you don't just read the book and end up confused what to do, but that, chapter by chapter, section by section, you take notes, think, and proactively develop a plan of action as you go along.

Trust me, the companion workbook will do more to spur you into implementation than the book alone can do. After the foundational thinking, you can get to work right away to review where you're currently at and plan how you can improve and transform the critical levers for your desired business growth and success.

First port of call is to synergise your business aspirations and area of expertise with your market and specific audience you wish to serve. This brand clarity is an early and essential point of leverage and where many business owners struggle most. It's the vital piece of the puzzle, upon which every other part of your business depends. Whether or not you take further steps to leverage your consulting, you can use these foundations to improve your marketing, attract more ideal clients and grow your client base and revenue.

I wrote *Leveraged Consulting* as a step-by-step process - of thinking, planning and doing - to help you create tangible and lasting success. Each step builds on the other. Too many business owners think they know the basics and want to jump straight to the moneymaking tactics. The thinking you do going through the early steps will totally influence how well you plan and implement the practical steps.

Taking an education-based approach to your engagement with clients, both your marketing and your consulting activity are part of a single continuum of dialogue with them. Without this, people won't necessarily or easily understand *why* your solution solves their problem or trust you're the person to help them.

In high-end consulting, you're undoubtedly helping clients with complex problems rather than a single deliverable. There are no set rules on the solution, only insights, guidance and decisions. This is where many people flounder with leveraged approaches, because providing advice in the form of information is seen as insufficient to help someone move forward.

However, education is fully capable of providing a solution. For instance, take this book, which has little interactivity compared to a course: my goal is to help you to appreciate the concept of leveraged consulting and how it can unleash you from the constraints of traditional time-intensive ways of marketing, sales and delivery of consulting and coaching type services. Only then will the practical approaches be worth learning about.

Before anything else, I need to support you to think through the problem, challenging your assumptions and perhaps your perception of the usual ways of doing things in your industry. I'm not just passing on knowledge and giving you cookie cutter model to follow. My aim is to help you decide which are the best strategies for *you*: your profession, preferences, skillset and the vision of success you have for your business.

I've integrated exercises throughout each section, because when you are pushed to review, reflect and plan, it's much clearer what action(s) you should take and therefore easier to make decisions about next steps.

Of course, a book is still one-way communication, but building in opportunities for reflection and planning moves it to maybe one-and-a-half way, because hopefully it moves you forward enough to prompt you to contact me and start a conversation!

PUTTING IDEAS INTO ACTION

The success of any strategy is in its execution. If you just read this book and you're not going to DO anything with the insights, reflect on the questions posed, or make any decisions, nothing will change. Likewise, if you start thinking this isn't going to work for you, because you think your business is somehow too different to others in professional services, you may miss out.

To reap the rewards of a new idea, you need to stay open-minded and you need to take action.

My aim here is to not to tell you there's only one way to build a "successful" service business. We may even have different sense of what "success" looks like. And certainly, your view of success, as we'll cover in the next chapter, is very individual to you.

What's intended here, is that the principles and perspectives presented inspire action. They move you towards new ways of thinking and doing things. It's not set in stone; you have to decide on the business model (and mix of strategies) that will work best for you and create a leveraged roadmap that takes you to your desired destination.

As I say to my clients, the vision and true purpose behind your business endeavour is yours to drive. Again, please don't wait for things to be perfect –

that was a big error on my part, which is why this book took so many years to "perfect" and it can never be perfect in everyone's eyes anyhow. It's better to take action, learn what's working and what's not than be forever theorising, procrastinating and perfecting.

Napoleon Hill advised: "Do not wait; the time will never be 'just right'. Start where you stand, and

> ※
> "One of the best aspects of letting go of perfection is the ability to say "I don't know how to do X - and I want to learn." – Dorie Clarke

work with whatever tools you may have at your command, and better tools will be found as you go along."

The plague of perfectionism can be rather paralysing to your business growth. As talented professionals, we don't just want to be good, we want to be great! We want things to work first time out of the gate. After all, that's what we're promised in the sales hype for the latest guru programme – follow my "blueprint" or "formula" and you'll be rich. Yeh right!

Rationally, I'm sure you see the flaws with this. Greatness takes time. Success takes time. A good idea becomes great when it's tested and refined. Success is something that evolves over time. Most innovations take at least 90 days (a 3-month cycle of improvement) to see real long-lasting results.

So, make a promise to yourself to take a step forward in your business every day. No matter what take some kind of action, even if it's imperfect action - it's okay! No great idea ever started out perfect.

As I say, I'm not here to say how you should run your business or give you "ground breaking" silver bullet methods. My aim is to shine a light on a new opportunity for working smarter not harder to achieve greater balance, revenue and growth in your business.

While some of what I share may seem like "motherhood and apple pie", but the fundamentals are super important and worthy of revisiting. Even if you've been in business a fair while, sometimes you need to put on a new thinking cap. I believe strongly that if you take these "teachings" on board and implement even a few of the ideas, you will be empowered to build a business you love, that your clients benefit from in multiple ways, and that is also wildly profitable for you.

Those who transform their business have been willing to take on board new perspectives, develop their understanding of key factors at play (some previously hidden), and take focused action to build leveraged systems.

With what I'll share in this book about the principles and practices for winning more and better clients using highly focused, education-driven approaches, you will have all the ingredients you need to create your own business system for the kind of leveraged consulting you want and the next level goals you have.

The foundations fortify the architectural design, and the natural step forward is to create an implementation plan of what you will do, when and how, and then take action to execute the plan and later evaluate the outcomes. People may understand *what* they can do, but aren't necessarily clear on their brand or message or the technology that underpins a tactic - or find it hard to stay focused doing it alone.

For start-ups, you can use the book as part of your strategic planning and to help you with clarifying your professional identity and brand. If you're already an established business, you can use the framework as a diagnostic tool to see where you might improve your marketing, sales process and/or service delivery.

If leveraged consulting resonates with the direction you want to go in your business, you may be ready to take action right away and apply the new approaches. There's further implementation assistance available within the *iSuccess Business Academy* – the culmination of my own leveraged consulting journey. As a reward for buying (and hopefully reading and digesting) this book, your first month's membership is covered so you can see if *iSuccess* is a good fit for you to move your leveraged action plan forward.

I teach people not just what and why, but how – the details that help you make decisions and push through tech headaches and marketing overwhelm, the stuff that otherwise will hold you back, keep you small and invisible, and drive you crazy. I teach time-leveraged approaches based on what I know, not what I think.

Putting yourself within an environment that guides, educates, inspires and supports you to innovate and achieve the success you want, alongside a degree of accountability… that's proved highly valuable to my clients.

I think a structured step-by-step, action-by-action path and supportive environment is as close as you can get to a silver bullet. At the very least, it's a targeted stream of silver bullets and that's what I've lined up for you in this book.

ACCELERATING YOUR JOURNEY

In the journey to leveraged consulting, destination and travel speed are up to you. This book is not intended as a prescriptive route to one person's view of success or how quickly it should be achieved. Rather, it aims to enlighten the possible directions for travel, to provide a source of inspiration and guidance for growing your consulting business in a way that's true to who you are, how you best serve and how you want to show up.

This is why we start our journey looking to the road ahead. You need first to see the bird's eye view of leveraged consulting and decide what success means to you. That is what determines which strategies are the best fit for your business growth. We then return to ground level to do the essential groundwork, lay strong foundations and identify specific design elements for the business model you want to build. In other words, we'll look first at the big picture and then get down to some practicalities in your business.

After this introduction, which has hopefully given you an outline of what's possible in the digital age, we'll build up the picture of how to achieve success with leveraged consulting taking you through some foundational thinking, some architectural planning and some hands-on doing.

Chapter 1 **THE POWER OF LEVERAGE** starts with understanding the opportunity that comes from leveraging your expertise, time and skillset within the context of growing a consulting practice. We examine typical income growth plateaus for solo professionals and small firms, and look at five points of leverage for building a successful and sustainable high-end client business.

Chapter 2 focuses on **LEVERAGED STRATEGY** where we look at the four areas you can create more leverage in your day-to-day operations to grow your reach and revenue in today's digital world. We emphasise that these are choices that should mirror and support your preferred ways of working and your personal and financial goals. We address the question of "what success looks like" to you to help you define your best business model.

In chapter 3, we'll lay the foundations for **LEVERAGING YOU** pinning down what you specifically bring to the table in terms of your "story" – what drives you, who you wish to serve and why, as well your experience and specific expertise. The aim is for you to gain absolute clarity on your professional identity and ensure your brand and messaging is authentic, unique and resonates strongly with a high-end target market.

In chapter 4, we get into **LEVERAGED MARKETING** - how to bring your unique value proposition to market. We'll go through the different channels you can use for people to find out about you and help you decide on the kinds of audience platforms you prefer and content you're most comfortable and/or proficient with to position you as the go-to expert authority in your niche.

Chapter 5 **LEVERAGED SALES** builds on these foundations to consider what and how people can buy from you. We'll look at packaging and promoting a branded offer to attract high-quality, targeted and responsive prospects into your business. Driven by serving not selling, you'll learn the *Engage-Educate-Enrol* pathway to drive your sign-up process and increase conversions. And we'll look at the simple technology tools and processes you can use to leverage technology, automate the sales process and ensure a dependable flow of signups into your high-end offer.

In chapter 6, we take things up a notch and look at **LEVERAGED DELIVERY**. You'll see the range of ways you can deliver your expertise beyond one-to-one, face-to-face services to increase your influence, impact and income. We look at setting up group events and creating digital products or blended programmes that allow you to with more clients in more ways. We look at some of the vital tactics for success in the online marketplace and cover off some key factors to consider when shifting your consulting business from local to global, from single stream to multiple streams of income.

Chapter 7 is where we're going to get super practical with **YOUR LEVERAGED ROADMAP**. We'll dive deep into critical levers for change and how to implement them, using an exclusive process improvement process I designed to support my clients called the *7 Dimensions of Success*. This also provides the basis for a super useful diagnostic to help you self-evaluate where you are with each component of your leveraged consulting journey and what your priority action points should be.

Please do take advantage of the free downloadable companion workbook. This will help you draw together the inspired ideas and action notes you glean from the book and support your self-evaluation activities. Then finally, I'll wrap up with how you can get further guidance and support from me to create a personalised success plan and take your leveraged consulting strategy forward.

Quick caution - this book is not for the faint-hearted. It's not rocket science or some heavy academic text, it's got both muscle and soul. I keep things strategic and super practical, but we'll also dive into sorting some of those self-sabotaging personal growth issues too. And, importantly, unlike the multitude of "self-help" books you could canter through, I'm encouraging you to take action. I'll give you insights, food-for-thought and a stepwise improvement plan. What you decide to change or do differently after reading will form your own personal roadmap for growing your consulting or coaching business in a way that fits with you as an individual and what you envision as success.

Second caution – well advice really. Although each chapter is self-contained, you'll probably benefit most if you don't dip in and out, because there is a logic to how the book is constructed. It's a structured curriculum and each chapter builds on the previous. The key principles will provide solid foundations for building your business and the practical parts will give you the know-how and a step-by-step plan of action.

Cautions and advices aside, whether you binge read, take your time or dip in and out, I hope you'll go on this journey with me and discover new ways of thinking about how to grow your business, strategically and operationally. Certainly, feel free to pick out the parts of the book that speak to where you are right now. Skim the bits that seem familiar or irrelevant, use them as reminders or maybe come back to them later. And I'm pretty sure you'll want to revisit some chapters once you've built up your roadmap.

My clients always come to me saying they don't know what to do or what will work for them or why things take so long to implement. More often than not, the problem they face is not a shortage of tactics but a lack of strategy, sometimes coupled with a lack of coherence, confidence and/or consistency. This is why doing the strategic groundwork and setting out the milestones for your success is so crucial.

If after reading the book, you decide to embrace the strategies of leveraged consulting in the digital age, then I have a couple of fast track opportunities in the final bonus chapter to help accelerate your journey. We will both have achieved a degree of success, if from our time together you achieve the following outcomes:

(1) You can see new ways to overcome current frustrations with your marketing and start to enrol more and/or better clients.

(2) You are inspired to redefine the level of impact, influence and income you can achieve for yourself and your business.

(3) You're empowered to believe in your own high value and potential as an expert, educator and entrepreneur, and to create authentic and compelling high-end offers.

(4) You come away with a set of clear action points and a roadmap that helps get you from where you currently are to where you want to be, in the short, medium and long term.

Chapter 1

The POWER of LEVERAGE

What Is Leveraged Consulting and Why Do It?

"Bring out the three old warhorses of competition – cost, quality & service – and drive them to new levels.

Jack Welch,

Winning: The Ultimate Business How-To Book

KEY POINTS

❖ A new wave of digital transformation is helping businesses to extend their reach and revenue as well as to meet changing customer expectations in how services and benefits are delivered.

❖ If you haven't figured out exactly how you can increase revenue without impacting costs, chances are you're stuck at a growth plateau.

❖ Unless you're differentiated, distinctive and offer something tangible, the only value propositions a client can judge you on is cost or locality.

❖ If you want to achieve growth in your business, you not only need clarity, uniqueness and strength of mind, you also need leverage.

❖ Leveraged consulting in the digital age aligns with seven massive growth industries. It's a "perfect storm" for building a high-end client business in terms of the opportunities.

❖ Every consultancy should have a high-ticket offer in their business strategy, so you can serve deeply while fully stepping into your power and the value of the results you deliver for your clients.

❖ Education-driven marketing allows you to rock your genius in an authentic way. You don't want to be your industry's best-kept secret.

❖ If you develop the resolve and determination to seek help, to learn, and to improve your business strategies, systems and technology use, you can achieve great things with leveraged consulting.

❖ Being strategic, entrepreneurial and leveraged in your client engagement & delivery models will enable you to break through the typical barriers professional service providers impose on themselves.

❖ Setting Automating much of the marketing & sales process of your consulting business improves operational efficiency and thus your productivity.

❖ When you blend digital with face-to-face support, you increase the perceived value of your programme – it's like your client is getting the best of both worlds.

❖ up a customer journey pathway for acquiring clients is the foundation for creating leverage in your marketing and sales.

❖ When you can deliver your expertise in different kinds of ways, digitally and remotely, this enables you to work with and impact more people.

REDEFINING LEVERAGE FOR CONSULTING

Leveraged Consulting in the Digital Age serves the solo professional or small firm – the "micro-business" if you like – who wants to build a successful high-end client business by working smarter not harder, and achieve growth by scaling not expanding. That means as you build your client business, there are critical stages where you will have to decide between growing at a regular rate or switching over to a more scalable leverage strategy.

The book aims to help you leverage your competitive advantage as an independent professional expert with regard to profile building, systems building, and assets building. It provides the lift and thrust to build, market, grow and scale your business. It offers a set of principles, practices and processes that harness digital technologies as critical levers to position, package, promote, sell and deliver your expertise in new, different or more efficient ways.

Leveraged Consulting in the Digital Age is not all about "going digital". There's certainly a big role for face-to-face communication in a service professional's business development strategy. But let's be clear: without a focus on the opportunities afforded by technology and the internet – often oddly termed "digital disruption" - this book would not be relevant to how we live, learn and do business today.

A new wave of digital transformation for professional services is helping businesses to extend their reach and revenue as well as to to meet changing customer expectations in how services and benefits are delivered.

There are multiple examples in our everyday lives of how companies are redefining traditional ways of doing business through new service distribution models: Amazon, Uber, Netflix, Udemy, to name just a handful. There are far fewer examples in the professional services industry. What this means for consultants, coaches and other experts is that there's a whole new world of business out there if you want a piece of it.

Leverage for independent service providers is a way for you to remain both profitable and competitive. Leveraging strategies are both upstream: how your business operates internally, such as your sales and marketing; and downstream: how you develop yourself and how you work with clients, that is your delivery or results mechanism.

While consulting remains an expanding industry, organisations today are either reviewing the way they use consultants or questioning the value and return on investment (ROI) they get from using them. Isn't it frustrating that you have all this knowledge, expertise and experience yet you can't seem to connect it with people who want what you have to offer?

Part of this, is the often intangibility of what consulting and coaching services deliver. Even in renowned firms, it's clear that their consulting is presented in a fairly generalist manner and their only offer is trading their knowledge and "done-for-you" services. This presents a constant struggle to win business, because such consultancy is simply a common commodity.

Unless you're differentiated, distinctive and offer something tangible, the only value propositions a prospective client can judge you on is cost or locality.

Successfully leveraged consulting businesses focus on micro-niches – that is, market segments with very specific problems. (Incidentally, just because it's a micro niche doesn't mean it's a small segment.) The point is, digital content can help you attract people who have a specific need and are looking for specific tangible outcomes.

Specificity creates a very exclusive *magnet* for attracting the right kind of clients to work with you. Once you have this dialled in, take your expertise and turn it into an effective programme of change for these people.

> ※
>
> "In any competitive marketplace, the thing you must avoid at all costs is becoming a commodity - a random, faceless provider who will suffice if the price is low enough. If there's no customer loyalty, you're always at risk of being undercut."
>
> – Dorie Clark, Stand Out

The challenge for all consultants and consulting firms today is not just how to survive or grow the business through existing practices, we need to be looking to how we adapt to new trends and develop new service delivery models. If ever there was a concept you absolutely must understand in order to be successful in a high-end client business, it is the *power of leverage*.

Few business owners properly grasp it, and even less use it well or to its full potential. This is compounded by very traditional models of leverage in business (mostly finance based) and in consulting firms (mostly people based). So, let's get a few provisos down first.

If you read any business textbook, leverage is usually talked about from a resource-based viewpoint, generally looked at as a strategy for growth achieved through asset or capability building.

Similarly, in the consulting industry, leverage traditionally focuses on setting up hierarchical structures to support a firm's client work – a kind of pyramid based on (alleged) importance and earning power of its staff, with the partners at the top and supporting directors and managers underneath. As the company takes on more clients, it must take on more staff and offices to support the work.

Neither of these is what I'm advocating here when I talk about "leveraged consulting". The key difference is the difference between growth and scaling - the increase in revenue without incurring significant additional costs.

If you haven't figured out exactly how you can increase revenue without impacting costs, chances are you're stuck at a growth plateau.

Why adopt a leveraged consulting model? Well, I'll give you three reasons.

First, it's about moving with the times and the responding to shifts in the industry. Second, it's about the opportunities afforded by what is now a global and digital marketplace for consulting, coaching and many other service-based businesses as well as retailers. And third, it's about finding a realistic and sustainable way to meet your personal and financial aspirations.

> ※
> "Conventional beliefs about our profession are wrong. These are paradigms - thought patterns that we take for granted and let limit us."
> – Alan Weiss, Million Dollar Consulting

If you want to achieve growth in your business, you not only need clarity, uniqueness and strength of mind, you also need leverage.

The businessdictionary.com defines "leverage" as: "The ability to influence a system or an environment, in a way that multiplies the outcome of one's efforts without a corresponding increase in the consumption of resources."

In other words, *leverage* is the advantageous condition of having the initial investment (of time, money, effort) yield a relatively much higher level of return (which are defined by our individual goals and measures of success).

A fully leveraged consulting strategy, illustrated in the flywheel here, incorporates three mutually reinforcing points of leverage across the end-to-end customer journey, that is your *marketing, sales* and *delivery* – all of which leverage *you* at the centre in terms of your purpose, professional expertise and personal attributes. This is driven by a seamless process of customer engagement and education prior to, during and after enrolment. (There's a reason for the white space in the inner ring – we'll fill that in later.)

Leveraged consulting in the digital age is highly client-focused. It harnesses online *marketing* on the front end so you can reach, engage and influence more people, and streamlines *sales* and *delivery* of online products, programmes and services on the back end so you can increase efficiency, profitability and impact.

All these require a firm grasp on your own professional identity, linked to that of your target audience, and your brand message, linked to what that audience wants and is willing to pay a premium to get. This is absolutely why we need to place YOU at the heart of this design.

(Of course, there are a great many other opportunities to use digital technologies to manage key business operations, which provide additional leverage in terms of efficient use of time and management of operations, teams and customers, but let's keep it straightforward for now.)

The limitation of this diagram is its lack of context - it doesn't illuminate the stepwise and iterative nature of growing a consulting business in planning terms. We need first to determine our *strategy*.

In relation to building a consulting business, I never found a full balanced picture of how all the moving parts fit together. What I mostly see is ad hoc content or courses on latest "hot" marketing or sales tactics or trendy course builder programmes. You know the kind: "100 Traffic Secrets", "Top Funnel Hacks", "Get 10,000 Facebook Fans", "Instagram Ads", "10x sales formula" or "How to Run VIP Retreats, "Best Quiz Building Tools", "Online Course Builders Lab" or "Product Launch Club".

Such training is all well and good, and many are actually very well put together by people highly experienced in the field. But it's only helpful if you *know* that this tactical solution is right for your business, is where you need to focus your efforts and is the best way to get the job done. The limitation and danger, however, is they are just tactics – they don't always help you review how it fits your business strategy and whether the approach advocated is right for you.

Because I've never come across a single, clear, coherent framework, I created one and decided to write this book. Built right, leverage forms the basis of how your customer engages with you, your brand and your work. It's simply the fundamentals of an effective and efficient client acquisition and fulfilment engine. The engine *fuel* is your expertise - and education is what makes the whole thing run right.

This is where things get exciting, because good educational content is the best quality fuel you can use to enrol clients. When you demonstrate and validate how you can help someone before you try to convert or sell them anything, you will attract them very strongly into your sales or sign-up process.

The reason I believe expert content is such an important element of a leveraged consulting strategy is two-fold. One, an education-driven approach more easily fits your professional values as a consultant or coach for how you help people. And two, it engenders the relationship building and trust that's needed to acquire a high-end client.

Research shows that audiences engage more strongly and are more often persuaded to take the next logical step with you when you share helpful content, explain your point of view and where it comes from, and connect on a human level. Your content doesn't even have to be polished; it just has to be valuable and authentic.

As you can guess, I haven't put everything on the picture; there are lots of other moving parts and I'll fill in the inner circle later in the book. But if I added a whole stack of other boxes and arrows right off the bat, you'd likely miss seeing the wood for the trees. This needless complexity is what gets us so overwhelmed and confused when we try to improve something or do something new.

So, for now, just think about your end-to-end process in this simplistic way (at least for now) helps you design a workable model. Your strategy and the business models you want to use determine its design – and ultimately, therefore, the level of leveraging power in your business.

But why do I need all this you may ask. I'm sure the end we all have in mind is to build and grow a successful business – and I'd guess that looks something along the lines of a *doable* business model, a *dependable* income and a *desirable* work-life balance.

EXITING THE REVENUE ROLLERCOASTER

Ensuring you have a consistent flow of income can be a huge stress for self-employed consultants. Compared to the comfort and stability of a monthly salary from an employer, working for yourself can feel like rollercoaster ride. The ups and downs certainly have your heart racing and adrenaline pumping, but more from anxiety than excitement. Perhaps you're able to use some savings to fill in the down periods, but it's not sustainable.

Competition is certainly partly to blame. The astounding growth rates in the consulting and coaching services industries globally means the competition for clients is challenging. Up against the big 4 consulting firms (or the big 10-100 in fact), it's become harder and harder for solo professionals and small firms to advance their authority, land clients and create a sustainable income. In an increasingly commoditised environment, the little players are losing out to the big names in terms of high-end revenue.

However, the reason many consulting businesses fail to earn consistent revenue is because they don't know how to attract and nurture the right audience for the kind of services and programmes that they are most uniquely equipped to provide.

Another reason is oftentimes, a solo consultant or coach thinks that growing their business means working harder, putting in more hours or hiring staff. And a third reason is that a lot of professionals simply hate selling, pitching and prospecting; and we don't tend to do (or do well at) the things we hate.

At the same time, many solo professionals and small consulting firms struggle to build a truly lucrative and fulfilling enterprise, because they lack the right strategic business model.

> ※
>
> "The primary outcome we all strive for is control. People think they want money, "balance" or freedom. But everything, at the end of the day, is about control.
>
> We don't only want money... we want control over our situation and our livelihood. We don't want balance... we want to choose for ourselves what we put all our time into."
>
> – Taylor Welch, Traffic & Funnels

Most consultants are offering a very broad spectrum of support, using very traditional business development practices to find and pursue clients, and limiting themselves to local clientele. Most are delivering an exhausting range of face-to-face, one-on-one or "done-for-you" services to the point where there's little leverage or scalability in the business model.

With leveraged consulting, attracting new clients comes down to how successfully you align your brand positioning with the needs of your target market. While it's also about how well you can systematise your consulting or coaching process in order to scale your business operation, in some ways that's more straightforward.

In a series of workshops that I ran a few years back for a group of (supposedly) successful business advisers, the number one challenge consultants and coaches faced was inconsistency in their income. Various frustrations attest to this one problem. I summarised the ten most common ones in a list – see below – and held a secret ballot for the groups to see which resonated most.

In every workshop, all of the participants could identify with at least the first half of the list. Most talked about the constant struggle to win business and work with great clients; others talked about income ceilings and cost per client acquisition.

COMMON FRUSTRATIONS AS YOU BUILD AND GROW A SERVICE BUSINESS

1. You're not getting enough enquiries, but don't really know how to do effective lead generation (e.g. making your website work for you).

2. When you do get enquiries, people don't seem to see the value in what you do or feel inspired to take action (so you hear "let me think about it" or "I can't afford it").

3. You know your stuff and that you can help your clients, but just can't seem to get your message across without feeling like you're selling (which feels icky).

4. You're fed up buying cold leads or appointments, where you end up justifying, convincing, chasing the prospect to work with you (which feels uncomfortable and desperate).

5. To get more clients, you take on less than ideal people or discount your fees, and end up with clients who aren't fully committed and so don't get the best results (which means you don't get great testimonials).

6. You want to develop clear, tangible services that are straightforward to deliver (i.e. offer great value to your clients without overwhelming them), but you're confused what to create or where to start.

7. You're juggling too many moving parts, ideas or options; working with clients has taken over your life and you can't fit any more hours into your day (which leads to overwhelm, procrastination or paralysis by analysis).

8. You'd actually love to have fewer but better clients who pay you more, and can't see how to make that pricing shift.

9. You're focusing on "closing' sales rather than attracting clients (which is exhausting and feels unprofessional).

10. You want to specialise, but have a fear of loss when considering "niching" your business compared to serving a wider audience. This is actually one of the hardest concepts to "get" about marketing.

Let's face it, most independent consultants have zero leverage in their business. They are buying leads and sales appointments, doing calls, holding meetings and delivering client work one-to-one rather than one-to-many through group events and programmes. This isn't helped by the fact that most consultants' business websites are not designed to "sell" either – they're just glorified CVs.

There's little point working tirelessly to attract prospects to your website if you don't make a clear call to action or offer, you have no means of capturing visitors' contact details or no structure to following up with them. And even if you do get a prospective client to call you to book a consult call, you're unlikely to sign them up if you don't have a framework for that call or you don't have anything tangible to offer.

A lack of structure and leverage punches massive holes in your business performance. Yet from my consulting work doing website reviews for small businesses, I see it all the time. So, here's a quick-fire checklist for you:

❖ *Is your website or social media sites giving you a vehicle for engaging your audience?*

❖ *Does it have a compelling brand message and generate leads for you?*

❖ *If you're capturing contact details, how watertight is your follow up and enrolment process?*

❖ *Do you know how many clicks you need to acquire one new client and what that means to you in time and money terms?*

In my experience, most of the challenges consultants face in producing consistent revenue is linked to *ineffective marketing* to attract the right clients and and/or low *profitability* of what you're offering. Most successful consultants are great at what they do, but lack a deep understanding of the psychology of buying and sales processes and pricing strategies. They may be enthusiastic and know how to engage their target audience in the subject matter, but "closing the deal" feels pushy, embarrassing and uncomfortable.

Quite often offering a discount or undercutting the competitor consulting rates eases the conversation about money. (The big consulting firms have business development and marketing teams to set things up, but if you're self-employed or a small firm, the whole lot is usually all down to you.)

As you probably know when you're on the buying end yourself, investing in a high-end service or programme is a big commitment. It's unlikely to happen from a standing start, which I why having a good relationship building process in place is so crucial. Your marketing must nurture your visitors' interest, build trust and goodwill and move them through a structured process of increasing commitment. This is most times referred to as your "funnel", "pipeline" or "ladder" as a metaphor for your prospecting process.

At the outset, people hear about you, opt into your list and stay in your marketing process until they decide it's not for them and leave, or they commit and take the next step, ultimately ending in a sale or signup. Your goal is to take someone by the hand so they always know what to do next. Keeping a good level of attention is also important.

This is partly about putting the structure in place as above, but a large part of effective marketing is down to producing good copy – how you set out and write your promotional material and webpages, including how you use text fonts, images and other media. The aim is to be attractive and engaging to the people who are a good fit for your high-end service, product or programme – your "perfect people" - and move them seamlessly and gracefully to the point of contract, purchase or procurement, i.e. sales.

The profitability of what you sell is determined partly by your pricing and partly by how leveraged your service delivery is. Let's say you win a client: how much are they worth to you in revenue (lifetime customer value) terms? Offering a high-end service can be great, because you only need a handful of clients to earn a 5-figure-a-month income and you may get at least one repeat contract with the same clients.

But many service providers get stuck in a typical time-based agency type model, where you're only offering one-to-one and "done-for-you" services or projects. Trading time for money puts a ceiling on your revenue unless you put up your fees or duplicate yourself with partners or associates.

Leveraged Consulting will help if you're experiencing any of the following:

❖ INCONSISTENT CLIENT FLOW

You don't have enough leads coming in, and, at times (or often), you doubt yourself or feel overwhelmed by all the different options to market your business to get more clients, consistently.

❖ INEFFECTIVE MARKETING

You're spending time and money on advertising that you can't afford in order to generate leads, because you aren't marketing yourself effectively to magnetically attract your most ideal clients to you.

❖ POOR SALES & PROFITABILITY

You just don't like the idea of "selling" yourself or your services. Maybe it's a question of how selling feels to you personally, perhaps self-worth or self-doubt, not wanting to blow your own trumpet, or maybe you just aren't sure what to say.

❖ POOR OPERATIONAL PERFORMANCE

Your business depends entirely or too much on you as the owner and you want to learn how to *leverage* your time and automate some of your key business processes.

❖ LACK OF TIME & FREEDOM

Your income is based solely on trading time for money, working one-on-one with clients and making sales customer by customer. You're finding it tough to know how to turn your current business into a profitable and sustainable enterprise, one you can streamline and scale so you can increase your revenue whilst gaining more lifestyle freedom.

Let's do an instant health check on your business right now. For each of the problems above, score yourself 0-5 where 0 means you aren't experiencing this problem and 5 means this is the exact situation that you currently find yourself stuck in.

If you scored 3 or more on any of these situations, then you undoubtedly would welcome a solution. As you go through the book, try to spot the leverage points that can stop the above situations arising. As we move into the practical chapters later on, we'll be looking to pinpoint the critical levers to work on in *your* business.

I want you to know with confidence where you should make changes that improve the situation dramatically for you.

To exit the revenue rollercoaster, let's go back to the three pieces of a fully leveraged strategy highlighted in the last section, and see how you can resolve the major problems.

No matter what your preferred operational model is, digital or face-to-face or a blend of the two, it's hard to grow and scale without leverage in these areas.

(1) **Marketing** - You're not visible or well differentiated in the marketplace and/or you don't have a compelling message or irresistible content to drive your lead generation and build a targeted list.

(2) **Sales** - You don't have a structured process for enrolling and onboarding clients, which makes things clumsy, inefficient and ineffective.

(3) **Delivery** - You're not flexible in how you serve your clients, i.e. the method and format by which you help them achieve a result they want.

Remember, at the heart of all of the outer three pieces of the puzzle is **YOU**. If you're not clear on your professional identity and/or niche: what you do, what you're about, what you stand for, who you help, it makes every other piece incredibly hard work and ineffective.

The chapter on *Leveraging YOU* is about positioning yourself as a leader, building a brand story, clarifying the "what" and the "why" of a need or problem you solve and being clear on the "how" in terms of the high-end expert service, product or programme that delivers it.

> ※
>
> "It's too easy to pretend that your wildest imaginings don't matter, to dismiss them as pipe dreams. The truth is that you can't break through to another way of living and expand your life and business if you don't admit to yourself that you DO desire success, recognition, growth and impact." – Anna Parker-Naples, author of Get Visible

You may need to work on increasing your leverage in all areas. But the important thing to know is that you are entirely in command of the influence, impact and income you can have. When you learn how to use the leverage afforded by digital technologies and digital media, you can position yourself better in the market place and create better processes to support sales and delivery of what you provide.

What good is your expertise if your ideal clients don't see you, hear about you or remember you; and if (due to location or cost) they have no realistic means of accessing your expertise to solve a pressing need they have?

Leveraged Marketing is all about visibility and positioning, relationship building. You need a plan for getting yourself and your message out there in the marketplace - becoming visible and slightly famous. This means adopting one or more platforms that you're comfortable (or could become comfortable) communicating through, such as writing, speaking, teaching. To do this effectively in the digital age, you have to do your chosen thing consistently. And trust me, the more you do it, the better and more polished you'll do it.

In truth, it doesn't matter too much if you speak from a stage or create online podcasts or videos; equally, it's as effective to write editorials in print publications as it is to post articles on a blog or via social media. The big difference between offline and online though is online has far more leverage in reaching a bigger audience.

As long as you're promoting your unique expert system, and the result you deliver for your specific target audience, you can position yourself with confidence, standing by the value of that result for the price you charge. Put another way, if you're getting a lot of objections like "I'll think about it" or "we don't have the budget", that is likely evidence that you're not communicating the cost to your prospect of *not* getting the result you deliver (and continuing to have the problem they have) as more expensive than the cost to get it.

In order to "sell" people on you and your expertise, and the value of what you do, you need to cultivate an engaged and responsive audience. And for that, you're going to need to specialise and create a unique brand message that speaks to the exact segment of the market you want to attract. The more specific you can be, and the more value you provide upfront, the more you'll stand out and get noticed by the right people.

It doesn't matter if you're a small business or a solo trader, a CEO or a freelancer, the importance of a strong consistent brand image and message throughout all your marketing collateral and your entire customer engagement process is not a step to be skipped or skimped on. A good brand allows people to remember what you're about – it should communicate your entire essence, purpose and values all at once.

> ※
> "The nature of selling professional services is promise. The first step in growing a service firm is getting clarity around your promise. It should be attractive to your ideal client and speak to what matters to them." – Randy Shuttuck

Problems with a lack of sales or ineffective sales process calls for a *Leveraged Sales* strategy. You need to have a tangible offer that matches what your ideal clients need and want and a structured enrolment conversation to discuss with prospects or applicants whether it's a good fit for their specific situation.

It helps to give your enrolment or signup call an appealing name. Rather than the norm like a "Free Consult" or "Free Session", how about a Strategy Session or Discovery Call. If there's a very tangible outcome you deliver, you can go one step further and name it something that matches exactly what they are wanting help with. For example, in my consulting business, one of my offers is called a Strategic Marketing Roadmap Call.

Now onto problem (3) - this is a lack of what I call *Leveraged Delivery*. You're operating on a time-based business model rather than packaging your expertise into consumables that don't require 100% of your one-on-one attention working with a client.

When you learn to deliver (some or all of) that expertise through education-based, results-orientated programmes, rather than direct "done-for-you" services, you immediately open up a whole new online and global market you can serve.

Your capacity to produce revenue is directly proportional to your ability to gain market share and this means responding strategically to changing times. With this in mind, let's turn to the market environment and the opportunities for professional experts to harness the power of leverage.

EXPLOITING MAJOR GROWTH TRENDS

Leveraged consulting in the digital age aligns with seven massive growth industries. It's a "perfect storm" for building a high-end client business in terms of the opportunities that the *positive* confluence of these present us with.

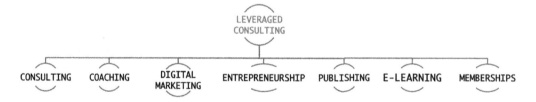

This line up matches perfectly with new ways that professional experts can market, sell and deliver services and digital products. As an independent business, you have the chance to harness these growth trends and align yourself with the storm (rather than being blown away in it).

With the right business growth model, one that fits service providers, you can make the shift to scale your consulting business into a thriving, digitally smart, value-driven enterprise, ride the tidal waves and take the world by storm.

Let's ponder each of the seven growth areas in turn. First, consulting and coaching, despite some reservations and shifts in focus away from management consulting towards more tangible implementation services, particularly technology consulting, both remain massively growing industries, globally.

Next, digital marketing, an industry unto itself now with the growth in new enterprise and entrepreneurship closely linked. There is an enormous wealth of information, training and support out there nowadays – almost overwhelming. Nonetheless, put simply, digital marketing allows consultants and coaches to build an online presence and engage an attentive, responsive audience. Offer out an expert report as a giveaway with a lead capture form and you have an effective and automated mechanism to generate leads, drive engagement and streamline enrolments.

The popularity of content and book publishing has exploded exponentially. Across the internet, there's now a plethora of publishing channels - blogs, article directories, video, podcasts, social media. You can video stream live and even run your own TV channel. You can self-publish and distribute books, both e-books and paperbacks through print-on-demand.

There's now an increasing volume of "indie" (independent) authors with experts deciding to go down the self-publishing route rather than traditional publishing houses. Both publishing houses and bookshops have had to adapt rapidly, but in honesty, they're all still playing catch up to the mega powers of Amazon.

Digital publishing has in turn driven enormous growth in demand for online learning or "e-learning". This is no longer the domain of universities, colleges and schools. In fact, Harvard's innovation as the first provider of a "Massive Online Open Course" or MOOC may have driven culture towards more access to high-quality educational resources.

Speaking, teaching and course delivery is quickly emerging as a hungry pursuit for independent consultants, coaches and other expert professionals. It's undoubtedly behind why LinkedIn – the social network for professionals - bought out Lynda.com a highly successful online professional learning platform – now a subscription service called LinkedIn Learning.

Which leads us to memberships. Rather than launching and selling products or courses one by one, there's a movement towards recurring revenue model of delivery. The advantage is you only need to acquire a customer once, and if they like your material and are getting value, they will continue to pay you month on month. It used to be that most continuity programmes kept their members for 3-4 months. Nowadays, however, we're seeing pricing strategies that use annual memberships to lock people in (at least for 12 months), and progression or community models that drive long-term retention.

Serving your audience through digitally delivered expert content and online support turns most of sales and marketing frustrations around. It also puts you on the right track strategically and operationally for transforming a small local services business into a high growth global enterprise.

That may not be your vision, but it is all to play for. Even exploiting a *small* piece of what's possible could make a substantial different to your influence, impact and income.

At the top end of the scale, implementing a fully leveraged strategy will require, at some point, a digital transformation that includes both technology integration and workforce development internally. But as a starting point, using digital media and tools to support your external engagement and how you build relationships is what will bring you the biggest leverage results.

Either way, you're going to need a strategy and a roadmap!

FOLLOWING YOUR INSPIRED PATH

In any business transformation or improvement plan, following an inspired path is a good way forward. Here's what I mean.

1 - Start with the end in mind and reverse engineer your route.

As we touched on in the introduction, decide on your vision for the future and what success in your business means and looks like for you. What kind of work do you prefer to be doing, what kind of clients do you like working with most, how do you want to engage with your audience to attract those clients, and what level of influence, impact and income do you want to achieve?

2 - Listen to your intuitive ideas as well as tactical ideas.

Since it's your values, personality, interests, passion, style, attitude as well as your subject expertise that will reveal the business you were meant to build. Your unique composition - your qualities, set of experiences and your "dreams" - as an individual is ultimately what should steer your business vision. It's what determines your true north and drives your direction of travel in the pursuit of success.

To help define your personal mission, ask yourself: what work are you most interested in doing, and why does it matter to you and the people you serve?

It's sometimes tough to find your true calling, but trust that everything in your life has led you to the specific type of work you do and the audience you're most inspired to serve. Your career and experiences to date has already created a deep well of purpose. If you can tap into what you enjoy and *want* to do as well as what you're good at and *can* do in terms of your expertise, this will create the vision and road ahead for you.

Revisit your mission often so it continually ignites your energy and motivation, and moves you forward to create an authentic personal brand based on doing work you actually love that gives you genuine fulfilment (i.e. you're not just doing it for the money!)

Concentrating on these foundational aspects of your business growth is important for building a business that is truly leveraging your expertise, personally fulfilling as well as financially viable. As we move into strategies for leveraging you in chapter 3, I'll help you discover your true genius zone or at least provide some moments of clarity and personal awareness to take you in the right direction.

> ※
> "If you want to reach your true potential in life, it's important your business or career is in line with your deepest values. It's the only way to achieve your fullest potential and feel a deep sense of fulfilment." – Eben Pagen

Running a business is hard and if you don't have a strong brand message that you're working from, it can feel like an uphill struggle to move forward in a meaningful way. This is why I believe leveraging "you" is a whole dimension worthy of its own chapter and because that's where I know a lot of consulting professionals get stuck.

I hope you can use that chapter to reflect on, rediscover or at least reconfirm, the inner truths of your business: why you started it, what your vision of work and life is, as well as to it to clarify your brand message in terms of the unique contribution you provide to the people you serve.

As you journey along an inspired, more profitable and rewarding path to success, these roots will tether you well. Given we now live in a very fast-paced, results-oriented environment, we often expect instant gratification in everything we do or experience. Unfortunately, when it comes to inspiration, getting back in tune with your authentic self takes time. It doesn't have to take years, but an immediate result is unlikely and unrealistic.

It's taken you this long to arrive where you are now - with all the plot twists, setbacks and baggage we all inevitably carry around with us. So please understand that it may take time to knock through the tough outer casing of your existing beliefs and issues before you can fully see your own inspired path to success.

Finding your own clear brand and marketing voice is a critical part of the process of value creation in any business, but with service businesses, there is no magic pill. However, I would like to emphasise that the journey of self-discovery can be enlightening, fun and liberating. I encourage you to keep your mind open to "new and different" and adopt a child-like attitude of wonder!

Of course, it's okay (and expected of you) to question and ponder, but rest assured that when you take action on the key things you're inspired to take forward, these insights will accelerate your business growth.

The way the book is structured, you'll be working through the same business diagnostic I use with my own clients to explore, identify and clarify your business vision and purpose, and to understand and diagnose probable root causes of your current challenges – some of which are definitely related to our own mindset and limiting thoughts.

Remember, your effectiveness taking action on any of the ideas and insights I share, and your ability to properly evaluate the benefits, is fully dependent on your willingness to keep an open mind and set aside some of your preconceptions about building a business.

Some people find this harder than others, as beliefs about everything, including how business works or how sales and marketing work, are deeply engrained in our conscious and subconscious thinking.

> ※
> "The human brain is drawn toward clarity and away from confusion." Donald Miller, author/creator of StoryBrand

Furthermore, most people overcomplicate their marketing; they fail to focus on the aspects of what they offer that impact people's lives; and they confuse prospects with too much irrelevant information, which makes them tune out.

In recognising the power of your personal role, visibility and influence on the success of your business, it's my hope that you'll get inspired and clear enough to identify what specifically you could change to build a business that meets your vision of success.

ROCKING YOUR GENIUS

In today's competitive marketplace it's not enough to be good at what you do. You have to stand out. Those businesses that hone in on a single idea tend to experience greater success attracting their best clients. Aim to work in your highest "genius zone" and truly believe in the benefits you can bring to your clients.

For professional service providers, this is your zone of excellence or core competency as an expert. If you're currently quite generalised, you will need to reinvent

> ※
> "Just one "big idea" for one marketing funnel can make you more money than most will make in their entire lifetime." - Todd Brown

yourself slightly and rebrand, because survival in an increasingly competitive marketplace means being super strategic and drilling down into a specialist micro-niche in order to stand out.

I'd argue that to be in real alignment with the bigger vision you have for your business, you need to identify an ideal offer within your genius zone that sits in at the intersection of what you do (your expertise) and what is profitable to offer the market (client needs) as shown in the figure here. If it's something you enjoy and fills you with passion and pride too, so much the better!

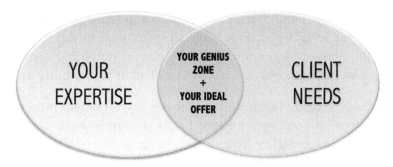

Once you have this dialled in, you can leverage digital practices to "rock your genius", grow your client base and scale your business in three key ways.

❖ First: Using your expertise to produce relevant and useful educational *content* that builds an audience and shapes your brand. This raises your status as an expert and drives your marketing and PR on the front end, so that you attract and win highly targeted clients and partners who are clear on how you can help them and trust that you can deliver.

❖ Second: Creating engagement and sales processes that power the hunger and demand in your clients' mind for the solutions you offer, because you're helping prospects understand the value of your help so much that they want to buy from you (and keeping buying) without you having to sell.

❖ Third: Developing high-value education-based *products* that solve your ideal clients' problems and support them in deeper and more impactful ways. These are your high-end programmes that you offer on the back end, which should serve your purpose and vision and determine your profitability.

The huge benefit of leveraged consulting is that it enables you to completely uplevel your business. You can move beyond a self-employed freelancer or small firm relying solely on local markets and regional networking and working mainly through one-to-one, face-to-face services.

When you know how to build a digitally smart enterprise, where you are sharing your expertise in highly *leveraged* ways across the entire customer journey, it creates the potential for higher and higher levels of influence and impact, and is a sustainable and scalable model financially for growing your business.

Every consultancy should have a high-ticket offer in their business strategy, so you can serve deeply while fully stepping into your power and the value of the results you deliver for your clients.

The way I personally see my own genius zone is in empowering fellow professionals and service providers to harness opportunities for reach and revenue growth beyond what you may currently imagine possible - to play a bigger game. I want you to achieve the kind of financial and personal fulfilment you deserve for the expertise and value you have to give.

It's a lofty aspiration, but I feel confident you have a brilliant opportunity in front of you to put the "big idea" of *Leveraged Consulting* to work in your own business. If you do, you'll outsmart your competitors by doing something distinctive and be able to take your business beyond its current level of profitability and reach.

What's important is to find your unique point of view on what you do, why you do it and stand true in your belief about the best way to help your clients or customers. That means bringing your ideas, insights and skills into the light, helping others get the results they want.

This expert-led and value-driven approach to business development suits consultants and coaches, because it means using your existing expertise on the front end to drive your marketing and relationship building with clients. As an expert, you undoubtedly have the capability for advising, teaching and guiding in your area of expertise – so educating will feel more naturally like consulting or coaching, rather than selling, pitching or prospecting.

> ※
> "You can't develop great ideas - or an audience, or a brand - if you don't start writing. Creating content helps you determine which ideas warrant more attention. It helps attract opportunities, like speaking invitations, so you can hone them further." – Dorie Clark

Education-driven marketing allows you to shine your light and rock your genius in an authentic way. Certainly, you don't want to be your industry's best-kept secret!

Many heart-centred retailers are looking for less sales-orientated approaches to attracting customers and helping them get the results they want. It's not vastly different. Education-based marketing is equally an effective customer acquisition strategy for direct sales consultants and small product-based businesses too.

Although on the surface, online marketers may seem sales focused, many are at heart also advisory service providers; their expertise is simply focused around an outcome of using a particular product or range of products can achieve.

At the same time, regardless of whether you're a service professional or retailer, there are new skills of entrepreneurship, customer engagement, marketing and enterprise building to learn. Looking at this holistically, here are some of my personal beliefs for how to build a great leveraged consulting practice, one that rocks your genius and wins you plenty of good business.

- I believe that a business built around your personal beliefs, values and expertise, fueled by education-based marketing, is the best-fit strategy for service-focused industries.

- I believe that creating a viable and novel idea that's applicable to a big and growing market segment can have a huge impact on your ability to attract business to you.

- I believe that self-aware and empathetic people make good marketers, because they connect well with like-minded others.

- I believe that business owners and solo-professionals that are good learners become good earners, because you have to work as hard on your *personal* development as you do on your business development.

- I believe that for things to change *you* have to change (your mindset, behaviours, practices – a Jim Rohn truism), because the universe responds not to affirmations per se but to forward thinking and action taking.

- I believe that having systems and processes is one of the biggest practical improvements you can make in your business operations to increase your clients' likelihood of success working with you as well as to increase productivity and drive your business growth.

If you can develop the resolve and determination to seek help, to learn, and to improve your business strategies, systems and technology use, you can truly rock your genius with leveraged consulting.

People who have travelled the path before me act as role models and examples of what is possible. Why would you not follow successful people in order to succeed in your business? Whether via books, audios, e-learning courses, events or via mentors, I've been an avid consumer (and buyer!) of knowledge and wisdom. And now I'm rocking my genius to pay it forward.

FIXING WHAT'S NOT WORKING

Left unchecked, the continued pressure to bring in new clients can take its toll on your state of mind. It's hard to win work if you're feeling stressed, on the back foot or pressured to "sell" yourself and your service. And it's hard to stay motivated if you're not winning work.

At the same time, it's also tough to step out of the familiar business development traditions of the consulting profession – that of networking sales appointments and glossy brochures. But, remember the definition of insanity? It's doing the same thing repeatedly and expecting different results!

Being more strategic, entrepreneurial and leveraged in your client engagement and delivery models will enable you to break through the typical barriers professional service providers impose on themselves.

The sad thing is many consultants earn significantly less than they are capable of earning. If that's how you feel, I know it's not because you aren't expert enough or well-known enough. And I doubt it's because you don't have a high value service or product to offer to your target market. If you're experiencing inconsistency, if people are saying no to you, if you're run off your feet, you need leverage in your marketing and sales processes.

If you're not earning what you feel you're worth, or feel there's a ceiling on your income, then it's likely you're placing limitations on your pricing and delivery capacity. Shifting your consulting from one-to-one tailored support to a more leveraged model doesn't mean giving up your existing practice working closely with a client on projects. It builds upon it - like an extension or extra storey - and provides a means to reach a bigger audience, add value and generate revenue in new ways.

At this point in time, I'd hazard a guess that the challenge you have right now is to make sure you do marketing that works: that wins you a consistent flow of leads and attracts the right kind of clients. As we've alluded to earlier, the number one reason why most professional service providers struggle to sign up new clients or create greater leverage so they can scale is because (in some way or other) their marketing and sales process is broken.

If you also experience a lack of consistency or volume in the client work you bring in, it's usually because of a poor offer or lack of systems. First get the process and conversions working, then ramp it up – that's my advice.

The reason you end up spending more time finding clients than working with clients is a lack of leverage. The reason people don't hire you or sign up with you is almost always a lack of clarity and relevance not a lack of funds.

Most consultants (and indeed many consulting firms) apply largely undefined service offerings to a broad market rather than highly targeted messages that align with the specific problems of their ideal clientele.

It's quite astounding the number of "experts" who struggle to articulate clearly the specific *problems* they help people solve or the *benefits* of their service. They talk about how experienced they are in their field, offer up all manner of accolades and case studies, but many have no clear offer.

On top of this, most do not have a clear *process* for what they do, or an effective *platform* for promoting and selling what they do. So not only are they unsure or unclear in communicating the *value* they bring to the work, there's no structure or system in place for engaging prospects (marketing), signing them up (sales) or when working with a client (delivery).

Sadly, the result is that many consultants and coaches end up at the "mercy" of their clients' whims, taking on less than ideal work, rather than being leaders and in-demand experts in their field. Yet, a lot of what's going wrong is straightforward to fix once you identify the root cause and put the right architecture in place to improve both your marketing offer and your sales system.

The figure here is a (slightly modified) slide from that same workshop series I ran for independent business advisers. It highlights the typical barriers to attracting and winning clients that leveraged strategies can help overcome.

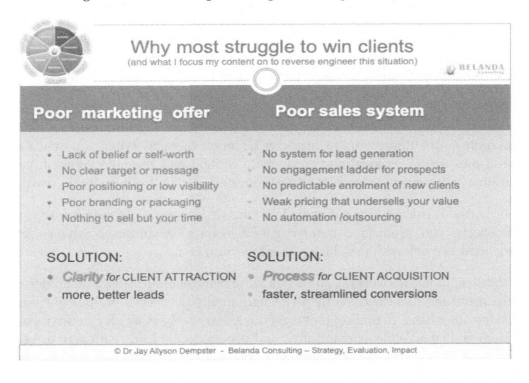

Good design enables you to build solid foundations for your end-to-end customer experience whilst understanding the principles that connect everything together. When you couple this with leveraged ways to *deliver* what you offer and sell – you have a complete pathway that takes your prospective client by the hand from the beginning to the end of their journey with you.

BUILDING DIGITAL CAPABILITY

Building your digital capability, in terms of the use of online platforms, content tools and automation, enables you to implement high-leverage business growth models. Having a digital strategy enables service-based businesses to leverage people, systems and customers and grow in a way that is doable, dependable, scalable and sustainable.

In the digital age, leveraged approaches lead to greater cost-effectiveness, influence and impact from your customer engagement efforts across the entire end-to-end process. A fully leveraged model is where you are optimising all the key elements required for business growth: you, your marketing, your sales and your service delivery.

Automating much of the marketing and sales process of your consulting business improves operational efficiency and thus your productivity.

Having a well-oiled, (fully or partially) automated client-getting machine working for you in the background 24/7 is incredibly liberating. No more remembering to order flyers, chase down leads and follow up on sales meetings. Leveraged consulting frees you to spend your time on strategic planning and high-end delivery work rather than low-end admin or development work, or just to create the opportunity to take a bit of time off!

Firstly, digital systems offer *streamlining* to your marketing and sales process - a structured and consistent way for you to rapidly build a platform from which to promote your authority brand, attract your target clientele. When you match an ideal message to an ideal audience, share content and promote yourself, you create a high-powered magnet to draw your perfect clients out from the crowd.

Furthermore, using online automated systems to generate leads and nurture your prospects, you produce a more engaged, responsive audience who is pre-qualified to speak with you, hire you or buy from you.

While traditional networking and advertising may generate leads, both tend to be expensive and don't necessarily yield high-quality prospects for your business. On the other hand, digital content tagged with targeted keywords can drive your "front-end" marketing - organically - and generate solid leads with zero or very low cost. While it still takes time and consistent effort, it's nonetheless cost-effective.

The difference between the traditional and digital methods is leverage. Networking and advertising are continuous operational costs to your business month after month, whereas with a good follow up system, content marketing can produce a continuous flow of leads long after the initial material is produced and published.

Secondly, digital products enable *commercialisation* of your knowledge and expertise, which satisfies a desire for cost-effective delivery (both for you and the client) and increases your influence, impact and income. A leveraged delivery model enables you to serve clients in new ways. Suddenly, you can grow your consulting business beyond the constraints of traditional revenue models like hourly rates and fixed fees.

Essentially what this means is you're leveraging your core knowledge assets by delivering your expertise in different forms and formats. On the "front end", this education-based marketing forms a core part of a "ladder of commitment" for your prospective clients. With their very first experience of you, hopefully they step onto the first rung of the ladder and continue to stay with you, step by step, until they ultimately reach the highest rung and sign up for one of your high-end programmes or services.

After seeing some positive outcomes emerging from your initial shared content and communications, you are building desire in your prospect to step up the next rung of the ladder. Your "back-end" products and programmes enable your prospect to continue the relationship with you and you're able to generate additional streams of income delivering your expertise in different ways.

Digitally, it's easy to create two or more products at increasing price points in the middle rungs of your ladder. These require a smaller commitment from your client. You demonstrate you can help them and they build confidence - a safe conduit - in moving towards enrolling in your high-ticket programme or service at the top. Given not everyone will be right or ready for your high-end offer, now or ever, this approach also increases drastically the number of people you can serve.

By packaging up a popular service as a programme or course and delivering it online, you immediately leverage yourself, your expertise and your time. Furthermore, having clear objectives and results ascribed makes this product both unique to you and very saleable to your target market.

Choose one area of expertise you want to become well known for doing well, create a signature programme around it and focus your marketing predominantly on that.

When you offer a high-end product or service, especially one delivered partially or wholly online, your pricing needs to demonstrate value for money and guarantee you can deliver the promised outcome for the client. For this reason, a high-end programme is likely to require a higher level of your time to deliver it, than a digital course or product which someone can work through on their own.

At the same time, an online programme will demand far less of your time than delivering an equivalent face-to-face programme. It's not all-or-nothing though.

You can blend accessible, own-pace digital material with the opportunity to work closely with you (at an event or using online communication tools).

When you blend digital with face-to-face support, you increase the perceived value of your programme – and your client is getting the best of both worlds.

That's not to say there's not a place for traditional consulting services. However, the competition to secure contracts is ever increasing, especially if you're not in a niche industry. Furthermore, cost pressures (particularly through procured services) means there's a tendency for people to seek discounts or avoid big contracts. What this means for you is more and more time spent "out there" finding new business and less time serving clients.

Undoubtedly, the information revolution is not about to end any time soon. It's a continuing trend – with more and more information being added every hour and available freely to searchers all across the internet. Anyone nowadays can stick up a blog, create videos, e-books, build social media profiles, etc) and market to the masses. There's an ever-expanding abundance of information at your fingertips.

I'm certainly not encouraging obsessively high content publishing and social media posting as the strategy here. Indeed, the challenge for the consumer of all this information is one of overwhelm. What I'm advocating an opportunity to engage and serve your prospective clients in new and more leveraged ways; to help them find a path through the overwhelm and confusion towards the solution they're looking for.

Getting yourself noticed by publishing viewpoints, "how-to" guidance, sense making and novel ideas can mean you gain traction in new market segments where people are looking for answers. Most striking is how great thought leadership can actually *create* entirely new segments.

As a professional and an expert in your field, you are in a prime position to help your target audience find a route through the maze. In the digital age, it's so much easier to connect what you do with a targeted and hungry audience. Choose one or two digital platforms that most suits your industry, your style and your skills, even if it's only to complement or supplement your face-to-face interactions.

DEVELOPING YOUR LEVERAGE CAPACITY

If you already sense that things have shifted in consulting and coaching, or if you're struggling to find and secure high-quality clients, it's probably why the notion of leverage appeals. You know it's not really just about marketing and getting more clients; in your gut, you know it's about strategy.

I strongly believe leveraged consulting offers a revenue growth model that has long-term viability. It takes advantage of several massive growth trends that are creating a new breed of business entrepreneur – the educational entrepreneur – and responds to the way that clients today wish to engage with and consume consulting or coaching services.

Massive growth in digital publishing and online learning are driving many consultants and coaches to become "educational entrepreneurs". This is not a term consigned only to the education sector. Rather than constantly reinventing your service to fit the unique needs of every new client, savvy consultants are creating packages around a core area of expertise that serves a specific and niche market.

Whether or not engagement happens online or offline, education is an incredibly natural extension to what you do as a consultant or coach. It's also an incredibly effective way both to communicate and to demonstrate how you can help your clients.

If you can help a potential client navigate through the vast sea of information, to understand why problems exist, to guide and support the implementation of tangible solutions, they are more likely to trust you and want to work with you. However, there's a notable difference between information and education.

Information alone cannot bring about the kind of transformational change for clients that education typically does. But a good learning design and consumer experience are paramount.

Information may open the door to a solution, but education shines the light on it. In fact, there's such as huge sense of information overload, overwhelm and confusion in the marketplace nowadays, that education actually feeds a massive need people have for clarity and guidance.

Creating and publishing education-rich online content expands both your reach (influence) and how you deliver results for your clients (impact), but also massively increases your earning potential (income).

Of course, there's no strategy for overnight success. I'm assuming that your current consulting work earns you a reasonable living, such that you are at least in a position to set aside some focused time to think and plan for growth. Although there's no one right approach to monetise your expertise as a consultant or coach, choosing a viable and profitable business model for how you market and deliver it is critical. That's the power of leverage in the digital arena.

Leveraged Consulting in the Digital Age is not based on the usual leverage model for consulting firms; that of building a solo practice, partnership or small practice into a large, corporate firm (although once you grow to a certain level, team management and organisational culture will become important factors).

I've based the book around leveraged models that specifically enable solo professionals and small businesses to reach increasingly higher levels of revenue without personal sacrifices of time with family and lifestyle pursuits. Which strategies you decide to adopt is completely up to you – some, all or none – you reap what you sow.

What I know from personal experience is that, in leveraging your expertise as an independent consultant, there's far more freedom and wealth earning six figures working for yourself than earning twice that working for someone else. There are less hassles and low overheads and after tax you get to keep what you make.

When you reach multiple six figures or seven figures working for yourself, there are no restrictions on how you spend the discretionary income of your business. This provides powerful opportunities both to enjoy the fruits of your labour and to "do good" in the world (if you so wish).

What you don't want is for your consulting work to feel like a job! Later in the book, we'll look more closely at what success with a high-end client business actually means. In brief, it's not all about marketing to get more clients. It's about optimising your marketing, maximising your sales conversion and increasing your profits.

Leveraging the power of digital gives you more ways to reach more people, deliver projects more efficiently and generate new streams of income, in ways that don't depend on you (the business owner or partner) being there (day in and day out). Your high-end consulting or coaching services should be the ultimate offer, but not your only offer.

Contrary to the whole load of work that you think business growth requires, to maximise your reach and revenue you actually need to use the golden rule of "less is more" - *narrow* your focus, *streamline* your process, *package* your system. You want to work towards achieving more with less – leverage - in terms of what you offer, to whom you offer it, and how you deliver it.

Leveraged consulting is most easily achieved by sticking to two main rules:

RULE #1 - Focus on <u>one</u> service area or result you deliver: such that you can find a way to standardise it and package it, so that you can market, sell and deliver it, digitally, even when you're not in the office or on client site.

RULE #2 - Focus on <u>one</u> perfect customer or client avatar: such that you create a rich expression of who they are and what they need, making it easier to find more of them, engage with them, build a relationship with them and decide on the best way to be of service to them.

For example, on rule #1, when I focused on strategic marketing for business growth as my one service area, I found I was actually leveraging my expertise across multiple strands: business strategy, operational improvement and evaluation, as well as combining it with my passion for branding and marketing. When I turned to focus on my ideal clients' and what they need to move the needle so to speak - rule #2 - it really helped to create the right kinds of content to drive my marketing and deliver my programmes.

You can make the shift towards leveraged consulting by thinking about it in terms of levels you want to reach. At a basic level, it can just be about finding ways to free up time spent on repetitive operational tasks by creating a system and automating it. For instance, you can use email marketing to deliver a sequence of welcoming and nurturing messages to follow up with a lead or to send a link to an online step-by-step guide for new clients.

Go one level up and you'll find you can leverage your time spent on non-repetitive, more creative tasks too. Some examples that technology can help with:

- Create content you can easily repurpose in different formats and share through different channels in a consistent and planned manner.

- Produce a slide deck of clients most frequently asked pre- and post-enrolment questions to save going over the same information with each one.

- Develop a structured checklist, course, quiz or action planner to make enrolment and onboarding more effective, engaging and efficient.

- Use simple document templates to ease collaborative work for a new client project, such as to gather key information, schedule meetings etc.

- Outsource tasks that don't have to be done by you personally and could be done by media specialists (e.g. graphic design) who do the work better and faster than you ever could.

- Hire a personal assistant or PA (who could actually be a virtual assistant or VA) to do bespoke admin or project management tasks.

At a more sophisticated level, leveraged consulting can be an entirely new business model where you leverage your expertise through branded, packaged products and programmes. This enables you to serve more people in more ways and achieve higher levels of influence, impact and income.

Leveraged consulting at this level builds your business beyond the limitations of physical location and customised services. When you think about marketing, selling and delivering your expertise online, a potentially global marketplace opens up of people hungry for the specific solution you can help them with.

The first gentle step might be to create a group version of your most popular service so you can service multiple clients at the same time. Running a programme like this leverages your effort and by serving more people, you can increase your income. A more ambitious leap would be to create, package and sell a digital product that generates an entirely new source of "evergreen" revenue, or at least makes any paid advertising you do cost-neutral.

With these simple shifts in your digital capability, the leveraged consulting model is a sustainable way of building your business whilst achieving the goals that you care about achieving for both your clients and yourself.

When you start focusing on the challenges you help your clients overcome instead of focusing on the services you offer, you'll notice a turnaround in both engagement and take-up. This is why a big part of the book focuses on brand messaging. In the wider sense, this means really pinning down what you do (in terms of the problem you help people solve or the benefit they get from working with you).

People buy from people, so an important element is your brand story so your target audience understand why you do what you do, as well as your how you do it. In your writing, presentations or conversations, talk about why you do what you do, your beliefs, passion and personal experiences. Being open and authentic in this way attracts a kinship with your ideal audience that's almost tribal in nature. It helps to highlight the relevance and value of what you provide and the outcomes you help deliver.

Clarity, relevance and authenticity is what will drive all of your marketing, customer engagement and sales. But communicating your unique value is both an art and a science in the digital world. While producing great copy is a skill most definitely worth cultivating, you first have to sell yourself to yourself.

What I mean by this is you need to have a strong belief that you can deliver what you promise. If you're not clear yourself about who you are or what you can do, i.e. if you aren't confident in your own value, you can't expect your prospective client to be either, and no amount of leverage will help.

This is super important because this aligning to your purpose and targeting a profitable audience is what leads to positioning yourself effectively in the marketplace. It's woeful to me how many independent consultants and coaches get totally stuck, perplexed and frustrated on this most fundamental element. And most times, they don't ever realise that brand clarity is the biggest blockage behind their lack of growth.

As your professional identity and brand message are so core to success (and not having this dialled in is the root of many other problems further down the line), I'm going to spend a fair bit of time on this groundwork and what I call "leveraging you". In the first sections of the book, we'll look to strengthen your beliefs in your value to the people you want to serve. When you can make this "first sale" of yourself to yourself, you'll make way faster progress with everything else you do to grow your business.

Yet, we must avoid making it *all* about you. You must also be able to look at your brand from the potential customer's perspective – they need to resonate with what you stand for. Top performing consultants are responding by focusing their marketing on the *people* they help, the *problems* they solve and the *results* they deliver - rather than on their CV or the features of their services.

These consultants have become (or hired!) good copywriters to get under the skin of their ideal customer, to be both like-minded and succinct. They capture interest by understanding the emotional triggers of their target audience, speaking in the problem language of their target audience, aligning with their hopes, worries, fears and desires.

Bear in mind too, that nowadays in the digital age, a "buyer's journey" isn't linear – in fact, it can be quite convoluted. People searching for your services will have been around the block long before they pick up the phone or submit an enquiry with you. By the time they happen upon your offer, they've often already done their research on you and your competitors, clarified what they need (or think they need) and narrowed down their options.

No-one likes to be sold to but everyone likes to buy. The experience of buying something you know you want or need brings a certain joy. But this feeling usually vanishes when someone tries to sell something to you.

Perhaps this is down to feeling manipulated or coaxed; or perhaps just a sense one's freedom to choose without bias is being compromised. Whatever the reason, pushiness is often what gives salespeople a bad name.

Yet, think of the power of customer reviews when deciding on a product, whether it's on products like Amazon or services like Trust Pilot. High numbers of high ratings and positive comments definitely sways us, if only because it underpins rather than undermines the decision to buy that we already made but need reassurance to add to cart.

When faced with decisions to hire a consultant or coach or buy a product or programme, prospective customers are scrutinising your offer in terms of whether

> ※
>
> "We tend to think our message is what moves people. But it's what we do first to create a particular state of mind in our audience that makes them receptive."
>
> Robert Cialdini, Pre-Suasion: A Revolutionary Way to Influence and Persuade.

you help them understand its value. They're asking: "Is this what I need?", "Does this solve the problem I have?", "How do I feel about this person/company?", "Is this a good fit for me?" and "What is the likely outcome or result if I/we invest in this?"

As a subject matter expert, you're well positioned to be a valuable resource to your target audience, because you're able to discuss industry trends, share best practice and engage in detailed discussions about how one solution might perform better than another. This shifts the emphasis to where it should be - on customer needs.

However, in your core messaging, remember that here again "less is more". In a world where people have so much information to tap into and are feeling overwhelmed by all the options and possibilities, you need to be laser focused and succinct. The old adage of "the devil is in the detail" does not apply to your front-end marketing - here too much detail *is* the devil and will destroy, dilute or dally your message.

I know that all sounds counterintuitive – and, as an educator, I've often fallen in the trap of wanting to explain *everything* rather than give a simple answer. But first you must *engage* your audience, reader or listener with a compelling message, a reason to spend time with you, before you get into any detail. When you're trying to catch someone's attention, the more you say the less people hear; the more you write, the less people read.

This is a super important principle for anyone marketing a product or service these days – start with why your audience should care. (And yes, a book or course is different to a piece of marketing, because it's a more deliberated engagement that someone has committed to, so you'd expect there to be plenty of detail.)

CREATING A CUSTOMER PATHWAY

Earlier I talked about a structured "ladder of commitment" that your clients ascend as they get to know you, and hopefully like you and trust you. Often referred to as a "funnel", this essentially sets out the customer journey. It provides you with a process - a client flow system – to streamline how you build an audience, nurture the relationship and encourage people towards a commitment with you.

I call this the *Engage-Educate-Enrol* pathway: the less your audience knows you, the more you need to focus on marketing activities that engages and educates them before you attempt sales activities to enrol them. We'll look at this pathway in more detail in the next chapters as we move into strategy and planning.

Right now, we're just looking at the broader leveraging principles involved in the process, and the digital approaches to implementing it, that of moving multiple one-to-one conversations (of traditional consulting business development approaches) into cost-effective yet powerful one-to-many dialogues.

Setting up a customer journey pathway for acquiring clients is the foundation for creating leverage in your marketing and sales processes.

Funnels come in all shapes, sizes and complexities, and this can make things confusing. A lot of people make it way more complicated than it needs to be (especially those selling solutions!) The main goal is to create a process whereby people start to see a solution. The success of your process is dependent not on the particular method of vehicle, but on people's ability to make progress in their thinking, planning or doing.

To keep things on the straight and narrow, and focused on consulting or coaching type businesses, in the next figure I've illustrated three principle ways you might engage, educate and enrol high-end clients through a *Funnel Offer*. Essentially, it's client dating! There's no end to the kinds of "date" you can set up – but you need to recognise they all have different levels of interaction. It could be a webinar or video series, a podcast, a course, or a free session - it might even be a book ☺

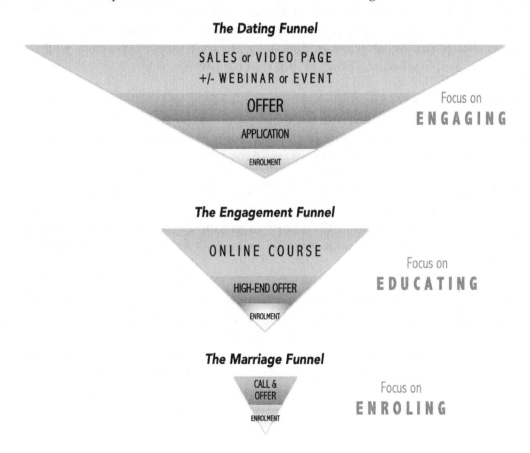

The Dating Funnel

SALES or VIDEO PAGE
+/- WEBINAR or EVENT

OFFER

APPLICATION

ENROLMENT

Focus on
ENGAGING

The Engagement Funnel

ONLINE COURSE

HIGH-END OFFER

ENROLMENT

Focus on
EDUCATING

The Marriage Funnel

CALL &
OFFER

ENROLMENT

Focus on
ENROLING

What is common to all is that your marketing or advertising aims to attract people into the widest end at the top by inviting them to engage in something relevant and irresistible to their interests and needs; then (to those who opt in) you provide an educational experience and make an offer to work with you. This leads to sales when some of those people decide to enrol on your programme or sign up to your service. The proportion of people who opt in at each layer in your funnel is what's known as your "conversion" rate.

More commonly for high-end offers, at the dating stage, there's no "click to buy" option; the final commitment is more likely to be "closed" through your final application and enrolment conversation. But having processes and systems in place can help do most of the heavy lifting to get someone to the point of a buying decision.

Which funnel offer you send people to ultimately depends on where people are in their relationship with you, i.e. whether you're communicating with cold, warm or hot prospects. It also depends on the extent to which you are prepared to embrace the power of digital platforms and develop the requisite skills of digital dialogue.

The cooler the prospects are at the outset, the wider and longer the funnel needs to be and the harder you have to work to develop a good connection. At the outset, when you are looking to build an audience, you need what I call the *Dating Funnel*. By providing relevant content in a group setting, this works well for attracting people who are a good fit, but don't know you yet.

In dating terms, you looked interesting but it's just a first date; you don't know each other at all and don't have any kind of relationship. You need to engage with them further, get to know each other, and do more nurturing to move your dates forward than people who are already familiar with you and what you're about.

In setting it up this way, you're able to fish in a bigger pond and expand your chances of attracting the right person and taking them on a journey building a relationship with you. Rather than hope to randomly meet potential clients in your local area, you use an online profile and great headline to engage the right people.

The best way to overcome a lack of prior connection is to provide a well-sequenced presentation, for instance by producing a sales page or video series and/or a webinar or some kind of event where you can make a presentation and personally introduce yourself and what you're about. Instead of a first date just the two of you, it's more like you're hosting a party and meeting people there. (If you choose to broadcast live, you could ask your guests questions and get some friendly banter going.)

With someone new, you'll want them to get a good vibe from you if you're going to click enough for them to want to take things further. You're just testing the waters with the people who are attracted to you, see if you might be a fit. If the match is good, your date will want to take the next logical step – to go on more dates as they move towards a greater commitment.

Creating the *Engage* part of the process and picking the right dating funnels is important for *attraction marketing* and *list building*. Promoting niche-focused, education-rich content attracts your perfect "type" (of client). There are such as various ways customers might start their initial journey with you in this way, some more hesitant or slow-paced than others. You don't have to do them all, pick those that suit you and you're good at.

- Consuming free content such as short articles, videos, social media posts;
- Opting in to your email list to get some special you're giving away;
- Subscribing to a free media channel like an iTunes podcast or YouTube;
- Buying low-end products like books and courses.

Being found relevant and valued by the right audiences begins the *Educate* part of the process with people you want in your *Engagement Funnel*. These are people who have already engaged with your expert content, know what you're about, and are following you in some way (via an email list, social media group or media channel). Focusing your content and communications on specific common interest topics is now the way to go. Prospects who are engaged and responsive will be the most open to deepening the commitment.

Warm prospects like these require less work to acquire as clients than cold prospects, because they've already pre-qualified themselves as a possible fit. A simple email invitation may be all that's needed to plan that special occasion. These are people who are likely to have already seen you in action and got to know you quite well.

But you want them to know you even better. If you're well well-known or and you have an active list or group, your funnel can be quite slim and compact. Hopefully the longer-term relationship they have with you means they now know you, really like you and probably trust you. These leads are moving from "warm" to "hot" and are usually pre-engaged and responsive to any offers you make.

The *Marriage Funnel* tests out how ready your person is for commitment. It really works with people you already have (or have had) a good relationship with, i.e. people who have already watched a webinar, been to a live event or taken one of your short online courses. These people may just need a focused "enrolment" conversation with you where you find out exactly whether they're a good fit and invite them to join your programme or sign up to one or more of your services.

Generally, these "hot" prospects know what they want and what you can provide and need reassurance about saying "yes' and signing on the dotted line.

OPTIMISING THE CONVERSION PROCESS

Comparing funnels, I hope you can see how the different shapes and sizes equate to the level of work you need to do to engage, educate and enrol a client. The height and width of the funnel is also representative of your conversion rate through each leg of the customer's journey.

In fairness, the diagram here isn't even to scale or you wouldn't be able to read the labels. If we're representing numbers of captured leads or prospects going through the funnels, I'd say the dating funnel with cold leads probably would need to be at least 20 times wider at the top than the other two funnels where you have an audience that is warm and pre-qualified. You might need 50-100 dates over many weeks, months even years, before you can seal the deal with someone.

In practical terms, this means you need 20 times as many people entering as cold leads into a dating funnel, because they need a longer process of getting to know you and seeing what you have to offer before they are likely to move forward. Notably, if your profile and what you offer isn't clear, that number will need to be much higher (i.e. a funnel with an even wider top end) because your opt-ins and conversion rates will be lower. The more well-targeted those entering are, the faster they will move through your funnel.

If you're just getting started generating leads, your new date/prospect needs to warm to you. You'll need to do some serious romancing – lots of gifts and loving gestures to show your audience you care and understand them in order to nurture and grow the relationship. You won't achieve it with just a single article or video; they need a continuous drip of great content and communication from you to stay in your funnel.

Depending on how aligned, targeted and positioned your content is, you can manage to get people to sign-up for a high-end offer in just one one-step.

To do that, you'll need a very well-crafted sales page or a video series, a webinar or face-to-face presentation - where you have more opportunity to build trust. But it's unusual if you're not a master marketer or salesperson.

On the other hand, if you've been "courting" your person(s) a little while, or you offer an online course as bait, the engagement funnel can be much shorter and narrower.

A good learning experience can springboard the relationship and trust building that otherwise would need to happen through a lot of "touch-points" using traditional (and often expensive) marketing and sales methods. And your conversions are likely to be higher because you need less people coming into your funnel. Those who go through one of your free courses or free sessions become pre-qualified and pre-sold on what you deliver and convert more readily.

The best way to lift your success rate in any of these funnels is to:

> ※
> "The role of marketing is to make selling superfluous... [in other words] The aim of marketing is to know and understand the customer so well the product or service fits and sells itself. Ideally, marketing should result in a customer who is ready to buy." - Peter Drucker

- Be aligned and targeted with your ideal audience so you're having an "on-message" dialogue and can generate high-quality, responsive leads;

- Become a well-positioned and visible brand in your industry or field of expertise so your prospects can easily get to know, like and trust you;

- Develop excellent enrolment skills, i.e. you can elegantly "close" your leads on your high-end service or programme.

The central premise of all three options is that you "woo" your prospective clients with relevant and helpful input before attempting to sell them on your high-end offer. If they enjoy and get value from your initial encounters and low-priced material, things may get a little more serious and they become willing to spend more time and money with you.

In marketing terms, we call this relationship building process a *value ladder*. It can be quite profitable if you work the numbers and conversion rates out. The conversion table below illustrates the likely income from one hundred opt-ins into your funnel.

Free giveaway opt-ins	Low-end product sales @ $297	High-end programme or service sign ups @ $5000
1000	10	2
-	$2.970	$10,000

Imagine if this is all you did every month. Even with these conservative conversions, that's a 5-figure income just from leveraging one funnel.

There are differing schools of thought on whether having a lot of low-end products works for a high-end consulting or coaching business. But it doesn't hurt or create too much work to create at least one stepping stone between your first date and your marriage proposal ☺

Whatever product or products you choose to create, make sure it is always of high relevance and high value to your audience and helps them with a key stepping stone to the full solution. Giving someone a "how-to' e-book, webinar or e-course that's put together in a hurry without much research, structure or testing may do more damage than good. It's certainly unlikely to attract people into a premium programme of high-end service.

Having said that, your webinar, video series or online course doesn't have to be fancy as long as it delivers value. The same with membership sites. It's all about giving people a success pathway so they see how working with you is making a difference and they're getting results. You can refine things as you go along to help them get there easier and faster - which adds yet more value. Getting people to pilot it and give you feedback will really help, so don't spend too much time perfecting everything before you launch and start promoting it.

> ※
>
> "The long-term health of your membership is dependent [not on how much content you provide but] but on your people's ability to make progress towards the result they want." – Stu McLaren, Tribe

A lot of people nowadays float the concept and structure of a new programme or service and even get people to sign up for it before it's even live. That way you can test out the level of interest and tweak your sales copy during a "launch" phase.

If you keep the content insightful and the dialogue helpful during this launch period, through an email follow up series or social media group, you can continue to provide value, develop the relationship and attract further interest. You'd be surprised how many people will readily pay $500 for a workshop or even $2500 for an online course, yet aren't ready to invest $5000 on your high-end consulting or coaching programme. And of course, some people will never buy – they just like to date but nothing serious ☺

Interestingly, what I've found on both sides of the fence - as a customer and as a provider – the decision to buy or sign up is not just about the money. It's simply about someone's readiness to commit to a course of action. Sometimes it's a mindset thing: about how they *feel* about you; or having a certain way of working, learning and developing; or moving on from a past bad experience.

The *Engage-Educate-Enrol* pathway as illustrated in the client relationship building funnels shown earlier, is an important part of leveraged consulting. At the end of the free thing, go ahead and ask them to sign up for your paid programme or service. In some cases, even before I get to the point of telling people about my programme, they'll ask "do you have a programme I can sign up for"?

REFORMING YOUR BUSINESS ARCHITECTURE

Any business nowadays exists in a highly competitive and changing environment, one that requires effective, responsive and well-managed processes and practices both to survive and to thrive. Relying on passion, specialist expertise, common sense and gut instinct to grow your business or streamline operations can only take you so far.

Having said that, it is important you build on the strong foundations laid down from what you have achieved so far. The power of any leveraged consulting strategy starts with leveraging *you-* as the expert(s) at the heart of the business.

What this means in practice is defining clearly (or reconfirming) your vision of what success means to you personally or for your firm, and particularly in relation to how you wish to serve and help people. This underpins all of your choices concerning the marketing, sales and delivery of what you do.

For those with a strategic goal of creating a value-driven, digitally-smart and profitable enterprise that will give you both financial freedom and personal fulfilment in the long term, you need careful planning to create the right architecture where you understand your target audience in terms of the business models, systems and processes you put in place. This includes ways of supporting how you:

- Align and target your purpose and profitability;
- Position and brand your professional expertise;
- Price and package a core offer around what you uniquely do;
- Systematise and scale how you promote and deliver it.

To harness the power of leveraged consulting, you'll need to implement an *Engage-Educate-Enrol* process to support client acquisition and onboarding that fosters trust and confidence in you. This will pay you back in dividends in terms of helping you to build an audience, convert the right people into actual clients and onboard them effectively as users and beneficiaries of your programme or service.

When you can deliver your expertise in different kinds of ways, digitally and remotely, this enables you to work with and impact more people.

Business design and understanding the critical levers for success is what ensures your marketing plan, sales process and service delivery suit your style, personality, resources and skills. Business growth is possible when you can identify what shifts you might need to make to take your business to a new level.

This moves us onto talk about strategy - onwards to the next chapter!

First, if it's useful, take a pause to capture any ideas and action points you have regarding the power of leverage in your business.

ACTION NOTES

_____

_____

_____

_____

_____

_____

_____

_____

_____

_____

_____

_____

_____

Chapter 2

LEVERAGED STRATEGY

Choose What's Right For You

"The significant problems of our time won't be solved at the same level of thinking that created them."

Albert Einstein

KEY POINTS

❖ Your leveraged consulting strategy must encompass developing the mindset, structure, systems and teams you need to grow the business.

❖ The important strategic question to ask yourself is does your current business (or business plan) represent everything you are capable of.

❖ Creating clear, strong foundations for your business will provide the steer needed to make smart decisions, both internally and externally.

❖ The reason so many small businesses struggle to grow is they don't have a strategic approach to attracting, enrolling and serving clients.

❖ When you focus your strategy on a combination of two, three or more global growth trends, it means you're at the forefront, ahead of the crashing waves, and fishing in fresh waters.

❖ One of the biggest challenges for consultants and coaches wanting to grow and scale is making the leaps in both mindset and infrastructure needed for stepwise innovation.

❖ The important part of creating a profitable business is how much time you're spending on what, relative to how much income you're making.

❖ Being strategic about business means joining up your vision - who you help, with what, why, and how - with the right branding, marketing & delivery models.

❖ The single most important element for reforming your business architecture is to get crystal clear on what you do, why and for whom, and then to create value around it and choose a vehicle to deliver it.

❖ From the moment that someone engages with you to the results you help them achieve, the impact you have on their thinking, business or life is what builds your tribe and fosters customer loyalty down the line.

❖ Business planning is not just about what you sell, it's about how you align, target, position, package, promote and deliver it.

❖ The best time to start building your digital platform was 5-10 years ago; the next best time is now.

❖ When you understand what's possible with leveraged consulting in the digital age and you're clear on your business strategy, you can make a bolder move to play your greatest game and achieve your true potential.

MAPPING OUT THE ROAD TO SUCCESS

Over the years, I've worked with hundreds of self-employed professionals and small businesses on strategic reviews and business plans aimed at helping them achieve greater success, be it in terms of operational efficiency, marketing, sales or revenue growth. The diagnostic we do identifies powerful turning points across a set of key dimensions to provide a digital roadmap for implementing more leveraged approaches.

What I notice is that many invest quite heavily in marketing tools, advertising and sales training (focusing especially on websites, social media marketing, email marketing, ad placements etc.). Yet rarely have they invested in the fundamental foundations for any of this to work effectively: message and process.

Two major areas I help them with that results in a stepwise jump in their success are clarity and leverage. Our most critical tasks are: (a) to develop a clear, unique and compelling brand *message* and (b) to improve the sales *process*. Together we create a structured and effective pathway to engage, educate and enrol more clients (and/or more of the right clients). This puts a system in place that works dependably and consistently to bring in high-quality leads and convert them seamlessly into clients.

There's also a third area concerned with the development of online education. While this is a fast-growing trend in the coaching world, it's a somewhat newer focus for the consulting industry.

While I've only more recently started helping others with this in the business world more recently, my professional career is in e-learning and digital capability. I've also designed and led blended learning programmes for university staff and students, and dabbled in the past with online coaching. Since online education is part of my own leveraged consulting strategy, I'd be not to add this into the mix.

I'm certainly ramping up my efforts to create courses and mentoring programmes for my business, which I can deliver online and that provide me with additional or alternative streams of revenue and are not dependent on physically going out to work with clients onsite or running classroom-based workshops.

I'll keep coming back to the fact that in this book is not advocating an all-in digital business. Neither am I saying go build and sell digital products. I continue to run both a face-to-face consulting practice and an online education business and creating opportunities that are a blend of the two. I'd never say to completely ditch working face-to-face with people, or indeed that you should give up delivering one-to-one services – this can be a vital component in your high-end business model.

Your business strategy and delivery models should suit what *you* do, what you *want* to do and how you wish to work. As the business owner, we have the power to set our own goals and metrics for success. What I am doing, and feel compelled to do, is give professional experts the insights to see what's possible in the digital age so they can solve current issues as well as open up new possibilities that ensure growth and sustained success.

I want you first and foremost to get a good sense of how you *might* leverage digital approaches to support and accelerate your business journey. What you define as success – the ultimate destination and milestones along the way - is entirely of your choosing. The next chapters will help you set out your stall, improve your client acquisition and create a roadmap to implement the approaches you decide are the right steps forward.

Consider where you are now and what your most pressing needs look like.

✓ Are you just setting up your own consulting or coaching practice and looking for help with business planning?

✓ Are you already in business and looking to get more clients but want to work smarter not harder?

✓ Do you find networking and sales daunting and you're looking for alternative ways to win business?

✓ Do you have a bigger vision for your existing business and want to grow your influence, impact and income?

✓ Are you overwhelmed with all the different marketing strategies, tools and tactics and want a simple way to decide what fits your business?

✓ Do you enjoy helping people, teaching, explaining, showing people how to do things and want to add more value to your existing clients or customers?

✓ Do you wish you knew how to create, market and deliver educational products, tools or programmes so you can create new streams of income and help more people?

In chapter 3 – Leveraging You - we'll explore what drives you personally – what is the main purposes and drivers for your business. Chapters 4, 5 and 6, are aimed at deepening understanding of how you can create leverage in your marketing, sales and delivery models. And in chapter 7, we'll use the *7 Dimensions of Success* framework from my signature programme to review the critical levers in your business design architecture and create your leveraged roadmap.

For now, we're going to focus on strategy.

Your leveraged consulting business strategy must encompass developing the mindset, structure, systems and teams you need to grow the business.

CREATING A LEVERAGED STRATEGY

A key goal of your business strategy is to help you achieve success. Right? But what does success actually look like? What is a leveraged consulting strategy intended to achieve and how will we know how far to go with it?

As business owners, we want to succeed - obviously. And anyone who picked out this book is looking for ways to be "successful". There's a reason the book *"Good to Great"* by Jim Collins is a popular read – it speaks to our desire for success, to improve ourselves and to seek excellence in what we do. However, most people don't know exactly what "good" looks like to them, let alone "great".

> ※
>
> "If you're starting small with no aspirations of becoming larger, or you can see the ceiling of success as soon as you start, you'll remain small by design."
> – Anthony Morrison, The Hidden Millionaire

I tend to look at business success in a very holistic way, beyond being all about profit patterns and year-on-year income growth. As captain of our own ship, independent consulting professionals can define our own business goals in terms of what success means to us personally and the influence, impact and income we desire.

The subtitle for this book incorporates an aspiration for success in growing a high-end client business, which may look on the surface like a money goal. But high-end is also about your expert status as a consultant, your ability to work at the top of the tree, so to speak. You deserve to get paid what you're worth, but you also merit the bigger influence and impact you can have in the world beyond your local face-to-face clientele.

I think *feeling* successful is in part about the personal satisfaction, the sense of achievement and fulfilment you get from the work you do, and in part about whether your income is sufficient to support the people, interests and pursuits you care about outside of work. While some of us certainly enjoy our work, I suspect that's not the whole story. In terms of success, we need to think beyond "work to live"; beyond the "doing" of work, beyond plans and targets, and move towards what the business brings to your life, how it impacts on you and whether the work fits how you want to live.

Maybe you feel you're successful in some ways and not in others or perhaps you're feeling that, so far, you're wholly unsuccessful. You might be close to what you deem successful and setting new goals, just starting out and don't yet have a clear roadmap, ready to quit, or up and down somewhere in between.

Think ahead about the kind of working model you want to create to grow your business. Building a workable and sustainable business is a marathon not a sprint. It means working slow and steady, but with the right business architecture in place, you can make headway towards success quite quickly.

Let me pause for a moment and ask you this: what would success look like to you? It's a very critical question. If you are a prospective client of mine, and after getting a picture of your current situation, I nearly always ask this question - right off the bat. If I'm doing a group workshop, we start by drawing a "rich picture" – a visual representation - first the now and then the future scenario as a basis for reflection and planning.

Often the person on the receiving end gives a lot of "umms" and "ahhs" … and waffles around some vague answer. And to be fair, it's tough to articulate a focused answer on demand, but that's what we unpick in the ensuing discussion.

Being able to visualise what success looks like will provide enormous drive and motivation when you need it (depending of course on how badly you want it!) Certainly, success means different things to different people. And please note too that your *potential* for success (i.e. your CV) and your *actual* success are two very different things.

The important strategic question to ask yourself right now is does your current business (or business plan) represent everything you are capable of.

Wherever you are on your business journey, what success means to you at each stage of your business growth, is often constrained by the set of limiting beliefs and conceptions we carry with us from our past experiences or even our upbringing. Along with fear of failure (or success!), this can mean we pass or procrastinate on taking action to test out a new idea or opportunity.

It's hard for you make changes in your thinking, business planning and process if the problem is hiding in a blind spot. If you're stuck or struggling, the answer may lie in various aspects of what building a business requires.

✓ *Is it in your vision or how you run your business?*

✓ *Is it your attitude to risk and trying something new to you?*

✓ *Is it that you've got a bit out of touch with what your market wants?*

✓ *Is it how you brand yourself and how clear your message is?*

✓ *Is it a lack of systems and tools or knowing which to use for what?*

✓ *Is it your efficiency and you feel you can't turn the wheel faster?*

What I'm saying here is that lack of success is often not due to a lack of capability, but rather a lack of a strong, in-focus picture of what success looks like in each element of your business (and life!) This is why having a business mentor or some kind of external review and challenge is extremely valuable for finding what's often in plain sight for someone other than yourself.

I know from bitter experience that, after a while, a lack of clarity on your best next move (or "flying blind" as Rich Schefren puts it) totally zaps your drive and enthusiasm. It can also cause paralysis by analysis. I'm an intelligent person and can work most things out quite quickly. But I spent almost two years in the desert of doubt, confusion and overwhelm, constantly changing my mind, standing in my own way.

Your intelligence, skills, experience, personality, creativity, connections or indeed "luck" do NOT determine whether you will be successful or how successful.

Actual success is determined in part by operational constraints and in part by attitudinal constraints, both of which can block your path to the promised land. The business model or marketing and sales processes you're using to grow your business – can be the weak links that really cost you! (Don't worry: the final chapter of the book includes an extremely practical tool for identifying your most critical levers for change.)

> ✳
>
> "Strategy isn't just something you obtain and apply from outside of the problem. It's about developing a set of thinking skills that let you solve your problems from the inside out." – Danny Iny, Strategy School

When all is said and done, your business success is about what outcomes are most important to you – and that is a combination of your personal sense of purpose, achievement and satisfaction, and your clients' sense of desire, achievement and satisfaction. If you're not sure, that inner game is what you most need to work on, preferably with a good coach or mentor in your court.

As we explore leveraged strategies, I urge you to have a go at defining *your* dream scenario for what "good" and "great" means to you in terms of success. Create a future vision of the influence, impact and income you desire, how you wish to work, and how you wish to live. That vision needs to be strong enough to drive you forward through testing times as well as provides measures for your progress towards achieving it.

Creating clear, strong foundations for your business will provide the steer needed to make smart decisions, both internally and externally.

The "milestones" on the path to success are worth defining too. These may be outcomes or benefits that emerge along the way, your personal sense of purpose, goodwill generated with your customers, or simply your bank manager or accountant saying you had a profitable year. Think too about the knock-on effect these successes have on your mood, and sense of progress towards your goals.

DEFINING & PLANNING BUSINESS GROWTH

"Growth" is one of the most challenging, daunting and oftentimes mystifying aspects of building a business. People get stuck at the start, in the middle and when they want to scale up. With this in mind, let's look at what we mean by growth in the context of building a consulting business, starting with the end goals at each stage, and how growth is typically measured.

The metrics (and nomenclature) for business growth may differ for specific industries and type of consulting, but here are some of the essential ones.

Metric	Evidence
Increased client/customer base	New engagements and retention
Increased productivity	Operational efficiencies that increase capacity or speed
Increased revenue	Pricing or new /products
Increased market share	New business from competitors
Increased market positioning	Consumer perception of the brand
Increased adjacencies	Expansion into related markets

Using a time-based model, the number of clients you can support coupled with your fee structure is, typically, what determine your profits. But if you can increase productivity – how effectively, efficiently and economically you work – that can give you a little more leverage in your capacity to serve more clients.

Developing a streamlined process for acquiring new clients, finding leveraged ways to serve clients, and using technology to automate key business processes, are all ways to enable growth.

The issue though is that when our client flow is good, we're usually too busy delivering projects to think about more leveraged strategies. There's no space in the brain let alone the diary to spend time improving our efficiency or planning for future growth. We don't feel we have time to hire and train people to take some of the pressure off us. And we often don't dare increase our prices for fear it will all come tumbling down.

For many, it's a case of surviving rather than thriving - keeping the proverbial head above water, working long hours, often doing more for less and feeling unfulfilled. Next level growth can feel like an unattainable goal.

To survive and thrive, you will most definitely need a plan for how you bring in new clients consistently and create sustainable revenue and growth. Leadership, marketing, managing a client pipeline and good communication are crucial parts of the consulting business. But developing the vision and brand message for your business from the get-go is critical.

Yet, so many consultants and small business owners don't do this foundation work; they jump right in and start on the hamster wheel. It's no wonder then that going solo running your own practice can create overwhelm and burnout.

The reason so many small businesses struggle to grow is they don't have a strategic approach to attracting, enrolling and serving clients.

If this sounds like you, then you may be either buying leads or have a burst of marketing that generates some contacts and appointments; you may even have tried some new fandangled marketing method you heard about hoping for a silver bullet.

From this, maybe you gained a new client or a group of clients and then you work with them (usually one-to-one and face-to-face) until that contract is finished before beginning the (dreaded) process of looking for more new clients all over again. It's a feast and famine cycle that feels incredibly stressful, emotionally and financially.

> ✳
>
> "A firm needs to have both little innovations that keep its core offerings fresh, and it needs big innovations that open up entire new service lines."
>
> – Michael Treacy, President of Treacy & Company.

For most solo professionals and small consulting firms, the problem is working out a viable growth strategy out of where they are right now. There's often a mental obstacle of thinking that the only way to grow the business is to duplicate what they already do, which is hard if there's no client flow system in place.

If you're not already working at the high-end, there's a counter-argument to taking on more clients as the first strategy for growth – you simply duplicate a low profit system. The best strategy is to work on leveraging you - increase your perceived value and charge higher fees.

Work on clarifying and building your authority status in a specific niche – your specialism or micro-niche – and invest in improving your positioning and visibility as the go-to expert for that one thing.

This goes beyond just a marketing ploy. It means developing your awareness and knowledge of what clients worry about and need most, which improves your brand messaging and market positioning.

As a thought leadership or solutions provider in one particular area in your field, you can attract clients willing to pay higher fees. And that means working on being a source of new ideas, innovating new service or product developments and building up your intellectual property.

When you focus your strategy on a combination of two, three or more global growth trends, it means you're at the forefront, ahead of the crashing waves, and fishing in fresh waters.

Half the battle with planning for growth is to figure out what's really going on in your business and what's holding you back. It's not always just an operational or tactical issue, it's often a mindset and strategy issue.

Understanding the problem within a holistic frame of "root cause" systems thinking is the best step to resolving it, because otherwise you're just blindly throwing tactical darts at a large dartboard without a bulls-eye.

But systems thinking doesn't always acknowledge what's going on underneath for you, on a personal level, knowing who you are and what you're about, and whether you're working in alignment with your purpose, preferred ways of working and moving towards your vision of success.

Two key things to do in your action plan:

1. You need to pin down what business growth means to you, what to measure in terms of performance and "success" in relation to your goals, and from there look at how your strategy might need to change in terms of moving beyond your current ceiling.

2. You need to correctly diagnose where any bottlenecks to growth lie – determine why something's not working so you can properly apply the best tactics to resolve the problem(s).

But remember to bear in mind that, rather than a tangible marketing issue or operational problem, it might just be a mental barrier or money block to working and earning in a different way. So now let's move on to ways in which you can move the needle for greater leveraged consulting.

MAKING MORE MONEY WITHOUT BURNING OUT

The principal mechanism behind any consulting practice is essentially to exchange valuable expertise for monetary (and non-monetary) rewards. Whether you're set up as a sole trader, partnership or limited company; whether you charge by the hour, day or project – *strategic* planning is crucial to manageable growth and sustained success.

Irrespective of industry, your strategy helps you define the type of clients you target; the services and products you deliver; how you will position and develop your brand; your price points for profitability; and your ambitions for scaling things up.

Your business plan should incorporate the key market assumptions, determine your unique value proposition so you stand out from the crowd, and balance potential risks against intended financial and non-financial benefits. It should also indicate the leveraged business models that will allow you to achieve certain income goals and preferred ways of working.

Building a successful consulting business means deciding on a business design where you're working in the industry and niche you wish to serve, have a consistent stream of clients and a price-point that meets your income needs and doesn't burn you out. That's kind of the ideal, right?

If your strategy is to focus on high-end client work that attracts high-end fees, which is perfectly valid when you're an expert professional in your field, it may take time to establish your place in the market, but you don't need more than one or two clients a month to make a 5-figure income.

Top tier consulting leverages your expertise – from your education and qualifications to your experience and capability. But if you're not positioning and promoting yourself in the right way, you can get stuck charging less than you're worth and doing work that isn't quite a fit to you.

Whether you're just starting up or struggling to gain momentum, having a clear strategic plan ensures you gain the traction you need to earn a living. Once you find your groove, eventually you'll need to bite the bullet and ditch any work you do at the lower tiers to free up time for high-end clients.

Leverage based on a growing reputation and attracting higher fees has become the quickest way for solo professionals and small firms to grow their income, but it still doesn't help with scaling up. However (and confusingly so), most consulting businesses are very conservative in their operating approaches and revenue model. Leverage in the consulting industry is based on traditional hierarchical business models and long-standing practices of the "Big Four" and adopted by smaller professional services firms with growth ambitions.

In the Big 4 model, the hourly rate still governs supreme, and while subscription services are growing (especially in the technology consulting arena), most revenue is generated from annual or one-off contracts. The machinery is a constant grind of business development, onboarding and delivery.

However, even if you hit your revenue targets, there's a problem with this model. If you only deliver one-to-one, face-to-face and "done-for-you" services, that means you're boxing yourself in a corner balancing growth (income) with capacity to deliver (outlay), which means recruiting more and more consultants, client managers and admin support, all of whom need managing.

As a solo professional or small business, growth in staff and workload is probably not the leverage opportunity you want to pursue. I've got around this in the past using an associate model, forming collaborations with other consulting firms or self-employed consultants in order to pull a team together and build temporary capacity when bidding for projects. However, there are challenges there also in terms of profitability, quality management, and scalability.

In most cases, a consulting business starts off by securing a few clients to validate market value and you grow your client base out from there. You're using your knowledge and skills to help your clients, probably working face-to-face on executive coaching, projects and/or "done-for-you" services. Your client pays you for the expertise and value you provide to them in relation to the outcome they want/expect. The outcome for each client is often very different, so you end up tailoring each project rather than having a core methodology that you can apply to all your client work.

What you do - probably (but not always) – is what you have already done in your job and career to earn a regular salary. Going freelance may simply mean being your own boss and doing that same or similar work on a self-employed basis. The initial goal is (at least) to replace your salary.

For some, your business may be based on other interests and experience you've gained helping people or serving a community, such as counselling, raising money, flower arranging, property searching, dog training… you get the idea. (A few of these may not seem high-end, but depending on your niche, customers and value you bring, they can become quite lucrative.) But initially (at least), your goal is to earn a living doing what you love.

Either way, you probably work on an hourly or daily rate basis or perhaps charge per package, assignment or deliverable. Essentially though, you're charging and contracting for your time, which is why we call it "trading time for money". If you stop working day-by-day directly with clients, you stop earning.

Starting up on your own-some is all fine and dandy until you realise that it's actually quite hard to find clients month after month; and it's even harder to get good clients! Finding clients to work with is actually where many consultants get frustrated; they struggle to attract the right clients to them and they struggle to consistently do business development alongside client service delivery.

In the early months, your "problem" is mainly how to get more clients, or better clients, or how to get a more consistent *flow* of clients. When a consultant (read also: coach, designer, therapist, trainer etc) approaches me for help with business growth, they are nearly all coming at it from the traditional viewpoint of one-to-one and mostly face-to-face work with clients.

While it can be profitable, there's an income ceiling. Growing the business with this model can start to feel like an uphill battle, especially if you're not getting good clients paying you decent fees. You're on the proverbial hamster wheel, working longer and longer hours without the financial or lifestyle freedom you wanted.

If you are successful at getting clients, with this unleveraged model, the only way you can free up time without loss of income is to increase your fees, bring in associates or create other streams of revenue. Most consultants are reluctant to increase their fees, for fear of then losing business, and most don't see alternative ways of earning revenue beyond one-to-one work. So longer hours it is ☹

With a time-based model and one-on-one service activities, success comes at a price. Eventually, if you fill your dance card, you'll hit a ceiling – even if you work every single day, there are only so many days in the week. Unless you're living off referrals (as I was for the first three years after setting up as a consultant), usually you spend only 3-4 days delivering paid work; the rest of the time you need to be finding your next clients(s).

> ※
> "When people talk about not getting stuck in the trading-time-for-money trap, what they really want is to adjust the relationship between time and money: how much time for how much money. They want to make *more money in less time.*"
> – Danny Iny, CEO Mirasee

Consultants in this situation (or close to it) are usually earning a decent income. If you charge say just 500 a day (be it £, $, €) and chargeable work is 3 days a week, that's 6000 a month, 72k a year - a decent income by most standards. If you charge twice that as I do, you can work less or earn more. But anything higher, you need a different business model.

Most consultants who are working week in and week out on client projects are burned out and yearn for more time freedom. So ultimately, lack of clients isn't the problem; lack of leverage is the problem. I've certainly felt that in my business, working on back-to-back projects to the point of utter collapse from fatigue and stress, which forced me into some major decisions about how I want to work. This is where my "leveraged living" began.

I love helping people who have taken the exciting entrepreneurial step to start up on their own and need guidance to get their branding and marketing working so they can attract clients. But it's even more exciting working with people who want to increase their influence and impact as well as their income – these leverage goals are what fire me up.

But it's frustrating how locked in people can be about how they build a business and how they use their expertise to be of service. There's actually quite an array of ways to earn revenue from your professional expertise – providing one-to-one, face-to-face services is just one of them!

One of the biggest challenges for consultants and coaches wanting to grow and scale is making the leaps in both mindset and infrastructure needed for stepwise innovation.

If you're relying on your income from services and you're working full out, you're going to feel you lack the time, skills and energy to do new things or do things differently. While I am bearing that in mind, I'd like you to look at strategy in terms of the long-term benefits of introducing leveraged business models before we tackle how you might eliminate any barriers. In my experience, when the "why" is strong enough, the practicality of managing the "how" becomes easier to plan.

In addition to the practicalities, in many cases, we also have to tackle our deep-set ideas about money and profit. We need to move away from the concept of daily rate or billable hours that impose limits on what we feel the market will pay (comparative to our competitors). And we need to overcome any fears concerning the complexity of the transformation required to step up to the next level of revenue growth.

The most important part of creating a highly profitable business is how much time you're spending on what, relative to how much income you're making.

However, at this juncture, I'm simply asking you to stand back for a moment and be open to thinking differently about how you market and deliver your expertise. Once you see that there are different business models you can apply to what you do as a consultant other than one-to-one, "done-for-you" services, you will see the opportunities for building and scaling a successful business more clearly.

EXPANDING YOUR REACH & REVENUE

There are many leveraged strategies that help you expand your reach (the size and location of your audience) and your revenue (the size and variety of your income streams). The foundation though is your professional standing – you, your expertise, your talent, your commitment and your intellectual property. Other strategies can be put into play to support your marketing, sales and service delivery, in order to ramp up the volume and speed of potential customers through your *Engage-Educate-Enrol* process – as described at the start of chapter 1. This includes implementing the digital systems, processes and people needed to reinforce your business operations.

The way consultants and coaches usually get clients and earn income are based upon one-to-one and face-to-face interactions – for example: sales appointments, breakfast meetings, client site visits, tele-coaching and so on. Doing any of your marketing, sales or delivery this way limits your capacity to engaging only a handful of people at any given time. If this type of interaction is your normal modus operandi, you'll know you spend most of your time preparing presentations, travelling, chasing and waiting.

If the people you do end up talking with are well targeted and you have a good success rate, this may keep your client engagements flowing. But success comes at a price: if not stress and exhaustion, doing this week in week out, it's the fact there's a ceiling on your numbers.

In the age of digital communications, I think it's easier for people to understand how you can expand your reach without changing anything much more than the medium employed. But you increase your revenue only by abandoning the norms of how consulting services traditionally operate.

Making the shift to digital marketing and automated sales systems means you have a client attraction machine doing the heavy lifting for you, 24/7 and 365. You achieve leverage in two ways: not only are you able to target and pre-qualify your leads so you have better meetings, but your time is freed up to do other things.

Technology supported systems give you back time in the week to do "billable" work so your revenue increases; but also, you have more time to do *income-generating* activities that yield longer term benefits to you: speaking, writing, networking, especially if you enjoy it.

Digital content creation and digital delivery transforms your business. It enables people to access your expertise who aren't yet ready or able to invest in your high-end face-to-face or one-to-one services. By creating and sharing high value content, you increase your capacity to serve more people in different ways.

DESIGN	DEPLOY	DEVELOP	DISTRIBUTE
One-to-One Services	One-to-Many Events	One-to-Many Programmes	One-to-Mass Products

increasingly digital

In a fully leveraged consulting business, in your strategic plan, how you operate and the kind of work you do, is really up to you to decide. Consider your goals in both financial and personal terms will help you see what is a good balance for you right now between your one-to-one work and digitally-delivered activities.

There are plenty of opportunities to reach, influence and impact higher numbers of people with one-to-many and one-to-mass products, programmes and events; but is this how you wish to run your business, does it suit your preferred type and method of working, do the numbers stack up to generate the income you want?

Digital products may well match your high-end consulting services if you achieve the necessary quantity of sales at the price you set. Customers understand that the level of interaction with you – up close and personal – is less, but they're also paying less. It's all about value for money in terms of the benefits and results they get.

With a good programme design, packaged and promoted well, you can provide a high-end experience for your participants, which mirrors working with you one-to-one but at a lower price point.

Regardless of the delivery method, what you do should bring about a tangible and highly valued outcome and personalised experience for your client yet allows you to reach and impact more people than is possible in traditional consulting practice models.

It's okay to integrate just those strategies that leverage *you* – in terms of improving your brand clarity to attract more and better clients – or create leverage in your marketing and sales through automation and structure. This can achieve quite significant improvements in how well you're able to generate leads, enrol clients and garner repeat business.

Nonetheless, there are far bigger gains when you take on board the fuller vision of leveraged consulting. When you make the changes in how you *deliver* your expertise, you can achieve a massive leap in income.

If you're a solo professional and want to move beyond trading your personal hours or days for money; and equally so for small firms, you need other kinds of leverage: leveraged delivery. You can increase your income substantially by creating, packaging and selling branded products and courses.

There's no magic bullet with leveraged consulting - strengthening one dimension strengthens the others. Being strategic means that your business gets stronger with each area of improvement in your digital strategy.

As you bring each area into play, I'm convinced you will see a substantial shift in the success of your business over the next few months and years. For now, though, I want you to remember one thing.

From the moment that someone engages with you to the results you help them achieve, the impact you have on their thinking, business or life is what builds your tribe and fosters customer loyalty down the line.

The guidance in the early chapters focuses on laying down good foundations. It will help you to clarify your core offer, build an audience, and boost your positioning and brand in the marketplace.

Being value-driven is an important mindset for success here. That means having a fundamental commitment to create meaningful outcomes for your clients. Usually, for service professionals this is second nature, but it doesn't always translate into how you engage with prospective clients.

Looking at your business through the lens of your ideal client (one you enjoy working with and is profitable) will enable you to identify your biggest bottlenecks to growth and pluck out the one or two key design elements that when optimised will enable you to make tangible gains.

This value-driven approach to business development is for service providers who want to achieve high levels of impact, influence and income from their expertise yet hate the whole sales side of pitching to clients and "closing the deal".

At one level, this may simply mean gaining greater clarity around your professional niche – even reinventing yourself around one micro-niche rather than trying to be all things to all people. On another level, it may mean discovering new ways to deliver your expert services and working from a different business revenue model.

Two examples that worked quite well for me and illustrate the points are:

1. Running *group workshops* in limited locales or onsite for clients can earn you a decent living if the numbers stack up and you repeat it several times a year, especially if you can offer attendees further opportunities to continue working

with you. But unless you can successfully franchise it out, this is not a leveraged or scalable business model.

2. A specific *niche product* can deliver repeatable training to the masses and if chosen well may make you competitive or distinctive for a while. But the real leverage is in the relationship you develop with your participants, which can support future engagement and sales.

BECOMING AN EDUCATIONAL ENTREPRENEUR

In adopting these kinds of leveraged approaches to build and grow your consulting business, principally means stepping into the role of "educational entrepreneur". The most apt definition for our purposes here is this:

An educational entrepreneur leverages their expertise by developing education-rich products and programmes to drive business marketing and revenue growth whilst providing a high-value customer experience.

Placing education at the heart of your business strategy has many benefits for leveraged consulting. Publishing expert content positions you, discernibly, as a thought leader in your field. You stand out as an authority helping people to understand changing contexts, gain new perspectives on the challenges they face, and to see how to get to the solutions they want.

The founder of Choose2Matter.org, Angela Meiers, provides a poignant summary: "Entrepreneurship is driven by the innate need to create, build, grow and impact. When we connect education and entrepreneurship, it's all about taking control of your journey to spend your life using your strengths and genius to make an impact."

What this means in context of professional services is a business strategy that is based on using education as a value asset. You use it to build trusting relationships, serve a specific need in the marketplace, support transformation and make a difference.

Even before someone becomes a client or customer, you can have influenced their ideas and made a big impact on their business and life. Your prospects are looking for leadership, empathy and integrity as much as expertise. And as an educator, you can deliver this far more effectively than any sales pitch ever will.

Leveraged consulting is about tapping into your zone of genius and most profitable market, and delivering what you do in a different (more leveraged) way. Most consultants and coaches are missing a boatload of money by not using their expertise to drive their marketing and new streams of revenue.

The combination of digital marketing and online learning is a remarkable opportunity. Both continue to be massive growth industries as people are out in droves on their computers, tablets and phone, needing solutions and searching for help, payment card in hand. Your job is to make it easier for them they find you.

Giving people something of value that helps solve a problem they have – i.e. expert guidance – is extremely profitable. By helping people get what they need, you're an ally - a partner and trusted advisor - rather than a tiresome salesperson. Rather than "done-for-you", your mission is to help someone learn how to bring about changes themselves, which yield the tangible outcome or gains they desire.

Education is an elegant bridge between engaging and enrolling a prospective client that progresses naturally through to working with that client. The education you provide can take many forms: such as writing, speaking, coaching, mentoring and teaching.

When you layer in expert interaction with your target audience, you're simultaneously providing a high value experience whilst building credibility and trust. Giving first makes it easier for the right people to say yes to working with you – by reciprocity.

In all my searches on the term educational entrepreneur (ship), while I've found a lot on both content marketing and course building. However, I've found very little about education as a business model for professional service providers who want to take a more innovative and entrepreneurial approach to growing their business.

There seems a general absence of support out there to help consultants and coaches break through the typical limits of one-to-one and "done-for-you" services. And there's even less support to help them design a cohesive leveraged strategy and business architecture to support a one-to-many approach.

If you do a search on "what is an educational entrepreneur" or "educational entrepreneurship", the simple definition that comes up twists the concept towards either education leaders who are entrepreneurial in bringing about change in their sector. Other interpretations of the term lean towards entrepreneurship education, i.e. the education of entrepreneurs or talk about the kind of knowledge, skills and attitudes needed to succeed as an entrepreneur.

While a few sources mention how to turn your expertise (even your hobby) into an education business, in my view, none of these capture the opportunity in the consulting industry; they don't express the full potential of business growth as an educational entrepreneur.

So, let me knock down a few misconceptions right off the bat here and define for the consulting professional what educational entrepreneurship is and isn't about.

First what it isn't. It is not about building an education business - although that may well be one part of what evolves. It's also not about churning out tonnes of "how-to" content across social media - although becoming a visible authority in a particular niche is certainly a part of it, especially if you're currently hiding your light under a bushel. And third, it is not about educating entrepreneurs or creating entrepreneurship training – although, as you'll find out, that audience has certainly been a focus for me personally.

What it is about then? Well, I describe educational entrepreneurship as an approach to business growth based on three mutually reinforcing points of leverage, all highly fitting with the consulting profession.

- The first is using education to add to your competitive advantage in terms of positioning you as an authority;

- The second is using education as a basis for marketing and lead generation;

- And the third is using education as a vehicle for delivering your subject expertise in new ways to generate additional streams of revenue.

As a solo professional, small business owner or partner in a consulting firm, whether you see yourself as an entrepreneur or an innovator per se, is probably debatable. But I'd hazard a guess that to some degree, you're already delivering some kind of education or valuable know-how in your client-facing activities, even if only in a face-to-face setting. What you may not have considered is how to monetise it.

Many of the larger professional service firms will have an educational element to their client work, even if it's just briefing sessions, demonstrations or workshops you run as part of your business development and client engagement activities. Perhaps you run training programmes, and these may form part of a professional accreditation depending on your industry. You may even have developed your own standard and certification. Again: what's possible depends on your industry and your leadership within that industry.

I'd argue that these initiatives definitely qualify as "edu-preneurship" – building a training wing on an existing business as an additional stream of revenue – I've done that too. If any of the above sounds like you, hopefully it's not a hard transition into seeing what you do as both educational and entrepreneurial.

I don't pretend this is an entirely new concept in either consulting or indeed marketing. But educational entrepreneurship is not explicitly defined as a business model for consulting firms, which tends to be dominated by service delivery, and to a degree subscription services, rather than product development. With respect to solo professionals, it will be interesting to see how the label "educational entrepreneur" catches on ☺.

BALANCING VALUE FOR MONEY

Obviously, we want our business to be lucrative, but our (other) primary goal is to deliver valuable and tangible outcomes for our clients. This way, they keep coming back and tell all their friends about us! In fact, you can grow your revenue simply by clarifying your *value* to the market place.

When your profit and loss account is looking worrying, it's only natural for you to rethink the balance of giving (value through service) and receiving (cash flow and revenue). For instance, when profit is down you face many difficult choices to bring customers back or attract new customers, such as:

- *Do you put prices down or discount?*

- *Do you reduce your costs or increase value?*

- *Do you do just enough to keep going or do you invest to grow?*

A key point here is how your business model affects your likelihood of burnout as we discussed above (e.g. working harder possibly for less) but also your brand (i.e. perceived value for money). Value for money is a really critical metric that positions you in the marketplace – that doesn't mean how cheap you are or whether you offer the most deliverables, it means whether your products and services are seen as worth the fees you charge.

Clarifying and articulating your value and the results your deliver is paramount. Put simply: if you offer a benefit to your client that matches a need, want or problem and they perceive that benefit is greater than the cost, they will buy from (or hire) you.

The "right" value for money strategy for consultants is one that strikes a balance between desirability in the marketplace, and the available services, quality, costs and competition.

> ※
> "Selling is easy when you're selling something people want. Easily the most important (and likely the hardest) part of your marketing is making sure your offer is dialled into the market correctly." – Taylor Welch & Chris Evans, Traffic & Funnels

Below are some examples from recent strategic questions I had from clients and the solutions we put in place:

STRATEGIC DECISION	TACTICAL NEED	IMPACT EVALUATION	CHANGE OUTCOME
Should I/we follow or deviate from our competitors?	How to differentiate our value and avoid reducing our prices.	Greater clarity and targeting for our expertise yield increased positioning in the marketplace.	Created an authentic and visible brand to showcase the distinctive benefits of our service.
Should I/we lower costs or increase our value?	How to serve both the customer and ourselves by delivering in a more cost-effective way.	Greater efficiency in our processes yields increased value whilst reducing cost to serve.	Moved from paper to digital to reduce costs and at the same time offer added value to customers.
Should I/we focus on being purposeful or profitable?	How to systematise and scale what we already do well.	Greater leverage of our time and expertise means delivering results to more people.	Developed systems for automating key business processes to allow us to grow.

There are clear ways to optimise what you are already doing to readdress any imbalances in cost-benefit ratios, so it's win-win for you and your clients. No need to start from scratch. However, here's a quick steer on the pros and cons of value versus money driven approaches:

- Creating more value always increases engagement with your brand, as people gain more trust and respect for what you do.

- Discounting on price lowers the perceived value of a product or service and yields only temporary engagement and loyalty.

- Cost efficiency drives can be a distraction for your business, pushing you to closer boundaries of quality and customer satisfaction.

- Cost reduction over time is likely to erode customer trust and respect for your brand.

Many service organisations in the public "not-for-profit" sectors have little choice but to instigate cost-cutting and added-value type change programmes due to reliance on government funding and requirements for regulatory compliance. As an independent in the private sector, you have more choices about your expert value, more control of your costs and more flexibility on your pricing strategies.

Have you noticed some businesses now offer a "pay what you want" pricing? There is no fixed price; you pay what you felt it was worth (for the quality, experience, service and so on). That's putting value for money to the test and relies heavily on delighting your customer!

Remember, there are millions spending millions every day. So, you might want to adjust your thinking around your pricing and immerse yourself in the land of the affluent!

GETTING GOOD AT STRATEGY

Strategy is about taking ideas, questions, options, and making sense of everything. It requires the thinking skills and intelligence to see how to do things better and the planning skills and discipline to actually take action to do them.

Raising your leverage capacity and achieving your true potential is not just about growing the number of clients you have. Choosing the right business model is critical to success – in the sense of what success looks like for you. The business strategy you decide upon is largely governed by the "leveraged" lifestyle you desire, how you like to work with people and what works best for getting client results.

When you start up in business, it's usual to develop a "business plan" and part of this is to set out your vision, the rationale for your idea and the market research that supports it. From there, you explain the specific products, programmes and/or services you will offer and why they're important to your intended market.

Most of the time, we're so busy hustling to find clients and then busy working with them, we often fail to make time for strategic thinking. However, when you do carve out some time to focus concentrated effort on strategic decisions for growth and identify the critical "levers" for change, this is what produces the fastest breakthroughs.

> ❋
> "[Great leaders] choose to exert only calculated force where it will be effective, rather than stringing and struggling with pointless tactics." - Ryan Holiday, The Obstacle Is the Way

I'd venture to say that in most cases consultants, coaches etc - as professional service providers - put their hearts and souls into helping the people they serve. However, running a successful business requires way more than just deep subject or technical knowledge and interest. You need to juggle getting the work, doing the work, managing the business, learning and improvement – simultaneously! And that requires strategy.

Leveraged strategies can be about doing the same things better, but it also is about leaving the comfort of familiar "hustle" activities – playing it safe if you like – and moving towards innovation and new opportunities for yourself and your business. This can feel like a risk, but is the only way to thrive in the battlefield of an ever-competitive market.

What if making a new opportunity work is not purely dependent on having a great strategy, but also your personal capability to implement it? Being prepared to challenge yourself and adapt to changes in the business environment is the sign of an entrepreneur who wants to go beyond their current level of play. And that's who this book is for. Are you willing to learn and figure things out if you have a guide to help you?

> ※
> "Strategy isn't
> something you have,
> it's something you do."
> – Danny Iny

Your current level of knowledge and skills have taken you to where you are today in your business. If you want to grow beyond that, to thrive and grow, you need to take the reins on your own success. The entrepreneurial capabilities that consultancy type business owners need aren't ones to leave to chance. However, just because we talk about business transformation – which I realise can sound a tad scary – it doesn't mean you can't take transitional steps towards it.

Let's just be clear on one thing though. With regards to strategy, there is an important distinction between business improvement and business transformation. In this book, we tackle both but they are not the same. A little bit of focused improvement work can be sufficient to move a lever or two, and the resulting change builds belief and the confidence to make further changes. Bigger changes require bigger decisions. In the main, transformation requires a leap of faith to a new way of thinking and doing.

With the technologies at your disposal today, you'd be amiss *not* to start rethinking your existing business model, building a digital platform to share your expert content and exploring new and improved ways to serve your target audience.

There have been serious shifts in customer expectations with regard to how they engage with businesses and brands, ease of access to information and expert support. The level of speed and convenience digital can offer are critical factors that drive decisions to work with you.

The best time to start building your digital platform was 5-10 years ago; the next best time is now.

A digital platform feeds two key functions. Frist, it provides you with a distinctive online presence so you gain greater visibility and credibility; and it integrates your marketing and sales process to help you engage, educate and enrol your ideal clients seamlessly and on autopilot. And second, a digital platform allows you to deliver consulting or coaching type interactions in highly leveraged ways through blended or wholly online programmes and courses as additional streams of income.

DECIDING ON YOUR POINTS OF LEVERAGE

At its simplest level, here's a representation of the different points of leverage that you can use to support how you attract and work with clients – namely, leveraged marketing, leveraged sales and leveraged delivery.

Placing this within our *strategy* (the outer shell), once again we place YOU at the heart of everything – you are your business. Now we have all the key vehicles of our leveraged consulting strategy (and indeed the structure for this book).

It's a structured and synergistic process, but you can decide to implement changes in your business architecture one step at a time. Let's look at the key vehicles for leverage at each point in turn.

A **COMPELLING BRAND MESSAGE & HIGH VALUE OFFER** that drives audience engagement...	so you can	**ATTRACT** laser-targeted, pre-qualified, hyper-responsive leads and prospects for your business.
A **RELIABLE CONVERSION PROCESS** that drives high-quality enrolments & sales...	so you can	**CONVERT** those leads and prospects into client partners who enrol in your programme with ease and grace and commit to doing their end of the work.
A **HIGH-END SIGNATURE DELIVERABLE** that can be accessed by clients predominantly online and drives revenue gains...	so you can	**DELIVER** what you promise to clients in a flexible way to help them get the outcomes, performance or transformation they want.

A further important point of leverage is achieved when you capture the *result* of all of the above working effectively so you can feed it back into the system.

A **GREAT CUSTOMER EXPERIENCE** that drives your credibility & leadership...	so you can	**EVALUATE** outcomes, garner testimonials and referrals that drives future marketing.

Now I appreciate strategy and planning isn't everyone's favourite part of the business. And if we're not tuned in or under pressure, it feels hard. Right now, you probably feel you already have too little time to maintain even "business as usual" let alone start innovating and making what may be perceived as risky changes with only the distant promise of transformation.

Business improvement and taking transitional steps may be all you're ready for now. And that's ok too if it takes you closer to the promised land. Just make sure you're realistic about your goals and the results you can expect making incremental improvements. If you're wanting to shift your whole business towards a more

> ※
> "Transforming your business isn't about doing a million different things. It's about finding one big thing and then leveraging that." — Frank Kern

focused, profitable and sustainable model, transitional steps may stretch the timeline considerably but you can still make it work.

Before thinking about which technologies best support our leveraged strategy, it's important to understand there are key distinctions between sales and marketing in terms of client engagement and the customer experience. This will be music to the ears of professionals who wince at any notion of selling, pitching or prospecting. Because here we're talking about harnessing the power of online platforms to build a highly targeted and receptive audience.

One of the biggest business building mistakes people make is to grow beyond your core, not *from* your core. Building out from your core expertise can be more systematic, high leverage and high return. On the other hand, looking at markets or products outside your core business brings high risk and no guaranteed leverage; certainly, it's not what this book is about.

This is why you're best to start by leveraging *you* and getting crystal clear on your unique value proposition. If you're at all unclear and confused about your foundations - your focus, your niche, your deliverables or your methodologies – chances are your prospective clients will be too. And lack of clarity leads to lack of business. So, get this as dialled in as possible.

Being a "generalist" is what forces consultants to work harder than they should need to, chasing after anything and everything. When you have a focus - a specialism - and a unique method that only you can do, it's a game changer.

For professional service providers, it's so crucial to find your unique value proposition and bring it to light. Because standing out and having a clear voice means that you have a clear and solid platform to rise above the noise of what is otherwise a commodity industry. There's so much hype out there especially on social media. If you can communicate with total clarity what you're about, what you deliver, you're going to get noticed and attract the right clients to you.

After my first year or so working in the business advice or business mentoring arena, I realised I was doing something different to other consultants and coaches. While they were buying leads and appointments and working on their selling, pitching and prospecting skills, I was having quality conversations with people who had signed up to get my information and applied for a strategy session.

You see, what I learned from my internet-based business is to filter prospects, so that those I spoke with or met actually qualify for my time. Rather than traditional sales driven marketing, I took a customer focused approach: engaging and educating my target audience, which attracted business to me rather than me chasing down leads and sales appointments.

Instead of "Ask and you may receive", shift to "Give and you shall receive"; it works very well for service providers.

From there, I started helping other consultants and expert service providers to make the shift, to think differently about how to market and deliver their expertise towards a more strategic, digitally-smart and education-focused business model. My consulting and coaching shifted towards supporting strategic planning and digital transformation, which has become my genius zone ☺.

DEVELOPING A STRATEGIC PLAN

Being strategic means being laser focused, selective and systematic about what you do, why, to whom, which governs how, where and when you market. A strategic plan certainly goes a long way to making your efforts both organised, manageable and prosperous.

A strategic plan for leveraged consulting focuses on five pillars: your vision, your business model, and the people, processes and systems you put in place to drive and support it.

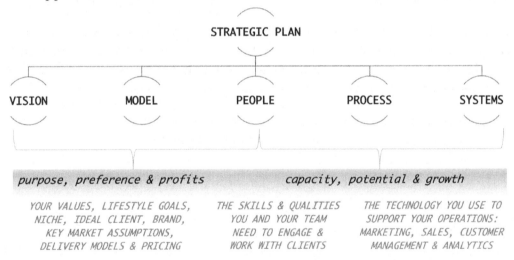

As the diagram here shows, what you want to achieve – in terms of your *vision* of success once again – is determined by the *purpose* behind your business, your *preference* for how you like to work (and perform best) and the *profits* you need to generate to support your lifestyle goals. How this happens is through your business *model*, the *people* you need (in terms of admin or tech support, sales advisers etc), to support the *processes* and *systems* you put in place.

The operations part helps you set out how you build, grow and scale your business to meet the vision and goals you have. Here, you can also partly consider "people" in terms of the audiences you have access to, online and offline, as well as professional networks and partnerships. Aim to be one step ahead of yourself.

Remembering the burnout warning, it's important you have sufficient *capacity* to do marketing, sales and delivery (and the admin running your business entails) at each stage of your business growth. Think also about your *potential* in terms of the marketing activities you enjoy and have skills to do well or who you need to bring on board into your support team.

Clearly in preparing the business plan, there are many elements you should ideally incorporate, especially if you're expanding your delivery model. But don't make it so dense you can't see the wood for the trees. In my experience of supporting small business start-ups and "solopreneurs", most business plans simply need to identify the core pillars of an effective strategy.

Being strategic about business means joining up your vision - who you help, with what, why, and how - with the right branding, marketing & delivery models.

Once you're clear on the why and what, create a cash flow forecast, which determines the targets for your marketing and sales efforts and the financial performance metrics. Ideally, you'd also look at the wider goals for your business and how you personally envisage success, as we've talked about before.

Contrary to this common practice in business, people who set up as a freelance consultant or coach, don't always plan their business with this kind of research and rigour. Did you? I certainly didn't go through it in such a structured way 12+ years ago when I first started out. (I think they call it "winging it" ☺)

So, let's do it now, just a simplified version. In relation to the diagram above, write down your thoughts on the following strategic questions:

---

1) *What's your vision of success? (I.e. how will you know when you're "successful", what are your measures?)*

2) *What's the core product, programme or service you offer (or want to develop)?*

3) *How do (or will) you deliver it (or how do you want to or prefer to deliver it)?*

4) *What are your preferred channels to marketing and promote it?*

5) *How do you handle the sales process to pull in customers/clients?*

Next, operationally, look at the key business processes and systems you need, especially how you will communicate your offer, manage relationships, on-board and work with clients. There's also the question of how you will manage risk, finances, people (if you have employees or associates) and admin.

Business planning is not just about what you sell, it's about how you align, target, position, package, promote and deliver it.

Once up and running, businesses tend to focus only on reviewing the numbers – the financial balance sheet - and all too rarely check back that the market assumptions they made initially in their business plan actually held true. For example, whether their brand fits their ideal customers or whether they are able to build relationships to support repeat business or rely on new clients coming in. We often soldier on and think that the problems we face are just the normal challenges everyone has running a business.

When a business is struggling or growth stalls, it's easy to focus only on short-term tactics to get more customers, such as price-cutting or promotional discounts or extras. It's much rarer to see service businesses focusing on developing new product offers; they tend to stick to what they know and already do well.

When you do branch out or kick off a new product idea or delivery model, you will need to dive into a lot more detail and use evidence to back up whether it has legs.

Let's call this your business design architecture, as depicted below. I know it doesn't look like a building, but essentially, the blue area represents your foundations and the top layer is what you want to achieve after constructing the middle bit. (Hopefully, the specific terminologies are fairly self-explanatory, enough for our purposes here.)

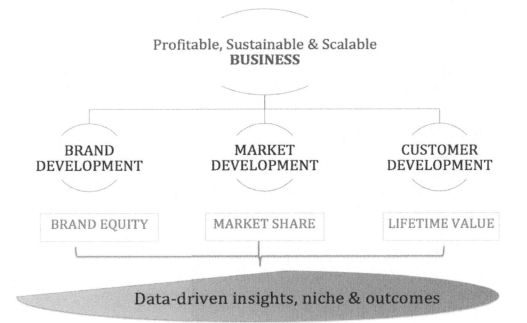

The key point is to see the *connectedness* between brand, market and customer development for your business. This is what makes the difference between haphazard marketing and an integrated, strategic plan for business development.

> ✻
> "Learn how to see...
> realize that
> everything connects
> to everything else."
> - Leonardo Da Vinci

In my business improvement consulting work, separating them out like this for my client can really help highlight where the root cause of a problem getting clients might lie as well as assessing opportunities for new (educational) products. So, I hope it's helpful for you too.

It's the holistic effectiveness of your business plan that will bring the outcomes you want. In building teams and systems, the individual components should be synergetic. They are also what determine your branding, optimal pricing and choice of platforms.

The single most important element for reforming your business architecture is to get crystal clear on what is at the heart of what you do, why and for whom, and then to create value around it and choose a vehicle to deliver it.

You can do this in three steps:

1. First, in your business plan: your brand, your marketing and your customer engagement - must first and foremost reflect your *core purpose* and your reason for being in the business you're in.

2. Second, you must create an audience that aligns with what you stand for, who you help, why you help them, and what you help them with.

3. And third, the value of what you do must be positioned, packaged and promoted as unique and premium.

MANAGING BUSINESS TRANSFORMATION

If you're not just starting up a consulting business, you'll know how well you're currently doing in a broad sense of client base, income and impact. Any existing business will benefit from an expert "review and challenge" from time to time, which is what I do in my one-to-one consulting and business mentoring work.

Unquestionably though, any improvement plan must be led by a good understanding of current performance, reviewing the effectiveness and efficiency of existing structures, processes and systems in place and knowing as far as possible the weak links in the chain.

With this in mind, I've included a self-assessment workbook for you to download and use to review your own business (see cover pages for the link). It's a good starting point to help you identify the points of leverage that can improve and transform how your business works. If you want to work with me directly on a strategic review and/or your implementation action plan, take a look at my fast track offer at the end of the book.

> ※
> "Nothing binds you except your thoughts; nothing limits you except your fear; and nothing controls you except your beliefs." – Marianne Williamson

Besides looking at the mechanics of your business, you may need to wrestle with some fresh perspectives on what your business is actually all about. This is where consulting meets coaching and why I see coaching as both a field in its own right and a sub-set of consulting.

Even marketing or sales (as terms and concepts) can end up being not what you think. Seriously true. Being self-taught, I didn't look at the basic principles and premises – such as "The 4Ps (or 7Ps) of Marketing" – until much later. I certainly had some major light-bulb moments and learned many lessons through my various network marketing and internet marketing endeavours!

Before any kind of change is possible, you may well need to put on a new thinking cap before you can embark on a new strategy or start implementing a different way of doing something. That's why I've started with ideas, frameworks and strategy in the first half of the book and then provided more pragmatic tools later in the second half.

When you can make the shift in both perspective and practical terms towards innovation, sustainable change is more likely to result.

Let's visualise what's needed for business transformation using a simple framework.

STRATEGY
- OPPORTUNITY
- LEADERSHIP
- COMMUNICATION

DESIGN
- LEARNING
- PROCESS
- IMPROVEMENT

CHANGE
- INNOVATION
- MANAGEMENT
- ANALYTICS

Firstly, how you feel about, react to and act on new ideas and opportunities and the ability to implement novel approaches is a positive business trait that demonstrates leadership and forms the basis of your strategy. After looking at the foundations for growth and "success", hopefully you now can see the importance of having the right revenue model and design architecture in place to support more leveraged approaches.

Secondly, for most businesses, even if you're freelance services provider or very small firm, doing something new or doing something differently may not seem like it requires some big transformation plan. Yet, I'd argue that with any change or innovation, there's more to it than just about implementing a new "thing". There's a mental shift that may need to happen too, even a cultural element, that requires learning as well as process improvement.

Successful transformation is actually less about taking on new concepts and more about knocking down (often tightly held) false beliefs, strengthening foundations and reforming the architecture.

And thirdly, nowadays, innovation is the mother of differentiation and the father of competitive advantage – people can't copy something that is unique to you. Businesses that have a culture of innovation tend to flourish in a competitive world, because they know how to increase market share, enter new markets and introduce new products or services.

Your commitment to learning and development will open your mind to a greater range of possibilities and opportunities to grow your business. Managing and evaluating change therefore feeds directly back into strategy and leadership.

Is your mind being stretched, even just a little? I hope so, because as a business owner, there are so many opportunities in the digital age that can benefit both you and your clients.

> ※
> "One's mind, once stretched by a new idea, never regains its original dimensions." – Oliver Wendell Holmes

When I introduce the ideas within this book to my clients, it gives me such tremendous joy and satisfaction when they suddenly "get it" then "get on and do it" and achieve great results using these strategies to attract and win new clients. To have that influence and impact when working with people, it's why I do what I do!

Leveraging your expertise by becoming an educational entrepreneur - through content sharing, writing books, creating courses, speaking at events - may be innovative in your industry simply because it's different to the norm. But really, it just means you are offering your expertise *in a new form*.

Niching down is a crucial driver of competitive advantage because it allows you to target a specific set of pressing needs and problems of a particular audience. These will be a group of people you personally feel compelled to help as well as professionally competent to deliver results for.

At the same time, there's advantage in being a contrarian in how you work with those clients. If you are marketing and delivering your expertise *in a distinctive way* compared to your competitors, you're ahead of the curve.

ASSESSING RISKS AND BENEFITS OF INNOVATION

Strategic innovation impacts revenue growth enormously in professional services. Being open to new insights and new ways of doing things is part of the roadmap to building a successful business. The choices you make and the mental resilience you need to succeed is in large part about managing risk.

A reluctance to innovate on strategy means you can get stuck at an income plateau.

While I can show you leveraged approaches that help break through typical income plateaus, bottlenecks and barriers to business growth, but only you can take the decision to innovate: be it to implement a new system, develop a sales webinar or create a new product.

In terms of strategy, moving into educational entrepreneurship as described above, you will need to be committed to pushing against the status quo, stepping out of tradition and moving with the times.

For decades, professional service providers have been either reluctant or conservative marketers. I see this with my consultancy colleagues both in the public and private sectors as well as the larger advisory-consulting firms, having worked in one of the top global companies (albeit I lasted only a year!)

> ※
> "Professional service marketing is certainly among the safest I've seen. Because it appears to take no risks, it's actually quite risky." – Seth Godin

There are three main reasons why our professional service providers struggle with business growth. Firstly, professional services are challenging to brand and market, because what you offer is often similar to your competitors and what you deliver is often mostly customised for each client. At the outset, as far as the client is concerned, the outcomes can seem intangible and largely undifferentiated.

The majority of firms are too flexible when it comes to strategic positioning; they offer a wide array of support and pander to tailored client requirements – typically in a "letter of engagement".

Furthermore, most services are delivered in a personalised way, which demands high levels of face-to-face interaction. This is both short sighted and time-consuming. Many aspects of a business can actually be systematised and thus offered to a variety of clients with personal interaction time used more for developing a good working relationship.

The second reason professional services struggle to grow is because consultants can be a tad old school. Many like to operate within a limited sphere of influence based on personal relationships, cosy networks and word-of-mouth referrals. Although time-consuming, these traditional "sales" methods do work, even more so when assisted by online activities.

This is all well and good if this brings in enough clients to maintain a comfortable albeit fairly limited monthly revenue and meets your desired goals. If this is you, you're probably not reading this book so I'm talking about perhaps some of your peers.

However, there are two limitations. Firstly, you're essentially delivering only within a small region of the country, so you tend only to market to local groups. It can seem fitting to use traditional face-to-face methods to build relationships and attract clients. But what happens when a new blood arrives in town and your competition starts taking significant market share?

The second limitation of sticking to local, traditional business practices is that when the market shifts, and you start to lose clients and client share, you don't have many alternatives up your sleeve.

> ※
> "As a dynamically growing consulting firm you must continually investigate, evaluate and decide on the applicability of additional models or working processes to use in helping clients. That's innovation for continuous improvement and versatility." – Alan Weiss, Million Dollar Consulting

The third reason for stalled business growth is in terms of delivery. Most consultants or consulting firms only offer one-to-one, "done-for-you" type assignments. This misses the bigger opportunities in the digital arena to reach a wider audience and increase your revenue in order to grow and scale the business.

The key to business growth relies on deviating from the norms of market positioning and traditional marketing, and implementing the right digital strategy for delivering tangible results for your clients in multiple ways.

Playing it safe tends to mean businesses focus on one of two things:

a) operational efficiency - doing more with less, including marketing and service delivery; and

b) customer satisfaction – getting the right balance in "value for money" terms.

While these are both important, for continuous improvement, only innovation can help you respond to future trends or push your business income potential up to the next level. These are key pivot points in your leveraged strategy.

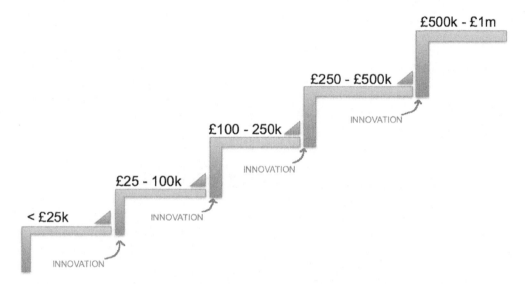

INCREASING YOUR CAPACITY TO SCALE

As we've discussed, the ultimate solution to growing a high-end client business is a strategic one not an operational one. Although you can certainly spend time optimising the *efficiency* of your business operations, that can only take you so far.

Bigger growth opportunities require strategies that are more transformational, because you need to build your business operation's capacity to scale and but ultimately enable greater reach and almost limitless revenue. As we showed in the figure above, service-based businesses come up against some typical growth plateaus, which require a change in strategy and innovation to move to the next level of growth.

With this in mind, I created the *Scale Model* to illustrate the different ways leveraged consulting strategies can support you in scaling your business. As shown in the graph that follows, income growth is stepwise as you move from a freelance, time-based model towards a fully leveraged model in a traditional way (which has limits), a transitional way (also with limits) and a transformational way (no limits).

Traditional leveraged strategies enable a solo practice to grow by developing teams and systems. Transitional strategies are based on shifting some or all of your work with clients from one-to-one and face-to-face to group-based and online.

Finally, we can choose to elevate our growth by making a more transformational jump to a product-based business model. A fully leveraged strategy is where you transform your business by building leverage into all of your marketing, sales and delivery processes.

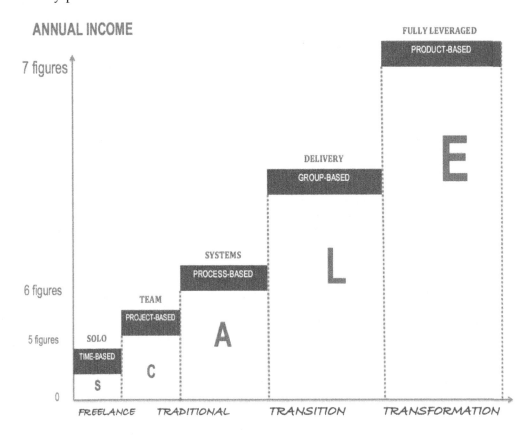

Which you choose to do, and in what order, depends to an extent on your aspirations, mindset and preferred ways of working, as an individual, with associates or a team, and with your clients.

Put in practical terms, most consultants will start their business as a solo venture (S), and as demand for their services grows perhaps adding one or more freelance consultants and a personal assistant to build a team (C). At some point, client and quality management becomes important for on-going success, which instigates the use of systems or further admin personnel and/or virtual teams to support engagement and delivery workflows (A).

Here's another way to view this in relation to your strategy and leverage tactics at each step.

STEP	STAGE	STRATEGY	BUSINESS MODEL	LEVERAGE TACTIC
S	SOLO	DUPLICATE	Time- based	Recruit more consultants
C	TEAM	ACCENTUATE	Project-based	Create a methodology
A	SYSTEMS	ESCALATE	Process-based	Automate your processes
L	DELIVERY	REPLICATE	Group-based	Develop one-to-many activities
E	FULLY LEVERAGED	ELEVATE	Product-based	Develop online programmes

For example, at (A) - automation will help you handle the marketing and sales aspects of your business efficiently and some parts of how you onboard, communicate and work with clients. But (A) is traditionally where many independent consultancies hit a ceiling, because the traditional enterprise model isn't scalable.

Growing the team and using systems can only duplicate or diversify what you already do. This is the traditional leverage model of most small to medium sized consulting firms. If you're having success in your niche as a solo practitioner and don't want to take on more staff, you can outsource or use associates to build a team around you and streamline your systems to grow upwards into (C) and (A) territory.

If you want to grow beyond your current level of *income* (but don't wish to increase your consulting fees or manage a team of associates), you will have to shift at least some of your approach to:

- Group-based delivery (L), which could be face-to-face, online or a bit of both; and/or
- Product-based delivery (E), which could be products, courses and/or programmes.

The added bonus of using an education-based approach and digital marketing is that you're already part way towards implementing L and E. You've done the mindset and marketing bits and now need to grasp the money and metrics bit to leverage your expertise fully.

Your audience reach is now far bigger than your local consulting or coaching could ever hope to support, which increases your influence. And your target market (who may or may not already be clients) can engage with you and get value from your expertise in more flexible ways and at different price points, which increases your impact and income.

You may decide on a deliberate transition away from one-to-one services towards one-to-many strategies or you may look at how these different offerings fit across your customer journey and funnel. In either case, the transformation you achieve leads you towards fully leveraged consulting and digital transformation for business growth.

> ※
> "If you're primarily service based there is such a huge opportunity to add more passive and scalable revenue streams driven by online courses. And you probably already have much of what you need in your service business to make the addition of courses much easier." ~ Greg Smith, Co-Founder & CEO, Thinkific

This pattern of growth is the same whether you run services face-to-face or via a technology platform, but obviously the opportunities to increase gross margin are way better with digital delivery. This doesn't necessarily mean one-to-many delivery cannot be high-end in terms of quality and price. And it doesn't mean giving up your face-to-face work. It means elevating certain time-intensive, high value "VIP" client work to premium "prices.

Strategically, there are three levels you can work at: 1, be the cheapest; 2, give the most value for money; or 3, solve the biggest (most difficult) problems. The latter is where high-end consulting services generally sit. The first two levels are exactly what you end up doing to undercut your competitors. When you operate on that "me too" level, it's hard work to gain market share without having first built up your authority status and reputation. You can also tip it in your favour by having a unique value proposition or offer, something very specific that you uniquely do (and do well).

Competing on cost is hard work. Discounts and extra bonuses can differentiate your offer from similar competitor as the customer is getting more value for the same cost. But they also cut into you profit margins. Giving "added value" such as a pre-workshop survey analysis or website review or free follow-ups is less cost conscious, as what you're actually offering would probably form part of what you normally do for client onboarding or retention anyhow.

Working at the highest level is where you're solving the most difficult problems. This should draw on your expertise and skills in how you engage, communicate and work with a client. This doesn't necessarily equate to spending more time or effort than your counterparts if you know how to build leverage into what you do.

What I'm saying is that when you design your consulting business from the perspective of developing a leveraged model, first you must decide on two things. The first is whether you really want to operate at the top of the tree - high-end – and believe you are capable of doing work at that level. If yes, then do you feel you're charging appropriate to the result you deliver? And the second is whether you want to work closely with a handful of people or influence and impact large numbers of people.

Here are some top-level questions you can ask yourself with regards to increasing your capacity to scale.

1. What level of influence, impact & income are you currently working at?
2. What would you like it to be?
3. What do you need to do to increase your capacity to work at that level?

I'm assuming you believe there's more potential to grow your consulting or coaching business, since you picked out this book. If that's the case, first please look at where you think you sit on the traditional, transitional or transformational spectrum.

To help with this, here are some of the questions we explore during my "Digital Roadmap" exploratory session with a potential new client:

❖ What's your current business model and how leveraged is it?

❖ What's your specific niche and how do you engage with your audience?

❖ How clearly are you promoting a core offer and call to action?

❖ What's your sales process and where are the biggest drop offs?

❖ How do you work out how much to charge and to whom?

❖ How does your price and value compare to your competitors?

As you dive in, whether or not you have definite and confident answers yet, those questions can quickly progress and deepen, because next I'd want you to turn things around and look at from the customer's perspective and see how your answers shift.

Let's focus first on what is the highly desirable outcome (i.e. a benefit, result, milestone or transformation) that you're helping your clients get to. Leverage your unique positioning to find out the words your ideal client uses to describe what they want (or don't want). Read posts on network groups, post questions, polls and surveys and listen more than talk.

When you do this, you'll learn people's "problem language" and the precise way they express their desires as outcomes and benefits. If you already have a good rapport with your target audience and existing clients, you can directly ask them what words and phrases would speak to them the most.

Second, use these same methods to determine what is the most effective and efficient way for you to deliver the solution or outcome they want.

Armed with these insights, you can really produce more effective copywriting to leverage your marketing and sales efforts as well as look at your delivery options to support what clients need. When you have these things nailed down and communicated to your target market, it avoids questions from prospects about how competent or cheap you are or about how fast you can do the work.

Drilling down further still: how does what you deliver relate to how much a specific outcome is *worth* to your client, how much time do you need to spend with them to deliver that outcome, and what forms of guidance and support are required to guarantee they achieve that outcome?

With this level of clarity, it's far simpler to produce good marketing to attract the right audience, nurture your prospects and drive sales. You need your ideal client to find you, engage with you, trust your confidence to deliver and get the promised outcome.

Once you have that worked out, which certainly is worthwhile spending a decent amount of time on and getting some help with, then strategically, the leverage capacity you need to build may become suddenly more apparent. And your confidence to make the leverage shift is likely to intensify.

EVALUATING OUTCOMES, BENEFITS & IMPACT

At this juncture, it's worth spending some time thinking about how you will measure success. Evaluating innovation and change programmes have been a mainstay of my consulting practice, so this is very close to my heart. But I promise not to get too technical on evaluation methodologies. We'll stick to the principles and look a little at metrics.

In your strategic business plan, however well formulated that is, you should at least have a set of immediate objectives and longer-term goals. See if you can correlate these somehow to a set of measures (or indicators for) the level of impact, influence and income you seek to achieve in the next 90 days, 6-12 months, and year-on-year in the future. That's your intended growth curve.

In terms of how you want to run your business, engage and work with clients, and other long-term "leveraged living" goals, the metrics are likely to be rather qualitative. You have to use subjective judgement as to how doable, dependable and desirable you feel your business is at any given point in time.

Quantitative measures are easier and, in the digital age, we certainly have plenty of analytics to help us – from tracking website hits and user behaviours to how many leads, applications, calls and clients you gain. These become your key performance indicators (KPIs). Identify the metrics right across the customer journey from end to end that will allow you to see exactly where your new approaches are making the biggest differences.

After making changes, such as to your business model, operating methods or pricing, or even just your marketing copy, or adding an email follow up, using a new signup process: look at your numbers. How have the quantitative metrics changed, how well are you moving towards your targets, and where are the biggest improvements.

This is where again how you're defining "success" starts to figure in terms of evaluating your design architecture against your business goals.

Leveraged consulting starts with you – and that means designing and growing your business from the inside out, identifying the central purpose for why you have a business.

Remember in the introduction chapter, read with the end in mind? The same goes for your business, evaluate with the end in mind – the end meaning your vision, your goals and targets (not the end of your business aha!)

That takes us full circle back to strategic planning and why it's essential you do the prerequisite research and preparation to develop a clear idea of your ideal audience's wants (not just what you think they need) before you build and pilot a service or product or decide on your business operating model.

What's neat though is that when you engage with your target market, you are actually continuously doing new market research and keeping up-to-date. You're reducing risk, validating assumptions and creating "proof of concept" for your offer. This is critical as trends and market demand changes over time.

By keeping it a pilot, you make it manageable to create and you have a small audience to interact with so you can therefore also continually re-educate yourself, deepening your understanding of your clients, their perceived risks and operating environment and therefore also about the challenges they face.

Armed with this insight, you can refine what you do and develop better processes, services and products to help your clients. This is in fact Kolb's theory of learning: Learn, Think, Plan, Do. After doing, you circle back: reflect, plan, do, to continue improving. Rinse and repeat.

It worked really well for the programme I created based on my own expert system. When I took the initial "imperfect" product into my market research, I found out more about what was making the biggest differences to their business growth. There were still areas where they struggled and as we worked through these together, so I refined my system, my marketing and developed a better programme.

DRIVING YOUR SUCCESS

Business success is by design, yet too many consultants follow a pre-formatted small firm approach or "play it small" strategy, or they just "wing it" without thinking clearly about what they personally want to achieve for themselves and their clients. Any business that achieves sustainable success has started with a clear vision for their long-term goals, and those are not just financial.

When you understand what's possible with leveraged consulting in the digital age and you're clear on your business strategy, you can make a bolder move to play your greatest game and achieve your true potential.

When you start your business, and as you look to grow, you'll be asking questions like: how do I find clients, what will I do and deliver, how many people can I work with each month, what tools do I need, what support might I need, and what income can I expect? These are useful proactive questions; they help drive your vision because they produce actionable responses.

Next comes the fear of selling and of course, of not selling! We all know that if you don't sell your products or services, you don't have a business. However, as a professional, like me you undoubtedly hate the concept of selling, pitching or prospecting, because we've all experienced the ugly high-pressure sides to it where you're battered intensively, insensitively and incessantly in a shop or over the phone.

Online nowadays too, you'll see a push towards manipulation using hype, scarcity and urgency tactics of countdown timers and "limited spaces", stacking with bonuses with inflated "value" tags and "one-time offer" upsells. (There's nothing wrong with those incentives if done authentically with your client's needs in mind; but often this isn't the case and so it just feels tacky and uncomfortable for the consumer.)

As a business, you know you have to win clients / customers to survive and grow, yet there's this sticking point of selling that I see holding back so many consultants and coaches in driving forward their success. You yearn for a better model for winning business that's more suited to your professional and personal values, ethics and style, but feel forced into the same corner of pushing to close the client on working with you.

At the same time as the sales dilemma is going on in your head, once up and running, some of you maybe find yourself working hard and making all kinds of sacrifices, yet still not building the kind of client base you need and seeing your vision of a successful business realised. You feel under constant pressure to bring in more money and deliver more value. I've been there.

This is all to your credit, nothing wrong with being a committed, hard worker wanting to serve your clients well. But the truth of it is this. It's unnecessary – you can work less and earn more - if you have the right business design based on the kind of strategies for brand clarity, leverage and scalability that I'm sharing here.

A successful marketing strategy in this sense involves identifying, anticipating and satisfying customer needs and wants and matching these to what you can distinctively deliver. This becomes your unique selling proposition. Continuing to graft to keep a handful of clients is not going to take you to the so-called "promised land" and it's pretty limited in terms of income, or having any kind of influence on your industry and impact on the world.

If you're even slightly uncomfortable with the idea of "selling yourself" as an expert or "flogging" your services, harnessing education as a business tool gives you a way to grow your client base with ease and integrity. By *reframing* your business model and how you share your subject expertise and use your consulting and coaching skills, you will find you can attract and work with clients with less grind and more grace.

Decide what it is you will do, and then do it. Avoid waiting for the perfect time to start implementing changes.

With a leveraged, streamlined process in place to optimise the flow of targeted, responsive leads, you're able to ditch the merry-go-round of sales hype and marketing overwhelm, and build a business that is enjoyable and fulfilling.

Coupling this with business processes that help you to leverage and scale your operation is a winning formula for successful growth.

So far, we've looked at the power of leverage and a leveraged strategy to build and scale your business, and reach higher levels of influence, impact and income. Use the space here (or in the companion workbook) to note down your main takeaways or "aha" moments about the concept of leveraged consulting or leveraged model(s) you think would serve you, along with any personal insights gleaned about the challenges, risks and benefits of innovation.

ACTION NOTES

_____

_____

_____

_____

_____

_____

_____

_____

_____

_____

_____

_____

_____

_____

Next, let's turn specifically to the foundations for leverage in your marketing, sales process and delivery model, which starts with leveraging YOU.

Chapter 3

LEVERAGING YOU

Get Your Story Straight

"Extraordinary accomplishment can result in failure if you feel no joy, self-acceptance or a sense of meaning."

Tony Robbins

KEY POINTS

❖ Those successful with a service business have usually understood the need to put themselves as individuals into the equation.

❖ Success is not all about improving the operational mechanics of the business. Most of the time, it's people's mindset that gets in the way!

❖ Investing in and growing your business should also include investing in yourself and growing as an expert, entrepreneur and educator.

❖ Productivity isn't about how much we do, how busy we are, or how much money we make, but about what we deliver – i.e. the value, outcome or impact of what we do.

❖ Talent management is at the heart of any successful business growth strategy, so why not yourself! As the leader and "captain" of your business, a clear & determined mindset is paramount.

❖ Most businesses don't give enough attention to good messaging and take much longer to grow. When your prospect is clear on what your offer is and how it fits their needs, they can more easily say yes to it.

❖ People don't buy what you do; they buy why you do it, and the results you can get for them when they work with you.

❖ Your unique expert brand needs to be so specific that it provides a badge of honour and distinguishes you from others in your niche.

❖ Take advantage of your passion, your story and your value by building a brand around your distinctive expertise insights and way of working.

❖ Consider your professional know-how and expert system not only as a service, one thing you offer, but also as one or more potential products or programmes.

❖ Leveraging you is like dating, it's attraction marketing leading to good quality conversations, continued engagement, and eventually a long-lasting relationship and partnership.

❖ In designing an expert signature programme, you're forced to pin down what it is you uniquely deliver, to map out the process of how you achieve that specific result, and then package it within a structured programme.

❖ A signature programme is something very tangible you can offer to your target market.

PUTTING THE "I" INTO YOUR SUCCESS

While we're often driven by external notions of success, the actualisation of it is very individual – it's about YOU, what you give and what you want. Independent client-focused businesses are more often than not driven by very personal ambitions. For the consulting services provider, I'd argue that authenticity, expertise and enthusiasm are all prerequisites for success. You'll notice that only one out of the three is about your professional know-how.

For many of us, a client business is not just a job where we get hired to do something. It's a representation of who we are and what we stand for.

Those who are successful with a service business have usually understood the need to put themselves as individuals into the equation.

This individuality is one of the key reasons for the "I" in my brand name – *iSuccess* – the diagnostic method I use for business consulting. In fact, I'm often asked what the "i" stands for, and actually it isn't one thing; it's a growing list.

Originally when I coined the term *iSuccess*, the intention was simply to bring together success principles for the *individual* with the practicalities and power of the *internet* to create a digital platform and system to support marketing and sales. However, as I began to work with clients from all kinds of industries, I realised the "i" goes way beyond these two terms as the table below illustrates.

✓ I (You as CEO)	✓ individual	✓ internet
✓ identity	✓ ideas	✓ influence
✓ insights	✓ ideals	✓ invigorate
✓ integrity	✓ innovation	✓ improve
✓ in-service	✓ inspiration	✓ invaluable
✓ irresistible	✓ information	✓ initiate
✓ ingenious	✓ integration	✓ ignite
✓ introvert	✓ implementation	✓ illuminate
✓ independent	✓ inducive	✓ intrigue
✓ intuitive	✓ impact	✓ income

I'm sure you'll discover there are some common themes in how you think about and talk about what *you* do. Can you come up with a unique set of words for the why, what and how of *your* business mission?

Bear in mind that your brand identity is more than the practical value of what you do or the things you produce. It's also a representation of your core values, your beliefs and your personality. This goes way beyond typical business mission statements. Your brand identity exists to solve a specific problem but it's also about making people feel a certain way as they interact with your brand as well as when they work with you.

I believe the raison d'être of a service-oriented business is usually extremely personal to you as an individual – au contraire to the line in the Godfather "it's not personal, it's business". More often than not, what you do is something you are passionate about as well as good at.

Certainly, if you started in business to help people and have an impact on people's lives, then success and a sense of achievement in your business is super personal!

Aligning with your purpose is a particularly important business dimension that you ignore at your own peril, because building a successful high-end business

> ※
> "No matter what you sell, you have so much more of you wrapped up in it (your expertise, talents and intellectual property). This can make it hard to separate the pragmatic monetary side of worth, with the worth that's wrapped up so tightly in your heart body and soul."
> – Karen Skidmore,
> **True Profit Business**

starts with you. Whether you're running solo or you're started up as a small firm, as CEO, Director and Manager not only do you set the direction of the sail, you also must design the boat and steer it forwards.

This means you need to work as hard on yourself as you do on your business. Learning and development is a cornerstone of organisational growth. Staying in good mental and physical health is equally important to avoid overwhelm and burnout.

As you're in the consulting business, you presumably haven't arrived empty handed. Your CV and skills audit demonstrate the knowledge, expertise, qualifications, and/or experience you've acquired in your industry/sector, in at least one or more subject or technical areas, and may already have experience delivering client work.

To play your top game, you should ensure you maintain an up-to-date sector and technical subject knowledge base. You also need to stay well versed in the methodologies of your industry and understand the ethics and empathies that underpin professionalism.

However, professional experts with a more technical mindset can get all caught up in the demonstrable elements of their products and process, and ignore the customer journey and user experience interacting with your brand. As a service provider, you need to connect with the emotive elements of what you do too.

I'd argue that continuous learning about your customers' needs alongside quality management are what determine the on-going success of any consultant's work. So just because you're looking to innovate - do something new or different – there's no need for you to throw out what you currently know and can do.

Unless you need to pivot due to changes in the market, your highest priority is to define clearly your individual expert brand and craft your core message. After this, you can build on it, adapt or refine it, whatever is necessary for you to stand out in a crowded and competitive marketplace. This aligning, targeting and positioning effort will be of massive benefit to how you market and deliver "that thing you do" and will put you in a much stronger position to innovate on strategy and develop contemporary delivery models.

When working on business improvement projects, many of my clients discover certain personal attributes, rather than operational processes, that are in fact what is holding them back. It can be limiting self-beliefs, mind blocks or stress around money or failure. It can be their attitude to risk or their tendency towards perfectionism, procrastination and/or overthinking that leads to a struggle with making decisions. This makes identifying and focusing on the most important things incredibly difficult for them.

Success is not all about improving the operational mechanics of the business. Most of the time, it's people's mindset and thinking that gets in their own way!

For others, growing the business has been more about getting that vital clarity on their unique identity and ideals. They've then gone on to become more focused and strategic, and less overwhelmed with the day-to-day running of the business - even feeling a sense of liberation enough to take a vacation!

Part of the educational role of a service provider is to help a client to push through personal barriers to getting the results they desire. This is why I always see coaching, mentoring and teaching subset roles of consulting as well as professions in their own right. For some individuals, the help that's needed is in clarifying their purpose, shifting or changing the way they deal with challenges, obstacles and failure, or about think about money and success. For others, it's more about improving their working practices, processes and teams.

As I mentioned in the previous chapter, my own approach to helping a client with their business strategy is to focus first on what success means to them and work back from there to look at the mechanics of their business processes, sales funnel, marketing collateral, skills, resources etc that will enable the goal to be achieved.

This evaluative approach is a key part of the roadmap to success that I deliver, but the real guarantee of impact is whether the right personal strategy is in place, not just how well it is implemented by the individual(s) concerned.

Leveraged consulting requires you to appreciate the wider set of principles at play for you as an individual as well as the tangible digital elements needed to grow a purposeful, profitable and sustainable enterprise.

The best way to serve a client is to help them gain new perspectives and know-how, but also a sense of opportunity, feasibility and urgency to implement solutions that achieve the desired outcome. Your story is an important part of your brand – it's often the undercurrent for why you started the business and who you choose to serve.

If you're feeling a little bit lost with where to start to leverage your expertise and create a unique and compelling personal brand, hopefully there are plenty of nuggets in this chapter to get you on the right track.

If you're not fighting demons from past experiences and are crystal clear on your professional identity, then feel free to skip to the next chapter. But if you have some uncertainty around what you bring uniquely to the table that helps your target market, and how to get specific in order to attract your ideal clients, then it's worth at least skim reading the sections here and picking out the insights that serve you.

CREATING OPPORTUNITIES OUT OF OBSTACLES

Setting up my consulting business was the result of a career change not of my own choosing – well at least not consciously. Rather than let situations define me or create barriers to future success, I leaned more into creating opportunities out of obstacles. And this kind of became my story.

I'd started up a home-based direct sales business as a side-line a few years before quitting the J.O.B. racket, because I needed a plan B after my daughter was born with neurological "problems". (At the time, we had no idea the impact this would have on our lives, but it certainly got me thinking what if....)

I knew I had an entrepreneurial streak so I started to explore "work from home" business opportunities whilst still having the so-called security of a "steady job". (Note that no job is secure these days anyhow!) I dabbled in a few different online businesses over the next few years with mixed success, but certainly learned a tonne about marketing. (Internet marketing was a whole new world back in 2004, but look at it today!)

When I was eventually pushed into a redundancy and no longer "employed", the idea of self-employment didn't feel so new and daunting as it might to some who didn't have this initial safety net. When I set up my consulting business, many people said to me "You're so brave." Or "I wouldn't have the courage." Or "I like the security of a steady income".

At first, I could have let other people's mindsets colour my own and gone looking for another job. But I set my mind on making it work and now going on 12+ years I have never looked back.

Ironically, one of those naysayers is now a happily self-employed consultant, travelling the world sharing her expertise via keynotes and workshops. Because she's an awesome networker and prolific writer in her professional field, she attracted clients like crazy. Frightening as it was at first, she broke through those personal barriers and consulting worked really well for her.

Nonetheless, in the main I'd say people who are averse to change or risk are not your typical entrepreneurial types - and that's ok, 95% of people never will be. There are those who stay in a job even when they feel underwhelmed, unappreciated or mega-stressed, simply because they hang onto what seems like the safer more stable option. (I understand: just try getting a mortgage when your income goes up and down from one year to the next, even though you're more in control of your "steady income" than you are in most jobs these days!)

Like a lot of things in life, there are choices if you want to see them. The point is: what happens… happens. Building success with any business means deciding to see or create opportunities where most only see obstacles; to see the benefits where most only see risk.

You can't always control what happens to you, but you can control how you respond – it's a matter of mindset, which ultimately governs your attitude and behaviour.

Whatever the case, it's likely that even though someone is not doing their life's work or achieving their full potential, many people's fear or sense of unknown territory is usually what holds them back in implementing a new opportunity.

(If you get a chance, look at *"Who Moved My Cheese"* by Spencer Johnson – it's a short little book and Youtube movie – a very enlightening story of four little characters and how they respond to change. Based on metaphors about success, what makes us happy, comfort zones, entitlement, challenge, and so forth, it's hilarious when you recognise bits of your own attitudes and behaviours in one or more of the characters!)

Starting my consulting business therefore provided an opportunity to break free from all the politics of corporate management. It came about because someone moved my cheese so to speak. It was something I'd thought about doing for a long time, because I knew it could create more freedom in my life. But I'd not had the courage to follow my entrepreneurial path until the situation presented itself and I reached a tipping point - more on tipping points and turning points later.

I like to say I took "voluntary" redundancy, because I kind of sabotaged my chances of staying on during a major restructure at the university where I'd worked my way up the career ladder for many years. I think I knew deep down that I wanted out, that the time was right to make the leap. As they say, the biggest opportunities and the highest level of personal growth happen outside your comfort zone.

Even though I got promoted several times, I had to fight for it every step of the way. They'd even put me forward for a national teaching award. Still, essentially, I was "let go" - let down more like - and I felt very angry and bitter about it for quite some time! (Incidentally, over the year that followed, every one of my team left too – very telling.)

The fact is I'd poured huge quantities of heart, soul and overtime into that job and such an experience totally knocks your self-esteem and confidence as well as your sense of professional pride. Maybe you can relate.

The best way I found to get over it – and get out of my own way – was to consider this a *brilliant opportunity* rather than a knock back or obstacle. That one shift in mindset gave me courage. I got back in tune with my own value and rather than just looking for another job, I took control of the situation and set up my own consultancy company.

As well as Mr Churchill's famous line, one of the quotes I always remember from my network marketing days was from Jim Rohn who said that "in life you will face only two things for certain: opportunities and obstacles".

> ※
> "A pessimist sees obstacles in every opportunity. An optimist sees opportunity in every obstacle." – Winston Churchill

We all sometimes need a little shove in the right direction. I used the obstacle of leaving my "not-so-safe-after-all" job to create a new and better opportunity for myself. I set my mindset to optimistic, choosing to see the situation as a good thing - an opportunity. I'm very grateful I grabbed it and, 12 years on, I've certainly never looked back.

INVESTING IN YOUR OWN EDUCATION

The fact that you're reading this book (and presumably others), means you see your own continuing education and professional development as important, and not something to be left to chance. This was my view too from the start of my entrepreneurial journey.

Throughout the book, you'll see acknowledgements of many experts who have guided me in my endeavours over my journey so far. I'm a big believer of the Jim

Rohn classic *"For things to change, you have to change; for things to get better, you have to get better"*. In other words, if you improve, your business will improve.

Investing in and growing your business should also include investing in yourself and growing as an expert practitioner, entrepreneur and educator.

I'm constantly expanding my education to support my practice. I read and study all kinds of things about business strategy, entrepreneurship, productivity, marketing, operational management, client relationship building, communication, leadership, and more. For me, my business education has not been quick, cheap or painless, but over time it's proved profitable. Continuous improvement adds to my expertise and skills and the value I give to my clients, and thus most definitely is worth the time, money and effort!

For instance, my goal is always to help my clients get better results faster. Even though my system works well and my clients get results and enjoy the process of working with me, I continue to refine and add to it, as well as develop my style and mindset.

In fact, personal development has been a huge benefit to me too; it's how I fuel my determination and persistence going it alone as a self-employed professional; it supports me in how I show up, handle fear and anxiety and celebrate success.

Five years ago, I spent 6-8 hours a day for three solid weeks toiling away on my laptop in my Devon retreat in order to shape this educational entrepreneur manifesto. Yet it's taken until now to produce the finished work, because I fell into the three frustrating traps, we all do: distraction, procrastination and perfectionism.

Nowadays, the sheer quantity of "how-to" and "self-help" content you can tap into all over the internet is quite astounding, but it also adds yet another trap to the challenges we face, that of information overwhelm!

Another trap is the tight grip we often have on our "to do" list, only feeling productive if we're busy or feeling disappointed if we don't get as much done or meet our objectives by our deadlines. It's worth noting the universal 80:20 Principle, which states that 80% of our results come from 20% of our activities.

Productivity isn't about how much we do, how busy we are, or how much money we make, but about what we deliver – i.e. the value, outcome or impact of what we do.

It seems savvy then that your "education" includes getting in tune with your own inner wisdom to bring clarity to your purpose, insight about what is important to you in your business (and life). Relaxing, going for a walk, meditating are all ways to let your mind wander freely, which allows your inner wisdom to rise to the surface. This is something I've come to do much later in my journey. Thankfully!

To be authentic with this book, I have to practice what I preach - to educate, not just write down everything that I know (tempting as it is to share and share and share!). My have been to distil what I know into its simplest elements, challenge perspectives, ask probing questions of you, find different ways to explain things and avoid producing some kind of prescriptive manual.

Next, we're moving into the more practical elements that help you to develop that all-important clarity on the key architectural elements of a well-designed service business.

Whether your goal is to start, improve or scale up your business, these are valuable cornerstones to build upon. When you get the architecture right, growth is not linear and gradual, it's step-wise and exponential.

TAKING LEADERSHIP TO A NEW LEVEL

When you look at any of the large professional services firm, it's not hard to spot those that are entrepreneurial and those that are not; they are the ones investing in their greatest asset – their people.

Talent management is at the heart of any successful business growth strategy, so why not yourself!

Since everything comes from your leadership (even if you're a solo-professional): the expertise, the vision, the great product idea, the marketing, and teamwork, but also the responsibility, accountability and action taking. That's why we should take great care of our own talent management, including our mental and physical wellbeing.

Have you noticed how much your mindset affects day-to-day energy and productivity? When we're in a positive mental state, we're super-productive and feel we can take on the world. But if for whatever reason you're a bit low, it's hard to focus and can feel like the world is against us. Well, I believe there are two types of people in terms of how we respond to change and uncertainty. However, when we understand our natural tendency and where they may have come from, we can start to retrain our brain.

Type A people will see (and even look for) the opportunities, they welcome challenges. They are the optimists and usually destined to do something significant with their lives through their work or business, or if not die trying so to speak. They're comfortable being out of their comfort zone and willing to take risks - at least to the degree of taking leaps into the unknown sometimes. Fear of failure may run alongside this, but type A will tend to "feel the fear and do it anyway"; or they are adept at living fearlessly.

On the other hand, type B people only see the obstacles and danger in everything. They are the cynics - they moan, and whine and complain and keep themselves small by negativity and inaction. Type Bs are very influenced by a fear of what others will say or think, slaves to limiting beliefs and childhood indoctrinations ingrained in our subconscious mind.

Of course, both types exist in all of us, it's a little conversation that goes on in our head – two little voices on each shoulder – "go for it" versus "don't do it". I do think you need a dose of healthy scepticism to assess the risks as well as optimism to make the jumps. Nonetheless, we certainly should avoid getting stuck, unable to take decisions.

When we procrastinate, inertia sets in - driven by fear, doubt and negativity. But when our motivation and determination are strong, we can change, take action and rise to the challenges we face. I'd nominate: belief, courage, drive, ambition, discipline and persistence as key driving attitudes and behaviours here.

For me, I'm definitely Type A – although I can't deny I do have a lot of type B moments. If I'm stressed out due to personal issues, lack of sleep, exercise and "me time', I can easily slip into Type B's fearful thinking sometimes for weeks! Can you relate?

When you're run down, problems feel ten times worse, because you lose focus and everything becomes like spaghetti. Take care of your body, mind and soul, so you're able to hear your inner wisdom.

On those occasions, I'll go away into my cave (yes woman have caves too!), detox, meditate and work on my mindset, so I can come back fighting fit. Or I'll spend days just doing what I want – walk, read, wear PJs all day, binge on boxsets, avoid social media and just "go dark". It's amazing how solutions and answers come to you easily when your mind and body are released of any sense of obligation.

At least being aware of the two inner voices is part of how our leadership develops. We can choose to listen to the one that serves us best. When you think and act differently; soon you develop a new tendency. I think this is where a business mentor or executive coach can be incredibly supportive and empowering.

What I'm emphasising here is once again is that your mindset is at the heart of achieving positive and lasting change. We need to mix the insights we gain from our learning with decisions and actions. For instance, this book is not intended as instruction or paint by numbers; it's not about me telling you what you should do in your business, or giving you lots of theory. It's about inspiring you with ideas and helping you make sense of them so you gain both light and power to choose the right options to support your goals, your business growth and your long-term success.

As the leader and "captain" of your business, a clear & determined mindset is paramount.

Starting out with your own consulting business, you will certainly embrace a little of your entrepreneurial spirit to set sail in the first place, and to steer your "ship" in a productive and profitable direction. But you also need personal accountability to see you through the lows and downers; and that sometimes means giving yourself permission to ease off the pedal and "float" for a while. Inspiration rarely visits when we push and force things.

As you build your business, a clear and organised mind will become ever important: the ability to focus, to create strategies and systems, to plan and execute - all vital skills for leading, organising, communicating and marketing what you do.

If you find you do need help with improving your mindset, strategy and/or productivity, it's most definitely worth diving into a few self-help books and programmes or investing in some mentoring to support you. This self-management is all part of developing your talent and your professionalism.

What you're "worth" determines your reputation, so you need to cultivate a consistently helpful attitude and a brand based on your beliefs, values, quality and relevance. Couple this with first-class service and products that get results for your clients, and you're set for success.

As a service provider, you're an expert, trading your knowledge, skills and experience in order to earn an income. Yet, now, you are also a business owner, and that means marketing yourself and "selling" you as a person as well as your services. It means dealing with a lot of other aspects of running a business other than your subject expertise. Scary stuff!

Having a clear steer on why you do what you do is vital to planning out exactly what is your value to your target market: what (result) you deliver & how effective you are in delivering it.

Many of you are experts in your professional field, but may be new to business development. I've found the hardest part of any new challenge is parting with your existing paradigms, for instance our notions of what business planning, marketing, sales and client management are all about.

The second hardest part is chasing too many tails and trying to do everything yourself; this leads to overwhelm and burnout. In fat, burnout is a worldwide problem for high achievers, ambitious professionals and entrepreneurs. It can occur for many reasons - a blurry or overly complex vision, too many ideas and not enough decision making or planning, a lack of support and guidance, which results in putting effort into the wrong things.

In his classic book "The 7 Habits of Highly Effective People', Stephen Covey urges us to "put first things first" - to prioritise your work, focus on what's important, i.e. the things that bring you closer to your vision of the future. What this is essentially saying is don't get distracted by urgent but unimportant tasks.

Covey tells a compelling story about leadership, that of a man hacking through the jungle with his team behind him; another man shouts down for him to stop. But the first man says "shut up, we're making progress!" even though from his vantage point the leader could see they were in the wrong forest.

Either way, we've all been guilty of falling into the "busy trap" when we should actually carve out time for creative and strategic thinking. Without a structured and balanced approach to business building (and indeed to marketing and sales), the stress, anxiety and panic can totally flatten you.

While I'd advocate you need to stay open to new ideas, insights and innovations, it's also important to review these critically and move on quickly. Look only at what best fits with your most desirable business strategy, add in some intuition, and really get to grips with personal strengths, preferences and resources you're able to draw on.

You lead with purpose, confidence and enthusiasm when you are:

- In tune with your vision and goals for your business.

- Clear on your expert niche and can position your brand message in line with what your target audience needs and wants.

- Consistent in how you communicate, serve and build relationships.

STANDING OUT IN THE CROWD

If we are to appeal to and resonate with our audience's deepest emotions and stand out in a crowded marketplace, we need to inject personality, empathy and commitment into our brand. Essentially, the best way to gain momentum in your business is to establish a strong "message to market match" and "unique value proposition". That means ensuring you send the right message to the right audience with the right solution.

Without those three pieces of the puzzle lined up and reflected in a compelling brand, attracting the right kind of business to you will be an uphill struggle. With a weak message to market match, you will feel like you're "selling" and end up with a lot of objection and rejection.

This is why in the *7 Dimensions of Success* framework I developed for my business consulting work, we set the "aligning" and "targeting" dimensions down first. They create the foundations for the rest of your business architecture. This groundwork is especially important if you're starting out, reinventing or revamping your brand or if you're moving into a new market.

I find many professionals struggle with tuning into the rudiments of what drives your business and motivates you personally, sufficient to bring this out clearly in your positioning and branding – our next two dimensions, incidentally. Getting to the heart and soul of our business can take a while because you don't always arrive at your "why" and "who" using deductive "right brain" logic. You need to tap into a much more deep-rooted emotional "left brain" layer, and many of us aren't used to digging to hidden depths.

We'll "dig" into this a bit more in the next chapter in terms of creating a value-driven brand for your marketing. In chapter 7, we'll then get very practical on all seven dimensions as we create your leveraged roadmap for getting some of the most critical "levers" in place that can drastically change the results you achieve with your marketing.

Essentially, you need to get to the point that what you do - and why you care about doing it - shines through all of your copywriting and communications. This is how you make your voice stand out in the crowd. Yet, it should also be something your *clients* care about and will pay attention to, so you attract the perfect clientele to you.

> ※
> "Copywriting is about communicating with the emotional part of a person's mind in a way that makes sense to the rational mind." – David Garfinkel, Breakthrough Copywriting

Some call this "tribe-building", which is back to leadership again. That may feel daunting – especially if you're not into big crowds like me - but really, it's just about making yourself known to like-minded people – waving the right flag on a tall pole, if you like.

Aligning with your purpose and targeting a specific audience who you can help with a specific need will create supreme foundations for standing out in a noisy world of others just yelling "hire me", "enrol with me". You need to get these first two dimensions dialled in before any kind of marketing, networking, promoting, launching or advertising begins. Improving the success of names for products, programmes and services, and how you package your offers, all stem from this.

First, get crystal clear on *one core concept* that you care the *most* about and that has a high level of interest in the marketplace. Once you're clear, it feels so much more straightforward to build out the rest – positioning, branding, pricing.

Most businesses don't give enough attention to good messaging and take much longer to grow. Before marketing, creating a website, building a list -

before you tackle ANY of that design or tech stuff - you need to lay down the foundations for your success.

This groundwork will help you create a strong and unique value proposition that your potential client is clear on. People love to read and hear what a business is about and the story behind it - what you do, why you do it, who you do it for, and how you do it. Story branding has become a very effective marketing tool, because your audience (aka tribe) can really get behind a story and feel passionate to share it with others.

Knowing and understanding your key audience is your most valuable asset, because in deciding on what to offer (and then when promoting it), you need to address directly the conversation that's going on in your ideal client's head. Aim to reach the point where you can articulate in no uncertain terms the problem your ideal client has and the solution they need.

From this clarity standpoint, you're showing them you understand where they're coming from and your message becomes more convincing. In other words, when you can clearly convey what you provide aligns with this problem and what you do delivers the outcome they want, you stand out in the crowd.

When your prospect is clear on what your offer is and how it fits their needs, they can more easily say yes to it.

We are all subjected to thousands of marketing messages just going about our daily lives. If you get your message spot on, your ideal clients will prick up their ears and hear you above the noise of other offers. If you confuse your brand name and key message with lots of other information and calls to action, nothing sticks in their mind. As the old marketing maxim states: a confused mind will always say no!

> ※
> "Choosing a crappy name -- or even a name that you don't hate but don't love -- will get you lost in a noisy marketplace. ...
> Even worse, the wrong name can be a major turnoff for your ideal customers." - Marissa Murgatroyd, Live Your Message

Focus on connecting with a key interest, need or problem your ideal prospect is walking around with, consciously or subconsciously. You'll find your most attractive proposition will likely be this exact one key thing. When you're able to do this, you can reinvent your business and brand your core offer through the lens of your perfect clients.

Make sure this one key thing is something you're so passionate about you can't stop reading about it, writing about it, talking about it, and finding ways to solve it. It's possibly something you have personally grappled with and worked through.

A key part of this is the premise that people are attracted to like-minded other people, like a club or trend where everyone wears the same badge, or hat. Simon Sinek brought this point into focus with his *"Start With Why"* message and his Ted talks have become legendary. I had the pleasure of hearing him live in Las Vegas back in 2010 when I'd started to reinvent myself and shift my business focus, and so attended some key international events.

In fact, I still have the "Token of Inspiration", a little metal coin of an inch diameter, which Simon personally gave to me when we were chatting after his talk (and probably 10s or 100s of others!). I've kept it on my desk ever since and it inspires me every single day.

The "start with why" idea really hit home with me. On one side of the coin is his "golden circle" (shown left), showing that "why" should be at the core of what we do and how we do it.

On the other side of the coin (shown right), it says *"Inspire Action"* - what a fantastic expression of his brand, which is all about ... inspiring action in others!

Being inspired by his concept, I took action! I dedicated a lot of time really peeling back layers to reveal my "why" - my inner purpose or "calling", if you like – before working on the nuts and bolts of "what" and "how". Even if you don't quite see yourself an "entrepreneur", think about what inspired you to start out on your own, who you love to work with and why that work matters.

This is critical foundation work because when you start with why (you do what you do), you have a much stronger and differentiated personal brand and can more easily market your services and products and attract business to you.

When you establish how to communicate with the specific tribe you wish to serve, starting with *why* you do *what* you do and then *how* you do it, your marketing becomes far more straightforward to create. Even if you don't quite see yourself an "entrepreneur", think about what inspired you to start out on your own, who you love to work with and why that work matters.

People don't buy what you do; they buy why you do it, and the results you can get for them when they work with you.

If you stay focused on your purpose when talking to prospects and clients, your business will feel right, because when you are working with authenticity and integrity, you won't feel like you are selling.

DEFINING YOUR PROFESSIONAL IDENTITY

The reason your *why* is so important to work on is that it helps you define both your professional identity and your personal brand - what you're all about, what you care about, and why it's important in your industry. This gives authenticity, authority and clarity to your brand messaging. Without it, what you offer will feel rather vague, commonplace and directionless to your audience.

I admit it took me a while to really home in on all this, because after a long and varied career, I'd become rather *multi-niche*. 99% of professionals stay in their "lane" – educators do education, designers do design, accountants do accounting, lawyers do law, plumbers do plumbing, engineers do engineering, and so forth. Well, I've never been able to stay in one lane.

I've been mixing it up, throughout my career. Even in the early years in the education sector, I've been a researcher, a teacher, a staff developer, a learning technologist, a project manager and a course designer. Likewise, in business, I've not stuck with one industry, but worked with people from many different industries, moving seamlessly between non-profit sectors, the private sector and third sector.

There comes a point when you wonder what you're good for! Because if you ever look at the job market, they want someone with a profession label who's stayed in their lane. But professional identity is increasingly being reinvented in new and different ways – the job market has yet to catch up. What you do is not limited by the labels of our profession, but by the nature of the work, the people you help and result you deliver.

For arguments sake, let's say you decide to call yourself a *Business Strategist* rather than a Business Adviser. Your industry is still business consulting, but this title is way more distinctive. How about a *Health Business Strategist* – now we're a specialist in the health business sector. It takes a while for this to sink in, because it's not what we see in job adverts or expect to put on your CV. But we're running a business not applying for a job. Your professional identity is totally yours to claim.

I know when you get the "what do you do?" or "what line of work are you in?" questions, it's so much easier to say to "I'm a lawyer", "I'm a designer", I'm a book editor. But if they're vaguely interested, the natural next questions are likely to be: "what kind of …" (ah interesting…) so "what does that entail exactly". With this in mind, how can you come up with a meaningful identity for what you do.

What do I do? (Thanks for asking….) *I'm a Business Strategist. I help people think differently about how they market, sell and deliver their expertise so they can grow and scale their business using leveraged strategies.*

Before arriving here, I've gone through some kind of professional identity crisis at least twice. That may resonate with your journey too, especially when you first set up your consulting business. Indulge me for a while, therefore, and let me give you my backstory and lessons learned that helped me reinvent my professional brand. I think it may help if this is a stumbling block for your right now.

My career has been diverse, working in universities and colleges I focused initially on e-learning as a specialist field then evaluation of e-learning projects then evaluation of change projects in general. As my career evolved so did my focus. Setting up direct sales businesses and establishing my consulting and training business, I felt I had other things to offer others that I was rather more passionate about. My experience positioned me quite well to help organisations and small businesses with strategic planning and process improvement, and thereafter I started to focus more and more on marketing and digital transformation.

It wasn't all plain sailing. After doing so many different kinds of work, in different industries and with different kinds of clients, I had a bit of an identity crisis. I'm sure this is why I started struggling to find clients. When you don't know quite what your "thing" is anymore and what you're best equipped to do in the world of work, you lose a sense of personal identity as well as professional specialism.

Sound familiar? If you're an accountant and you've always been an accountant perhaps not so, but if you're a "jack-of-all-trades", you need to decide what you will be master of – and focus your reinvention on that.

Think of each stage of your career history as a leg that supports the chair you sit on as a professional expert. Even though you may have started over in some areas, each leg you add brings greater stability to your status when you sit on top of it. But it doesn't always feel that way, does it? Like me, you may have felt (or still feel) a loss of identity.

If you've switched focus once or a few times as your job and talents evolved or the market changed, use it to your advantage in how you can serve your clients, but look at what you're king or queen of, sitting on your chair with all its legs underneath.

Anyway, hopefully you get the picture, our professional identity evolves and we have to redefine, reinvent and rebrand ourselves from time to time – or we leave it to chance and it can feel quite overwhelming and frustrating.

For instance, my academic career and business career developed completely separately to each other, and at first, I wanted it that way. However, I ended up with two professional identities and in fact two variations of my name. It became quite tricky later on when I wanted to reconnect the two. It's a case in point of how to manage multiple identities. My full name and title is Dr Jacqueline Allyson Dempster. I shortened Jacqueline to Jay way back in college so to anyone who knows me from my academic career, I'm Dr Jay Dempster, which carried through to my consulting business in the early years.

On the other hand, when I first started a network marketing business, I guess I was a little self-conscious about what work colleagues would think, and so wanted to keep it separate. I started using my middle name Allyson (named after June Allyson) and the Jay Allyson brand was fashioned.

A similar situation might be book authors using a different pen name when they want to write in a new genre. Or if you changed your name when you got married or divorced, this may complicate things in terms of what you call yourself from there on. You need a way to stay connected to how people know you in the industry and the reputation you've built up. Keeping the two names separate for professional and personal purposes can be one way around this. You can be Dr Jones at work and Mr or Mrs Smith on the home front or it may make more sense and lead to less confusion to use Dr Jones-Smith across both.

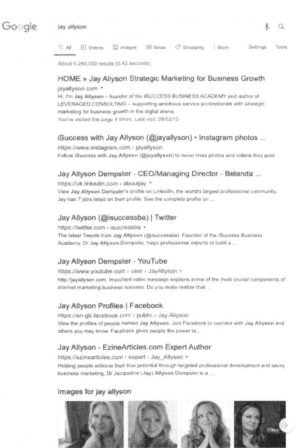

Using two names for different industries worked well for me for a while. It kept my business coaching identity nicely disassociated from my academic education identity. My logic was that if people searched online for Jay Allyson, they'd only find my business-related stuff and wouldn't be confused by references to my academic publications. Plus, Jay Allyson is just a nattier easy-to-remember brand name.

There's another important reason I decided on using "Jay Allyson" as a business brand identity going forward - online I'm unique! Having a unique name is definitely useful as a marketer, less so in academia. Every email address and social media account I have is "jayallyson" not "jayallyson9" or "the-real-jay-allyson", which you end up with if there are already lots of people with the same name as you.

Annoyingly I messed up when I was trying to merge my two Twitter accounts: in switching out the names, I accidentally released "jayallyson" as a profile username and it was snapped up by someone called Allyson Jay who eerily actually looks a little like me! I may get it back, but for now I'm using @isuccessba. Since my display name is still Jay Allyson and I have nearly 12k followers, I still get found on page 1 of google.

There are many experts far more prolific than me who you can google for more examples. My point is this "page #1 ego board" isn't to impress you (and) but to impress upon you that even with the messes I got into, nothing is impossible in terms of professional identity! Having a digital presence is a great advantage for building a distinctive brand and becoming "slightly famous", as I'll talk more about later.

Hop on over to google and *look yourself up*. When you search your own name or company name, you should own the top spot. And if you've been in a business a while, then you should dominate the whole first page with your websites, social media profiles and content. If that means adding a middle initial or brand name to make sure you don't get lost in a page of other sites and profiles with the same name, why not give yourself that advantage and claim a unique identity.

Your social media presence acts as a digital shop window and any links needs to encourage the right people to enter your world. The chief focus of your professional branded website is then to communicate clearly who you help, why you help them, and the benefits/results people will get from working with you. This is the real embodiment of your professional identity, and promotes your unique expert status.

CLAIMING YOUR UNIQUE EXPERT STATUS

Ok, so going back to how you raise your leverage capacity that we looked at in the previous chapter, let's assume you've decided you want to work at the top of the tree. If you're building a skyscraper, it follows that you need strong foundations and a big part of this is to get super clear and very specific on what exactly you do. As you may have found, that's harder than it sounds!

Your unique expert brand needs to be so specific that it provides a badge of honour and distinguishes you from others in your niche.

One way to achieve this is to build a brand around a "core concept", as we talked about earlier. This is usually a key thing you're known for doing; it should be a simple idea, complex to solve; transformative and of premium value to your target clientele.

It's like that as a consultant, it's hard to pin yourself down to a single distinctive expert area. You probably rarely do just one thing, you have a menu, a "smorgasbord" of possibilities. All the talk about pinning down a specialism, sub-niche or micro-niche can feel uncomfortable and constraining.

For me, having different niches and client types used to feel discordant in terms of the (dreaded) question "what do you do", until I found the common theme and focused on a specific field, that of helping businesses grow. Nevertheless, I always got frustrated that "I have ALL this expertise and knowledge, how come I can't get more clients?" That's because I wasn't focusing on one core niche but rather working in lots of different roles plucking at all the various strings on my bow.

One of the hardest concepts to accept in marketing is that generalists get lost in the crowd. Essentially, you need to specialise – pluck out a specific strand where there is a big need or problem, then build a distinctive offer around it, which is aimed at the specific audience who has that need or problem. This is how you attract your most ideally suited and profitable clients or customers. Your identity and brand should match and speak the language of what these clients are looking for.

How I do this is by packaging up my services into structured and branded programmes that deliver a specific solution to a specific problem. That may be delivered in different formats, for instance as a one-to-one consulting project or as a group workshop.

Another way to look at defining your unique expert status is to consider the specific solution – as an outcome, benefit or transformation - that you uniquely provide. Even if you're using PRINCE2 or something standard in your industry, find a way to differentiate what you bring to the table, perhaps simply a novel way to represent your methodology visually. This becomes your unique expert system.

Next, look at the vehicle for delivering this solution, i.e. how you work with your clients, such as one-to-one consulting, virtual coaching, an online course, a physical or digital product.

Being clear on your core business (why, what & how) means you can design your architecture accordingly: create a platform, target your audience,

position yourself, package and price your offer, build and scale around one unique solution you deliver.

To start you off working out your own unique expert status, here are three key questions to address, which should cohere to form the vital core of your business brand and messaging.

---

1. Why did you start up your business?

Why did you choose that particular industry? Are you qualified in a key demand area? Do you simply prefer working for yourself than for someone else? Or maybe you just want to work in an industry you enjoy? (You may even have re-qualified or trained to do so.)

2. What problem that people have is at the heart of what you do?

What motivates you or has you excited about your service or work with clients? If income were not the driver, what specifically would you choose to do and why is that important to you and your clients? As well as consulting or coaching, how have you already been helping people with this: writing, speaking, teaching?

3. How are you special in what you do and how you do it?

Do you believe you have something of distinct value to offer people? Do friends or family often comment on your skills and qualities and you wonder if you can turn that into a business? Do you have an innovative way of delivering your product or service? Can you articulate what that is exactly? Do you already have a platform online or offline? Do you have an existing audience / email list or following on social media?

These kinds of personal questions may seem a bit "fluffy" in business plan terms, and I'm not saying making money isn't important; of course, it is. If you don't make money, you're not really in business. If you're doing what you love, but spend more than you earn, it's a hobby! Even charities and social enterprises have to make money, in order to survive and expand so they can impact more people.

If you're struggling to pin down exactly what you do and articulate it clearly right now, don't worry. We'll get deeper into this in later stages of the book.

Finding your purpose means thinking about why you do what you do: why did you get into that your specific industry, what do you like about it, what gives you satisfaction, how do you see the benefits to people from what you do?

Essentially, what is mean here is that your business is an expression of what your work is about and what your sense of worth is to your clients – it's for you to define its purpose and value. When you think in these terms, you end up operating in a very different space.

If you're conscious of your "why", you'll generally be more focused, more disciplined, more productive, and more likely to get out of your comfort zone when things get tough or you need to innovate.

With clarity on the *value for money* you deliver, you can more easily epitomise your vision and naturally become more charismatic and persuasive, more magnetic and effective when marketing your services. This is also how you stay totally authentic in claiming your unique expert status.

Take advantage of your passion, your story and your value by building a brand around your distinctive expertise insights and way of working.

> ※
>
> "No other person ever has, or ever will, have the unique blend of talents, strengths and perspective that you have." – Marie Forleo, B-School

When you do this, you raise yourself high above what the "me too" competitors in your industry are doing, because what you do, why and how you do it is inherently unique to you.

What's exciting is that as individuals, we have this great opportunity to create a business that is an expression of who you decide to be in the world, and the influence and impact you wish to have. Working in alignment with your "calling" means you operate your business in less of a "selling" mode because you are committed to a bigger vision, something of value beyond just yourself and your income.

TAKING CONSULTING INTO MARKETING

Professional service providers are first and foremost experts in what they do; they may also have had to develop consulting or coaching skills as part of their work with clients. However, consultants certainly do not start out as business managers or marketers (unless that's their field of course!) But what if you could leverage both your expertise and consulting skills as part of your marketing and sales process - that would feel natural, right?

The *Engage-Educate-Enrol* pathway you learned about in Chapter 1 is all about doing just that: setting up a structured process to attract your ideal clientele to you, in a way that feels natural to your everyday consulting or coaching practice. After engaging and educating your prospects, when you eventually invite someone to have a consultative *enrolling* call with you, it's in the spirit of providing further service.

The dialogue should be non-directive and non-salesy; it allows you to have a personal meeting of minds, demonstrates your professionalism and understanding of the problem(s), shares some of the value of your expertise and, most importantly, builds rapport, confidence and trust – all at the same time.

When you structure the consulting or coaching conversation towards identifying the gap between where they are now and where they want to be or the result they want – you highlight a course of action or plan. People find that very helpful and will thank you for it! Don't give too much away though, because the natural next question is whether they want some help to implement what's needed.

> ※
>
> "It's been said that buyers of Consulting do not travel the Internet looking for consultants but people with a problem do search the internet for a solution to that problem. If you hone in on that problem in your brand message, they will find you." – Alan Weiss, Million Dollar Consulting

As we talked about with the dating funnel earlier, this fits with what's known about the "customer journey", as show below. People need to know, like and trust you before they will take things further with you. These stages are necessary for creating and cementing the kind of relationship that leads to a sale, i.e. the point at which they become a client or customer.

It's especially important to nurture this journey when you're offering high-ticket services and programmes. And the best way to nurture is to be caring and giving.

STRANGER
interested but doesn't know you, curious

PROSPECT
likes your stuff, very interested, intrigued

LEAD
trusts your stuff, engaged, partially satisfied

CLIENT
buys your stuff, engaged, satisfied

Now, I understand that giving away your intellectual property for free (on what we call the "front end") may seem counterintuitive if you're in business to earn a living. Yet in truth, prospective clients are way more likely to see you as a trusted adviser if you first confirm you can help them before you try to sell them anything.

Think about the steps you go through in your consulting or coaching work with a client to help them achieve the desired result – this is your "expert system". The sequence acts as an educational tool for your prospective client to work through the problem in partnership with you as the expert guide.

You see, information or knowledge on its own rarely produces enlightenment or understanding, only a promise. And people are either very sceptical these days of marketing hype or they chase after shiny shortcuts or tactics that are the heralded as the "next best thing".

Apart from purely "done-for-you" services where there's a brief and a deliverable and little conversation, consulting and coaching provides the client with real dialogue – engaging and educating your client on how to solve a complex problem. What if you use that as part of your marketing with potential clients?

For me, I first used presentations, guidance templates and diagnostic sessions as a means to lead my prospective clients towards an understanding of the problem and why they have it, and how they can resolve or rectify it. This provides added value and I later realised these consulting materials were very effective as marketing tools to attract new business.

Having a clear and structured educative system is very pragmatic way to move people forward to understanding the problem or need they have and identifying the right solution for themselves. Once they have that enlightenment, so to speak, it's far more likely they will make the decision to buy your product or service in order to get the solution they desire.

Creating a branded expert system is a great way to promote your leadership in a specific problem.

Believe me, there's a tonne of ways to build your business upon educational principles and marketing practices that will feel completely natural to you as a consultant or coach, because it's inherent in the expert thing you do. I never "sell" because I don't associate selling with the type of consulting or coaching work I want to attract, which is a collaboration not a transaction.

MAPPING OUT YOUR EXPERT SYSTEM

The way you go about working with a client is your "expert system" or methodology – a step-by-step process for delivering a specific result they want. Your expert system should start from where your client starts and provide a means for them to achieve the outcome they signed up for. Notably, your expert system is entirely unique to you, which is why it's often referred to as your "signature" system or programme – more on that in a bit.

Even if we don't necessary refer to them as expert systems, consulting methodologies (techniques, tools and frameworks) are quite common in our industry for tackling a particular challenge, problem or client engagement – think McKinsey.

If presently you don't explicitly think of what you do in systems terms or deliver your client projects in a structured way, mapping out in tangible terms how you get a client from A to B is a useful exercise. Think of it as a mindmap with your core concept at the centre and plot a route through the themes.

The unique core of your business as what the Japanese call your "reason for being" – your "ikigai". You'll find this at the centre of the four elements of ikigai:

(1) What you love or enjoy doing

(2) What you're good at

(3) What people want (to get done or know how to do), and

(4) What they will pay (you) for.

I love this approach to identifying your expert system because it's the big cohering idea that underpins your business brand. This is so critical for effective marketing and developing a signature programme or service.

(The time spent identifying my own centrepiece was so worthwhile because it allowed me to bring several areas of expertise into a single concept as part of the reinvention and rebranding that I mentioned earlier. It also allowed me to see when to say no to things that didn't fit with my core business!)

Once you have your core concept and methodology documented, you can use this in tender bids and presentations to potential clients as well as part of your induction of any new partners or associates you decide take on. All great leverage!

Sharing the methodology that you use in your marketing and sales communications helps to clarify the start-finish points and demonstrates to a potential client that you understand the problem and can deliver a positive outcome (to justify the cost of working with you).

Someone's work with you does not necessarily start only when they sign up as a client. You can kick off their journey as part of your marketing. If you create content that speaks to the conversation going on in your prospective client's head, education-driven marketing draws your ideal client towards you like a magnet.

It starts the process of working together (before they are even a client) and builds trust in you and your approach before you ask for a bigger commitment.

For instance, part of your consultative or coaching process is likely to be providing industry insights, introductory material on specific topics, a diagnostic or review, and maybe a checklist. You can use this kind of education-rich content as an entry point - a first step towards working with you on a deeper level and a first taste of what you do.

All your content should mirror your values and beliefs, which hopefully your clients share, as well as pull from your knowledge and expertise, which hopefully they seek. It should provide high-quality, relevant and useful guidance, which demonstrates you're someone who can help them.

Putting an expert system into play in real client work is a great way to find out two crucial things: firstly, how your target audience receives it, i.e. do clients enjoy the approach, and secondly, do they achieve better and faster results using it compared to other things they've tried. Additionally, there's the question of can you teach them to use it independently of you being there in person.

The next natural step is to put the expert system you use in your client services into practical forms that others could learn from – i.e. products. (I did this in the form of articles, guides, tools, infographics, templates, checklists I now use in my courses, and ultimately this book. This creates lots of expert marketing collateral and also fulfils my enjoyment of teaching.)

FINDING A DISTINCTIVE HOOK

In a crowded marketplace, consulting type services can be invisible, intangible or seen as a commodity in the eyes of your customers. Your marketing therefore needs to tackle head on the doubt in any potential client's mind about your expertise, service quality and ability to deliver. Based on what they see, read or hear, potential clients will ultimately decide whether they think or feel you'll be a good return on investment.

Everyone's looking to find a good new angle or "hook". With so much information and so many marketing messages and sales ads, it's increasingly hard for any business or personal brand to stand out in the crowd as unique and special.

Perhaps because of the growing confusion and demand for simple solutions, there's now correspondingly also an abundance of tactical "if you do this one thing" advice out there. In many ways, this serves only to further perplex and confused us - and your prospective clients too.

> ※
>
> "Marketing in a post-TV world is no longer about making a product attractive or interesting or pretty or funny after it's designed and built – it's about designing the thing to be virus-worthy in the first place." – Seth Godin, The Purple Cow

But ideas – and remarkable ideas in particular – are the cornerstone of the innovation and differentiation necessary to gain competitive advantage in business. Good ideas can spread like a virus, especially on the internet. Great ideas travel and get passed around faster than covid-19! I'm guessing you've heard the term "viral marketing"? It's the epitome of a successful idea, that once it takes off, propagates and intensifies audience engagement. Sometimes people become "accidental leaders" because an idea or opinion – something they said or wrote – resonated and took off. Suddenly, almost overnight, they became the authority figure on that subject!

As the market keeps evolving, successful businesses think ahead to hot new topics, work on how they can stand out and get noticed – i.e. lead the herd, rather than follow the herd.

Every good idea will still need positioning and promoting to rise above the general noise, since identifying the next new trend or hot topic a very tough game to play in any industry. What you can do is maintain your finger on the pulse, find out what your market is asking for, synthesise current ideas and put your own spin on it.

GROWING YOUR INFLUENCE, IMPACT & INCOME

By providing guidance and consulting on your expert system, you are creating a step-by-step process that helps people understand the problem and how the solution is reached. In so doing, you're also positioning yourself as the expert to help them implement it.

As people engage with your material, they will self-select on whether you, and what you offer, are right for them or not. But not every potential client will be ready, willing or able to pay for your high-end consulting or coaching, even if they're convinced you can help them achieve results. This is where developing educational products at different price points comes into play.

There's a relationship between demand, price and quantity, shown in the graphs here. Willingness to pay is the area *under the demand line*. In other words, it's where people will buy a given quantity at a given price.

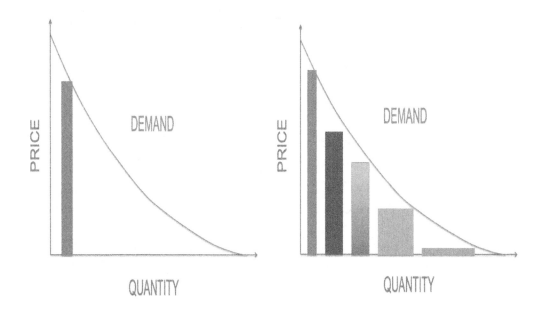

This is a concept I gleaned from an article by one of the team at *Thinkific*, the platform where I host my online courses. They were talking about content strategy, but creating products at different price points is equally applicable across your whole business.

The point here is this. If you only have one offer (whether it's a product or a service) at the high-price end (left side of the graph), you're not leveraging yourself enough. You're missing out on serving all the potential people (on the "empty" right side of the graph) who are willing to pay for your help, but only ready to invest in a product at a lower price point.

Typically, only a segment of your potential market will buy high priced consulting or coaching services or programmes. That means a lot of that area under the line is going to waste; people you're not serving unless you have other low-cost options. This is where a diversified product strategy provides greater leverage. We'll go into this more in chapter 6 when we look at leveraged delivery.

When you add free or low-priced options - a free weekly article, a podcast, a book, a course, you will serve more people and increase uptake of your high-end offer. Depending on the volume of sales and the rate they convert to higher price point sales – lifetime customer value - you could end up making quite a tidy profit. It could be a steady trickle or a great gushing stream of additional income.

Everything in your mix is mutually reinforcing across the customer journey; it's a funnel into the next funnel and essentially an "upsell" to a higher priced option to continue learning from and working with you, and getting results. (If any of these terms are unfamiliar or baffling, don't worry, we'll be going through this in more detail in later chapters.)

The logic is that if someone likes your free stuff and it helps them with a first step forward, they're more likely to buy your entry-level course. If they find this valuable and it helps them, they're more likely to buy a premium product like an online group programme or live event or take up one of your high-end one-to-one services.

This is what's known as a *value ladder* and is often deemed the most effective way to nurture prospects towards a high-end commitment. Now, not all business strategists agree that a value ladder with multiple products at increasing price points is necessary or even a good idea. Some advocate keeping things very simple: a free training webinar that generates leads and offers a high-end programme - a one-step funnel.

Personally, I advise somewhere in between – three steps - a lead magnet giveaway, one low-cost option and a high-ticket service or programme. This is because until you're certain of your conversions from clicks to paying clients, a low-cost front-end product can help fund paid advertising to drive traffic to your sales page and into your funnel.

Regardless of whether it's a free or paid product, one thing is clear. Education-focused products make great business tools – they can help you build your audience, grow your email list, and increase revenue from the sales generated across your entire offer matrix. Entry-level products are a great precursor to your work with clients and a very persuasive demonstration of your expertise in helping them.

Your product can be anything, from a slice of material you probably already use in your work with clients "behind the velvet rope", such as a diagnostic, a short consultation session, a worksheet, tool or template, right through to a full blown 12-week online course or 6-month coaching programme.

For example, you can add value to a standalone course by adding in greater access to you, the expert, and a more personal interaction and individual support – what you might call "done-with-you". The benefit is it accelerates the learning process and you get results faster with your direct assistance.

The low-cost options are preliminary steps in your expert system where you are educating the client, engaging with them, developing a two-way understanding. The higher price options get down to business and show them how to do things or provide "done-for-you" services that lead to the result they want to achieve.

Remember our relationship funnels in chapter 1? Education is intended to entice and engage your ideal audience. It's the best "attraction marketing" you can put out there. Your packaged content should mirror the steps of how you ordinarily build a consulting relationship – pose questions, talk about experiences, explain problems, teach on the solutions, show examples of what you do.

Leveraging you is like dating, it's attraction marketing leading to good quality conversations, continued engagement, and eventually a long-lasting relationship and partnership.

In fact, now there are many quiz or survey tools you can use to ask diagnostic questions that, as a consultant or coach, you'd typically want to ask a new client. They help provide context and segment your audience so you can provide them with relevant guidance based on their answers.

This is actually a key part of good learning design. Start with what comes naturally to you and build a product from there. Just remember that your primary objective is to educate, inform, and impact the people you are serving.

It's not technically difficult to get going with these tools, so don't be put off the idea. Through this responsive process, you can powerfully show your potential client you understand their situation – where they are and where they want to be (i.e. the desire - a solution or resolution that you know you can help them as they work at deeper levels with you.

The media you use can be anything; it could be a survey or online poll with feedback on the responses, a set of powerpoint slides, a worksheet, infographic, mindmap or flowchart, an audio (podcast), a video (webcast), a webinar or virtual "live" workshop.

The natural next step after showing them a roadmap to get from the problem to the desired outcome is to ask: would you like some help to implement this approach to achieving that result?

DEVELOPING A SIGNATURE PROGRAMME

How you help your client implement your expert system and achieve results can be packaged and presented as a "signature" programme, which immediately distinguishes you from your competitors. This is why creating an expert system is an idea you should take on board as soon as you can. (It actually took me a couple of years to realise this myself. I already had an expert system that worked brilliantly for my clients, I just needed to package it!)

In designing an expert signature programme, you're forced to pin down what it is you uniquely deliver, to map out the process of how you achieve that specific result, and then package it within a structured programme.

Having a signature programme doesn't mean you can't be flexible in your approach working with a client. My signature programme is based entirely on my expert system. I use this structure as a framework for my consulting diagnostic process and also as modules in the *iSuccess Business Academy*.

Having a professional methodology - including visuals, tools, templates, checklists and so on - gives you and your client a clear and intentional step-by-step process and confidence in your ability to deliver on your promise. The customer wants to feel they will receive great "value for money" (i.e. when the value of the result you get for your client is matched with the price that they pay for it).

Unless you are brand new and don't yet have your working methods clearly defined, you will undoubtedly have some kind of system for how you deliver your service whether you're aware of it as a tangible process or not.

In my consulting practice, I was intuitively mapping out a process in my head. Because what I found working with clients is that, at the start, they had a misconceived idea of the fundamentals. They only knew the *symptoms* of their problem and did not understand the root causes to see why a solution is a solution.

My signature programme is intended to enlighten and educate so clients are equipped to know what to prioritise and can select and implement the best tactics move forward without the usual stress, indecisions and overwhelm. For instance: say the problem a business owner say they have is poor sales, that's quite a broad problem. The client may incorrectly assume that sales technique or team performance is the issue. If they went with that as a solution, they would be investing time and money training their sales team.

However, once we delved deeper into the situation with a few key questions, it was easy for them to see where exactly in the process they were losing sales. It wasn't the sales team; it was the offer. We then worked on improving message-to-market match. I asked them to look at their data right from the beginning of the process – rather than only focusing on "sales" on the back end. Looking at the right data, we could clearly see the root cause was a low performing website not the sales team on the phone who were doing their best to convert the wrong audience to their product.

My expert system is the process by which I diagnose the root cause of my clients' challenges and help them identify the priority areas to change and develop solutions for. The solutions are to align their purpose, positioning and branding with their target audience to create a much tighter message-to-market match. But first they need to understand what drives conversion rates.

You undoubtedly have an array of tacit insights and personal qualities acquired from your career and/or lifelong learning. Your signature programme will be unique not only because it's based on your own expert system but also because it's tried and tested through your professional experience working with clients.

Your signature programme packages your expert system – its framework and practical methodology – and provides a vehicle for delivering it. It's something very tangible you can offer to your target market.

Your signature programme should feed an urgent or recurring desire your clients have, not your ego as an expert "know-it-all". (In in my enthusiasm, I'm close the edge on this one as I love to share my lessons learned!) What you should aim to offer is an educational experience. It's not an excuse to do a brain dump and call it a "course". There needs to be a learning pathway, a structure and an experiential element for your participants.

 (If you haven't yet used your expert system to solve real problems and get results for clients, or if you're changing the format for how you deliver it, I suggest you run a pilot to test and refine the methodology. This will also generate testimonials for marketing your programme in the future.)

By offering prospects a valuable, transformational programme as your core offer, you're giving them the support they actually need so you can make an impact on their life and/or business. At the same time, attracting high-end clients and having a tangible results-driven product can transform *your* impact and income.

Packaging your expertise into a programme of support or a product gives you far more leverage in your consulting business than negotiating a certain number of days one-on-one work with a client. Say your monthly income goal is 20k: instead of having to sell hundreds of consulting or coaching hours at a few hundred pounds or dollars an hour, you only have to sell a handful of programmes at 5k.

If creating a signature programme seems daunting, don't worry, because I'll be helping you with this in later parts of the book. For now, let's move onto specifics with our next pillar - leveraged marketing.

Just before we do, here's a prompt to capture the key ideas and "light bulb" moments you got so far. Use the space in the companion workbook to add more.

ACTION NOTES

_____

_____

_____

_____

_____

_____

_____

Chapter 4

LEVERAGED MARKETING

Attract the Right Crowd

"The really eye-opening thing about entrepreneurship is it starts with one basic premise: find something people need or want, and give it to them."

Derek Murphy,

Guerrilla Publishing

KEY POINTS

❖ People who like what your brand stands for are the people most likely to pay for your services and products.

❖ Attracting clients to work with you relies heavily on the clarity and elegance with which you present the problem and your solution.

❖ Work out how you can help someone do something better. People don't improve by knowing more, they improve by doing things better.

❖ A strong brand message needs to represent your professional and personal sides and embody your values, beliefs, expertise and culture.

❖ Storytelling is gaining credence as a mighty powerful technique for brand development and its use in marketing is growing.

❖ Business is constantly reinventing itself, which means consultants need to be constantly reinventing themselves too.

❖ Only when you own your expert process can you create an authentic brand and start attracting the clients you really wanted to work with.

❖ Always ask yourself, does the professional label you give yourself bring you in close alignment with the particular group of people you feel most compelled to serve.

❖ Look at the intersection where your interests, expertise and talents fit together - that's a very powerful way to define your personal brand.

❖ To traverse the complexity that the digital age has procreated, what people most want now is a roadmap for success to clarify, systematise and streamline everything; to leverage not burden your business.

❖ Challenging the hard wiring is essential to transforming practice and what enables a shift in perspective is real education.

❖ If you want to make more money and serve more people than you currently do, you need to find more ways to engage, follow up and deliver to more people.

❖ When you can set out the key parts of what you do working one-to-one with a client as a tangible step-by-step process, you have an expert system you can turn into an educational programme.

❖ With digital marketing and web analytics, it's now easier than ever to access robust data across your end-to-end customer journey.

MARKETING IN A CROWDED MARKETPLACE

Every day, millions of people in almost every country across the globe consume digital content and at the same time are bombarded with thousands of marketing messages. We now live in an environment where both online information and digital marketing has become ludicrously abundant and worryingly merged. Competition for attention is rife.

People are constantly on their computer or phone searching for information that addresses, improves or solves a problem they have. They read articles and books; they watch videos and TV programmes; they listen to podcasts and audio books; they attend workshops and masterclasses; and they sign up for courses or coaching programmes.

Such consumption drives production of yet more content and as businesses tap into this vibrant marketplace, growth in online information is exponential. In marketing in a crowded marketplace, authority, relevance, distinctiveness, quality and clarity are paramount.

Just as in print, the authoritative status used to be somewhat assumed and we rely on our tacit knowledge and common sense to sift wheat from chaff. Nowadays, however, there is increasing scepticism and most audiences are pretty discerning of the quality and providence of the content they consume. And importantly, they're looking for like-mindedness, understanding and leadership.

Consultants are well-placed to satisfy these criteria to provide expert knowledge, learning, know-how, guidance and advice. High-end clients are an engaged and intelligent audience who know what they want. They have a specific problem or challenge and are looking for specific answers and specific solutions for how to do something (or do something better). And in the main, they have money to invest for the right solution.

Consulting firms market themselves based on the "solutions" they provide or help deliver. We may help clients to understand what's needed and/or implement what's needed. Ultimately, what we deliver is a beneficial outcome that they pay us for. Some will "do it for you" (e.g. agencies, designers, tech services), whereas others will "do it with you" (e.g. consultants, coaches, therapists and so forth).

When you learn how to clarify the one specific thing your ideal client wants that you can deliver, you stand out and your marketing becomes highly leveraged. Using digital tools, it's way more straightforward to

> ※
> "Lack of clarity in WHAT you're aiming to create, WHO you're creating it for, and HOW you're going to do it is why most people fail." - Mike Klingler

craft, package and promote a unique message and push it out to the world.

By publishing high-quality, digital content, you build credibility and trust. Your material becomes a magnet, consistently attracting leads for your business, pre-qualifying potential clients, and creating new streams of revenue. Aptly tagged keyword content and automated systems help you segment and draw the right people to you, as they decide if you're a good match for what they want, need and desire.

Online, you can create branded and easily shareable educational content with which you can vastly increase your audience reach and your earning potential.

MATCHING YOUR MESSAGE TO YOUR MARKET

Before you start promoting anything to anyone, you must leverage your unique message so it matches the right audience. That means defining who your offer is aimed at, why it's of value to them and how it will impact them. Use this as a steer to create consistently powerful, compelling marketing messages.

Segmentation and differentiation in the marketplace are frequently overlooked as innovations in strategic business planning, yet a lack of these can easily render your service a general commodity rather than a unique rarity. This makes business growth very difficult. You can focus on one segment or more than one, depending on your business plan, but specificity is quite critical to effective marketing.

Successfully aligning what you do with a specific target market who can truly benefit is key to building an active and responsive list of prospects. As people move forward with you, it shows their interest and commitment, and you can start to test their willingness to spend money with you.

Having subscribers such as people who have joined your email list or social media group/following creates an important asset for your business and also means your marketing can be much more tightly targeted and controlled. Eventually, when you've built some rapport, you can start to make offers to your list that will lead to sales with more elegance and less effort.

In essence, people who like what your brand stands for are the people most

> ※
> "Building your email list is literally the foundation of your entire business. When you grow your email list you are growing a business asset you can use to get instant views on your content, videos, products, launches and more!" – Carrie Green, Founder of the Female Entrepreneurs Association.

likely to pay for your services and products.

When people engage with you and your content, it's a good indication that they resonate with what you stand for, and probably resonate with you on a personal level too. If they have a particular desire, need or problem you can help with, they will want to learn more about what you do (and can do for them).

If they have chosen to engage with you, they're already primed prospective buyers. The metric here is not only the *number* of people who join your email list, follow you on social media, join a group you lead, but also those who comment on your post, turn up to your live event or webinar or buy and leave a review for your book. This is your tribe - a targeted, responsive and profitable audience you can build a relationship with.

Once you've identified your ideal audience, it will make it much clearer what kind of content will grab their attention the most. When you understand who your perfect prospect is and what they want and need, you will know what to say, what to do write, and what to create.

Think about these three questions in relation to your best clients:

1. What questions do you consistently get asked?
2. What are the major pain points or needs?
3. What do they sing your praises about the most?

You can test your theory by creating content, sharing it with your audience and seeing how people respond. Join a few social media groups online where your likely audiences hang out and see what they're posting or asking questions about. Ask people what kind of content they would find most valuable or create a poll of topics and invite them to vote.

These are all great ways to:

- Identify the select group who are the best fit as potential clients for your business;

- Understand what problems they are struggling with the most so you can match what they want and need to your marketing messages;

- Ensure you are creating content that grabs the attention of your perfect people and focuses on the solution they desire;

- Craft a compelling and irresistible giveaway to offer (as a "lead magnet") in exchange for their name and email address.

Clearly, producing content does require an upfront investment of time, but the perpetual flow of leads and long-term gains can be substantial. Through your content, your prospective clients will start to appreciate your deep understanding of the context and trust you know what you're talking about! The solution to most of your clients' wants and needs comes down to clarity.

Attracting clients to work with you relies heavily on the clarity and elegance with which you present the problem and your solution.

In my consulting business, invariably, my clients want help to improve efficiency, increase sales, get more clients or improve marketing ROI. These "desires" distil into how to get more clients or customers. However, they don't see what else needs to happen. Even if I could wave a magic wand and they get all the clients they want, their operational set-up is unlikely to support a sudden explosion of new business.

Bear in mind that the solution your clients want and what they actually need is often in their blind spot. For me, sharing content around systems, automation and customer support is unlikely to hit home for my ideal clientele. But talking about strategic marketing, business growth and leverage opens doors.

CREATING A VISIBLE BRAND

No matter what business you are in, no matter how intrinsically motivated you are or how good you are at what you do, you need to acknowledge and accept that you must also be in the business of marketing. And, in some shape or form, that means creating a visible brand.

It's less daunting than you think. Start by aligning the purpose of your business with your target market, understanding their needs and wants and building relationships as a trusted adviser, an educator and change agent as well as a provider of valuable services or products.

Creating a brand around your purpose, expertise and signature programme is, I believe, the most crucial element of marketing success for independent consultants. Building your brand around a specific and unique *value proposition* positions your expert status with four important benefits:

    (a) It fuels both our ego and our mojo, which let's face it, just feels good;

    (b) It differentiates you from others in the same space;

    (c) It naturally segments those who resonate best with you, personally;

    (d) It leads to positive enrolment conversations that convert to clients.

For me, although I've reinvented myself a few times, having an online brand presence has always been a very significant vehicle for building my business. Before deciding to work with me or join my team, many people say they looked me up on social media, read something of mine or heard me speak and saw me as the "go-to" expert in that niche. Some remarked "you're everywhere!" That's positioning and branding for you.

While some have the opinion that social media is a waste of time for securing consulting work (or for anything!), I'd argue the opposite. Although the direct benefit of a particular online platform really depends on your target market and where they hang out, writing good content and interacting in networks definitely does get your name out there.

Your digital presence and visibility in turn attracts guest posting, speaking engagements, collaborations and other opportunities, online and offline, to grow your audience. From there, a lot of work can flow in.

So how do you go about creating a brand around your expert status? Well first, you must decide what's your best "go-to" specialism. In a consulting or coaching type business, your value originates from a specific area of expertise or passion you have, so often that's the easy part. Your specialism should undoubtedly be something you know lots about, you're good at doing, and you can help people with. It's probably best if you choose a topic you enjoy talking about lots too.

Although you may have trained, gained qualifications and developed expertise in a particular vocation (e.g. chartered accounting, cognitive behavioural therapy, business improvement), it's generally the case that we enjoy doing the things we're good at and care about – it puts fire in our belly. And we get really good at the things we enjoy doing, mainly because we tend to do them more often. This becomes your "sweet spot".

If there's a profitable market for what you do, planting a seed in this sweet spot is the best way to nurture your business growth. This holds true whether your talents are in business, health, accountancy, finance, book publishing, web design, nutrition, photography, media production, hairdressing, floristry, personal training, yoga, and so on, you name it.

BEING AN ATTRACTIVE PROPOSITION

A business's success depends on good ideas, authenticity, connection and results. A positive brand based on value ignites enthusiasm and drives all your profits. This isn't something you should leave to chance or expect to build without careful consideration and planning. Most recognised experts achieved success less so from "doing their job well" and more so from putting new insights together from disparate ideas presented in novel and meaningful ways.

From my very first modest "signature" programme, *Mindset, Marketing & Money Breakthroughs* – I've stood for helping people bridge their performance gaps – to break through barriers to success. You can't do this kind of work and deliver results with information alone, which is why coaching and mentoring has always been a big part of my courses. Good educational design is critical to how I deliver value and it's what I'd aspire to become slightly famous for!

Work out how your expertise can help someone do something better. Because people don't improve by knowing more, they improve by doing things better.

Earlier, I revealed (and don't mind admitting) that my first attempts at retail (direct sales) businesses were not particularly successful, probably because I never liked the traditional notion of "selling". I did a lot of soul searching and work on my mindset and studied sales techniques, but for me phone prospecting, sales pitches, retail events and sales presentations were all wretched experiences. If I'm honest, it felt desperate and cheap. I didn't last long doing those traditional methods!

In the professional services industry, that kind of sales driven attitude is just counterproductive. Nevertheless, what I learned from doing those businesses, and then again building internet-based businesses, has allowed me to understand the importance of knowing your target audience. It's led me to some absolute truths about why, when and how people buy things. And it's not from hard sales tactics, that's for sure; in fact, mostly the opposite is true.

> ※
> "Sales miracles begin when you make the transformation from party crasher to the guest of honor." – Rich Schefren

Through my own experiences, seeing the struggles of fellow consultants and online entrepreneurs, and what my small business clients had also been doing, I saw how the old paradigms of sales and marketing don't really work too well these days – especially not in the digital environment where social connections and trust are critical.

Branding is a core element that underpins both business strategy and marketing. Professional services need to market excellently, so they need a strong brand to attract the right audience. And you just can't dabble in anything you need to do well.

The psychology of sales and marketing became a fountain of knowledge I greedily drank from. I focused on marketing strategies and pushed sales techniques aside for quite a while.

Marketing a business online transformed the way I approached business development even further, and I started acquiring "leads" and "prospecting" people in a different way. I stopped handing out business cards, hanging around events with leaflets, saved a tonne of money by not buying leads or chasing down appointments.

In fact, I side-stepped, or more accurately hurdled over, all that horrid salesy nonsense - targets, pipelines and pitches - and developed a "success blueprint" for building a business via "attraction marketing" – showing people you can help them by actually helping them – which proved a much more enjoyable way to engage and win prospective clients.

I had in essence become an educational entrepreneur and as we progress further to explore other opportunities for leveraged consulting, I hope you will see how this can help you too to make a breakthrough to success.

My educational objective here is to help you achieve greater clarity and focus on why, what and how you wish to help others through your business services and products. From there, I can help you to build a structured, targeted, professional and education-driven system of your own, which enables you effectively and efficiently to attract, engage and serve your ideal clients.

CRAFTING AN AUTHENTIC MESSAGE

Your brand message should capture:

-   Your expertise
-   Your professional identity
-   Your personal goals and motivations
-   Your story
-   Your ideal intended audience's persona
-   Your personality and style (or that of the CEO).

These all form the backbone of your professional brand. Some of what's in the list may be a surprise, because they're quite personal. Nonetheless, they are all equally vital elements that will help you to more easily engage, win and serve more of your ideal clients.

A strong brand message for a service business needs to represent your professional and personal sides, and embody your values, beliefs, expertise and culture.

In my case, my brand today integrates various different professional identities. Having spent 20+ years as an education and e-learning specialist and 10 years building internet marketing businesses, it seemed silly not to use my expertise to create my own programmes rather than marketing other people's. I developed my unique brand around entrepreneurship and marketing, building from results I was getting in my local one-to-one business mentoring clients and leveraging my time by creating online materials, and eventually, whole courses.

My brand emanates from the one question I'm always asked, which is "What's the secret or the "right" approach to growing a successful service business?" My answer is never about tactics or the next best marketing tool or trick - it's about creating a strategic path to success.

The overarching strategy, I've come to depend on every time, is to get super clear on your purpose first then put education at the heart of your business development process. When you engage, inspire and serve your clients, they get excited about the possibilities and are then naturally open to working with you to implement the steps you show them to achieve the results you promise.

I believe that your brand – i.e. who you are, what you do and why you do it – comes directly out of your professional journey and your personal story. The biggest struggle I see with professional service providers when they start to develop their brand and marketing is that actually, although they may have managed to reinvent, redefine or reaffirm their expert niche, they haven't really pinned down their professional identity or, cliché as it sounds, found their true calling.

Cultivating a professional identity means narrowing your niche into a unique speciality. You will need to do the groundwork: consider the wider influences that make up your expertise. Your life and eclectic set of experiences combine uniquely with your insights from different disciplines and can mould your niche into distinctive territory.

Being distinctive is less about having an original concept and more about synthesising an original solution to a common problem. What do your clients misunderstand about a concept, what mistakes do they make and how can you help bring an idea to life, illuminate the problem and redirect their thinking?

This is the first phase of *codifying a system* that helps solve a fundamental problem - a framework or model, principles, stages, methodology and touchstones. This helps people to see a structured way to move step-by-step through the complexities of an idea and showing how it works in practice.

Professionals with a long career history can often lose sight of who they are, and what exactly as an individual they bring to the table. This often results in them losing sight of their goals and motivations, what wisdom they've gained over their lifetime, and what experience and expertise they can share, in terms of a specific offer.

Not knowing your true purpose or calling, and losing a clear sense of what drives you and makes you relatable, totally impacts your ability to connect with a specific audience and position your brand in the marketplace.

Doing work to reflect on and identify your personal struggles and successes is a pivotal part of any brand development exercise, because as a consultant-coach, your story – or journey - is a highly effective way to engage and connect with your target audience and to win customers' trust. Creating content, sharing your experiences and interacting with your target audience is essentially a way to put out a beacon so that compatible people can discover you.

STORYTELLING TO INSPIRE & MOTIVATE

Crafting your story is a great way to create a compelling business brand, because personal stories are powerful for connecting with people. They bridge the gap between your expert status and advice and where your audience or client currently is, and they help change someone's perspective and understanding of a problem or potential solution that you offer.

Storytelling is gaining credence as a mighty powerful technique for brand development and its use in marketing is growing.

Let's start at the very beginning…. Think about your own story behind how you ended up doing what you do – it's most always unique. Ponder for a few minutes what the journey is that you are on, what's the desired destination, the point of it all; what obstacles have you encountered along the way; and what inspires and motivates you most to reach your goal.

Since your story forms part of your brand that represents what you do and why you do it, I feel it's helpful (rather than narcissistic) to include mine in my own book, particularly since I'm assuming you are a consultant or coach like me, and want to achieve greater "success" as do I.

Stories come in all forms and another way to bring a point to life is to use metaphors and analogies. I love them and use them often, if you haven't noticed that already! However, the focus of a story should be on the customer and the customer's journey – where the brand story is simply positioning itself as a trail guide.

> ※
> "If you can dream it, you can do it!" - Walt Disney

The concept of leveraged consulting as an educational entrepreneur was actually born out of my story – and as I share it, I hope it illustrates how to find your "sweet spot" and then how to leverage it.

A sweet spot is what Rich Schefren terms one's expertise and special gifts - that one thing that differentiates you and your service business from the rest in your industry. You might call this your "genius zone". It's often a result of the particular journey and different paths you took. This all forms part of your brand story too and will always be unique to you - it's the story of how you ended up doing what you do.

For me, this came to light as I was trying to align my expertise with a business brand. Because my career is long and varied - I've worked in educational development, professional development and business development - I always felt I didn't have a specialism and was operating in two separate spheres and professional identities. I'm what Rachel Henke aka *"The Niche Expert"* would call "multi-niche" – for me it was just a giant branding mess!

So, I redefined my specialism around business strategy at the intercept point of my three main areas of expertise – operational improvement, digital marketing and e-learning - which are all critical areas for strategic business growth. Suddenly, I'd found my niche.

As an educational entrepreneur, I believe in sharing both the business and personal side of one's own journey. People get a lot of value learning from other people's experiences and your audience will resonate more with you when they understand your past struggles and the similarities with their own. It's one of the reasons I'm such a big fan of autobiographies of successful people, because their stories are inspiring and revealing as well as motivating.

In fact, storytelling has created a whole niche of its own in the business world. Jimmy Davis calls it *My Story Marketing*, Donald Miller calls it *Story Branding*, just do a search on those terms and you'll see its prominence in brand marketing.

My is a long and twisted tale. I spent years on what seemed at times an insurmountable learning curve! Most of the time, I felt frustrated trying to work stuff out for myself. I'd get so stuck I even felt like giving up completely; there always seemed something new to take on board and I felt I would never be that "expert".

I'm sure how, but throughout the ups and downs, I remained steadfast on the pursuit of building a business around my expertise, because I felt I had all this insight and capability inside me that I believed could really help other people.

My own entrepreneurial journey began in the midst of a high-flying career in the university sector. I started a home business part-time in the direct selling industry. This was my plan B to change my lifestyle, give myself some options, and have more freedom to support my kids. In truth, I also wanted to live a more "extra" ordinary life.

I don't mind sharing that part of the longing was a growing disappointment in the politics and structures of large corporate organisations, which put the reins on my creativity and drive rather than pushing and nurturing my innovation and entrepreneurial capabilities.

However, the main driving force was when my daughter was born with a severe brain disorder (which we really didn't understand the consequences of until several years later and how this would impact on our family, friends and careers). I just knew I needed a new plan.

My very first business was in direct selling for wellness products, which actually worked well since I was coupling it with weight loss coaching, adding value rather than just "flogging" products - an early example of my educational entrepreneurial tendencies.

Three years later, with my home business as a safety net, I grasped an opportunity from a rather self-inflicted redundancy at the university I'd worked at for 13+ years, and I set out on my own as a self-employed consultant - exciting and scary!

After struggling to make the income I wanted from direct sales locally, I became obsessed with figuring out how to market my business online. I studied with some of the top "gurus" from around the world, attended some excellent (if expensive) marketing events in far-flung and luxurious venues. But still, it took years to realise the keys to success, which I'm revealing to you in this book.

Way back then, if I'd had the big picture that I have now, I might have grown my business so much faster without the cost of all the different products, tools, courses and events, which had only served to confuse and overwhelm me.

In essence, I distilled all that know-how into what worked to get me results and implemented a structured, consistent process for growing the successful service business I have today. And part of the story is to emphasise that I'm still on a journey of learning, listening to the market and redefining myself to stay ahead of the crowd.

REINVENTING YOUR PROFESSIONAL IDENTITY

Let's talk about professional identity again for a moment, and why we need to constantly reaffirm or reinvent ourselves.

Business is constantly reinventing itself, which means consultants need to be constantly reinventing themselves too.

As we touched on earlier, sometimes when you've evolved your professional identity over time, you find yourself in a fog because you can't work out who you are anymore, what you believe in, what you stand for, what you care about. Call it losing your mojo, call it losing focus – sometimes you just lose the plot. When this happened to me personally a few years back now, it was very frustrating and sad, because I've always been such a driven and optimistic person.

And it's not a simple 3-step formula to get it back, despite what some online courses will sell you on. It's a strategic review at a very deep and personal level – it's tough, it can take time and you can't force it. I know, because I've had to do it, and it took me many years. If this is where you are, I don't want that for you. This is why I do what I do.

Only when you fully own your expert process can you create an authentic brand and start attracting the clients you really wanted to work with.

In order to get into this on a deep level necessary to help with your business branding, I'm giving you three pieces of advice on professional identity, which may either go against the grain or feel quite liberating!

#1 - Stop labelling yourself with any specific profession or title that traps you in

the commodity box.

For instance, when someone asks "what do you do", you may be used to answering: I'm a "Business Adviser", I'm an "Accountant", I'm a "Physiotherapist" or I'm a "Yoga Teacher". But that's your professional trade; it's not *what you do* in terms of what you achieve for your client.

Such mundane labels don't encapsulate the *value* of what you deliver to your client. Your unique blend of knowledge, skills, experience and expertise has the capacity to take you way beyond stereotypes for such occupations and how you work with clients.

If you stick with these labels and don't clearly articulate what you *actually* and *specifically* do for your clients, i.e. what they get or progress from working with you, this will severely limit how your business can grow and scale, and how you're able to adapt to changing market needs and demands.

> ※
> "If you've been struggling to come up with the perfect witty job title, I dare you to stop the insanity and focus on talking about what you DO, instead of trying to fit yourself into the box of a title." – Rebecca Tracey, The Uncaged Life

Instead let's identify "what you do" in different way: you work with a particular type of person or organisation who has a specific type of problem that you help them to solve. That's transformative work, right?

#2 – Don't dismiss all of your prior experience when you start down a new path.

I made this mistake myself when I was just starting out as a "success coach" (industry label). I completely separated my professional career from my network marketing business. I thought that my Bachelor of Science degree, my PhD, my teaching qualification, my years of experience in academic development, my e-learning expertise, had nothing to do with the new direction I was taking (it was just a plan B back then).

Moving into a new field, I felt that I was starting from scratch... and that really affects your confidence! Until I embraced all of the achievements, insights and life experiences that I've accumulated over the years, and saw this as a professional journey, I couldn't come to appreciate how unique I am. That's not to brag, it's just that now I realise there's not a single person in the world who has the same experience and the same perspective as I do.

Your professional identity should represent what some might say is your "expert brand", your "true calling" or soulful business (which in my experience often stays hidden, or hides in plain sight, for many years.) The act of writing and producing content around ideas in your field clarifies your thinking too, and helps your unique perspective come into the light.

Always ask yourself, does the professional label you give yourself bring you in close alignment with the particular group of people you feel most compelled to serve.

As you move forward working with your clients, you may branch out from your established field of expertise. As you learn and develop, you may find new areas of expertise emerge where you feel you can satisfy your target market's needs in more ways than your original niche. You may start to bring your distinctive personality into the mix.

On the downside, all this shifting around can often end up confusing people (including yourself!) about what you're really about. It's important to continuously reinvent your professional identity so it remains a coherent blend that is uniquely yours.

#3 - Identify how you can use your unique expertise to help with a pressing

problem that people are looking for a solution to.

Let me illustrate this one with the story of three of my "professional reinventions" that rode the wave of market demand.

Originally, in the early 90s I was working in the field of e-learning – mostly doing curriculum innovation working with academics to integrate technology into teaching and learning. My uninspiring and non-specific label: Academic Development Officer.

(In 2000, I did get promoted to Head of Educational Technology, and again in 2004 to Head of Educational Development and E-learning, plus I was nominated for a National Teaching Fellowship Award - all before essentially being made redundant in 2007 – so peculiar how the world works!)

Reinvention #1

Due to the swell of national digital learning programmes I was involved in, I positioned myself as the person good at large scale projects: designing them, writing bids to fund them, managing them and evaluating them. My expert brand evolved from curriculum design and teaching development to leading innovation.

By the time I set up my consulting practice in 2007, I found I had a lot to offer the sector in evaluation design, which suited my clients' need to demonstrate deliverables to funding bodies. A lot of people were struggling with this and yet public accountability dictated they had a clear evaluation plan. I had a lot of work coming in because I claimed this as my expert niche.

Reinvention #2

Five years later, my public sector clients were becoming concerned about efficiency and value for money (public accountability again) and my evaluations shifted towards process improvement, looking at operational management, identifying bottlenecks, duplication and waste in core business processes.

I reinvented my brand once again and started helping my clients develop "lean" processes. I trained in Six Sigma Black Belt to further my expertise in this field, thus building on my consulting and evaluation skills and adding this new service.

Reinvention #3

In the background of my consulting work, I was still pushing forth my internet marketing ventures, coaching people who wanted to build a successful online business. A lot of this focused on getting them business-ready with a personal brand, and that meant working on their belief system, their self-esteem, as well as teaching them the nuts and bolts of marketing, helping them set up social media profiles and so forth and having better sales conversations.

I don't think at the time I realised how all my other education, evaluation and business skills made me different to all the other team leaders out there calling themselves "success coaches". I'd spent a decade asking high-end clients "what does success look like' in order to map the key aims of a project or process to short, medium and long term outcomes. This is not dissimilar to goal setting, business modelling, market research, analytics, customer experience and ROI type of work.

Slowly, it dawned on me how these two worlds aligned so I reinvented myself once again towards business improvement, and finally strategic marketing for business growth, which is now the principal focus of my professional brand.

Reinvention #4 is the path I'm now on with this book, alongside my online courses and the *iSuccess Business Academy* membership. Although it bridges my consulting work and my online business, I've kept to my "brand name" Jay Allyson. Being set on impacting a global digital audience, to me the fact that this variation of my name is unique online makes this perfect sense. In any case, my social media accounts carry my full name in brackets and search engines are clever enough these days to find me whichever variation of my name is used, which is very helpful!

REALIGNING YOUR AREAS OF EXPERTISE

If any of my reinvention stories sound like your career trajectory too, I'd definitely recommend doing some mind mapping exercises to recentre your professional identity around your expertise - what you do, what you're good at, and what you enjoy doing, rather than particular job titles – it's actually very liberating!

Look at the intersection where your interests, expertise and talents fit together - that's a very powerful way to start defining your personal brand.

Draw a large circle in the centre of a page – leave it blank for now – and create spokes out of it like a bicycle wheel. At the end of each spoke set out each of your expert areas. You may have to play around with it and want to add spokes to each spoke, but that visual picture gives you a way to hone in on the common theme – this is your unique sweet spot.

Some of my early mind maps were terrible – they really showed up how confused I was about who I was professionally, what I did or wanted to do. I ended up with three things - education, enterprise and evaluation – and I still couldn't work out for ages what was the cohering sweet spot - the "educational entrepreneur" is a phrase I coined much later.

Nevertheless, after getting this far in self-discovery, I made the decision to amalgamate my professional identities. I included my full name on social media sites like LinkedIn and Facebook and on my consulting website and brought my business and educational expertise into alignment.

In fact, it seems a quirk of fate now I look back. Because as well as helping my small business clients create education materials, I was helping education sector corporate clients with business improvement.

Talk about karma! As a result of interweaving the two, I found a common ground offering strategic marketing support to both. (As an aside: did you know the word "karma" literally means "activity" and the basic understanding of how karma or the law of cause and effect works is that "what you sow, you reap". That's pretty cool!)

Certainly, it's felt like karma in my case, and maybe you can see it in your story too, that none of your past learning or experience is lost; it's all what makes you truly unique expert! In my "Jay Allyson world", after doing years of content marketing, coaching and mentoring entrepreneurs in my groups, I started creating webinars, designing courses and running workshops. The materials I developed for these were exercises, worksheets, checklists etc, and I realised I was drawing a lot on my education and professional development background.

> ※
> "My wake-up call was when I realised clients don't pay for coaching. What they invest in is content: exercises, tools, templates, systems – that help them create clarity, make decisions, get into action and increase their income." – Kendall Summerhawk

As time ran on, rather than separate and different, my skill sets were becoming more mutually reinforcing and powerful than I'd appreciated and it was no longer helpful to keep things separate.

Once I realised this, I started working with regional business programmes, helping small and medium sized enterprises (in the UK, we call them SMEs) with strategy, marketing and growth plans. And a key thing most said they got from my approach working with them was clarity from working through the checklists and exercises that helped them develop a simple roadmap for what actions to take and how to measure the results. It's why I've taken that same approach in my marketing (as indeed in this book and my courses).

SUPPORTING THE CUSTOMER'S JOURNEY

Perhaps because of the growing confusion and a demand for simple marketing solutions, there's now correspondingly an almost overabundance out there too of tactical "if you do this one thing" advice. It's certainly the case in the coaching space, maybe less so in the consulting niche. I really think this is counterproductive to everyone.

For me personally, the offers all start to look alike and just serve to distract and further perplex. I've rarely seen a course that provides the education and mentoring support you need to solve complex problems that you ordinarily hire a consultant to help you with.

To traverse the complexity that the digital age has procreated, what people most want now is a roadmap for success to clarify, systematise and streamline everything; to leverage not burden your business.

This is the "customer journey" and to tap into it, you just need a logical sequence you take your prospects through. This is the *Engage-Educate-Enrol* pathway I talked about in chapter 1. The process is simple – capture interest, give value, offer premium. I've created an example in the figure that follows.

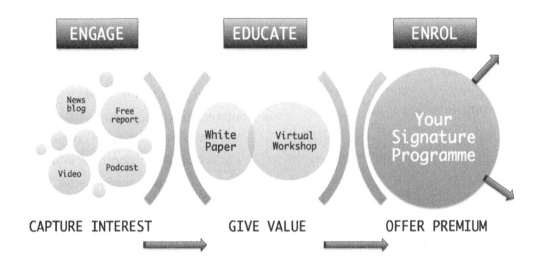

Your expert content – in whatever medium – is the fuel that engages your prospect and educates them to connect the dots between what they're (sometimes desperately) looking for (i.e. what they want as an outcome), and what you offer. It may be the timing isn't quite right for them to make a decision on whether to buy your product or services, but by engaging with them, nurturing their interest and continuing to give value, over time you strengthen the trust relationship.

Even if you still do your enrolment call over the phone, an online marketing system can streamline 95% of the relationship building: automating how you deliver regular content, capture leads, develop your authority status in your prospects eyes, and presenting your sales page and offer.

And it doesn't have to stop there. A single core service or signature programme can be sliced into multiple pieces of content in various formats (articles, checklists, videos, audios) and all used as free giveaways or low-end products to tease and tantalise your prospect as they move through your process.

This content gives you huge leverage for growing the business and your overall revenue; we'll tackle this more fully in chapters 5 and 6.

BUILDING TRUST WITH POTENTIAL CLIENTS

When you use this kind of value-driven path in your marketing, you build and nurture a trusted relationship with your target audience from the outset. You become a beacon for integrity and a magnet for new clients.

First comes *perceived* value - your front-end marketing or promise - which gets your foot in the door, starts the engagement and converts prospects to clients. Real value is the outcome you deliver on the back end - your paid products, programmes or services - and what keeps your clients coming back.

The truth is, nowadays you can create amazing marketing funnels online, but if you can't persuade people to buy your stuff or hire you, it's a waste of time, energy and money. It's actually not even about how good your product or service is, the crucial part is how well you can communicate its value to, and impact on, the customer.

How about if we mix up the notion of perceived and real value? What if we give some real value for *free* on the front end by providing great educational content or support that helps your potential client solve the first part of a problem they have.

> ※
> "Most service organizations build their promise based on their capabilities rather than on the goals, opportunities and challenges of ideal clients." – Randy Shuttuck

Do you think that might draw the right people in and make them want to work with you as opposed to someone who shares only perceived value through a fancy marketing website?

It's a basic human need to be understood, to feel connected to people with common values, and to be acknowledged. Your clients are no different. Some would argue that marketing is about engaging people in order to "sell" to them, that it's a transactional model of engagement – i.e. the marketing results in a transaction of some kind, a sale of your services so you get what you want – an income.

However, I believe a more effective model from a leveraged perspective is to think of marketing as a *transformational* model of engagement. People may be attracted to what you do and why you do it, but the perceived value is far higher if they feel you can help them move where they are now to where they want to be, because of what you know and are able to do.

This is where content marketing has changed the whole game of prospecting for consultants. It enables you to shift people's perspectives, open up blind spots and generate confidence in you and the solutions you help people with.

Your potential client can check you out way before you ever have a conversation with them to "close the deal'. If you give people great insights about how to deliver results long before they become your client, they

> ※
> "With content planning, it's is about getting intentional and strategic, with everything you post." - Laura McDouall, Tell My Story

get to sample your expertise and approach – the whole "try-before-you-buy" tactic.

INFLUENCING WITH EDUCATION-RICH CONTENT

When you create a positive reputation for your expertise, your influence increases and your income follows. If you stay authentic to your purpose and goals, and create your professional brand around this, your clients become a loyal fan base.

As your fan base grows, so does your influence and you create a tribe of like-minded people. As your audience and your following build, you end up becoming slightly famous for what you do, how you show up, and how you help people.

A good personal or professional brand is capable of magnetically (i.e. good copy) and organically (i.e. organic traffic) attracting clients to work with you, hire you or buy from you.

To me, the spirit of entrepreneurship goes beyond just making money; it's about making an impact.

> ※
> "Your personal brand is what other people say about you when you leave the room. It's essentially your professional reputation." –
> Dorie Clark, Stand Out

The majority of entrepreneurs do it wrong and have a backwards approach to creating and marketing products and services; they don't work from the inside out. The educational entrepreneur takes a very distinctive approach compared to traditional business development and sales processes. To understand it requires a new perspective on client engagement, which for many is a challenge in itself.

If you're reading this because you're looking for ways to leverage your professional expertise or talents, it's probable you're currently working harder than you feel you ought to or need to, and making less money than you know you could (or should) do.

If you find yourself in this situation, it's not a good pressure to be under. Yet, the root cause of this situation is not solely an operational problem, it's likely strategic in origin, and can stem from your current perspective (call it belief, attitude or mindset) about business and sub-elements of it, especially marketing.

What I've found over the years is that in successful entrepreneurship, business development is inextricably intertwined with personal and professional development. It's a holistic system and works particularly well when you're in the service industry, because essentially, you're also in the people business and your business is built around YOU.

So, at this junction, my question is this:

❖ *What are the benefits of shifting from how you currently operate your business as a consultant to operating your business as an educator?*

While you can use this book as educational tool - a step-by-step process - for building a more successful and sustainable service business, first you need to become open to the idea of there being different strategies for growth. Then you need to think about what is required to make the shifts, and what are the steps you can take.

Remember the SCALE business growth chart I shared with you earlier? It's actually a roadmap; it maps out your possible routes for implementing increasingly leveraged business models that progressively increase your profitability and earning potential.

When you design the right vehicle – your business model - you put yourself in the position to move up through the typical income plateaus I see with consulting and coaching based businesses and can achieve much higher levels of success.

The next question is: where are you on the journey right now?

Acquiring a new perspective can open up previously limiting blind spots. This I learned from Rich Schefren's "The Future of Marketing" and I'm paraphrasing here. How will you shift your perspective so that you pick the best strategies, tactics, tools in the marketing and systems at your disposal, which in the past you were perhaps blind or confused about or thought don't apply to your type of business (something I hear all the time!)

Are you willing to shift your thinking so you can start to leverage your own capability and drive to achieve the big vision for the business you want?

Because I take time to understand my client's mindset as well as my client's business, I'm able to identify what's holding them back getting the results they want. I take a bird's eye view and I see things that they don't see. What's interesting though is that when they see what was previously hidden (in their blind spots), they are much more willing to make the recommended changes to improve things.

As Rich points out: the question is why they can't see what I see? I see my expertise and experience as shining the light on a new path. True, part of that is that they're too close to see what's missing or off-balance, which is quite common and that may just be the only thing.

But most often it's because with their current perspective, they can't distinguish elements that are creating barriers for them - they are either too deep trying to hack through the forest or they are in fact in the wrong forest (to use a metaphor from Stephen Covey's "7 Habits of Highly Effective People").

I'm sure it's the same in your business. As the expert, you can help your clients or customers to "see" the light, but only if you take an educational approach – you can't just tell people or give them information about something new and expect a light bulb moment.

Here's where it gets a little deep, hold tight!

CHALLENGING OUR BRAIN'S HARD WIRING

Consultants often get accused of getting paid to tell clients what they already know! But their true value is helping clients to see what they know in a new light, to acknowledge their blind or weak spots, and create new perspectives, to reconceptualise even. This is an important step in someone's learning. Importantly too, their enlightenment creates confidence in you and trust in the advice you're giving.

This happens to me all the time now. I've learned to get out of my own way, to open my mind to new ideas and let insights come to me, naturally. Others cannot provide you with a recipe (as I'd previously hoped they would; years of self-development and marketing courses taught me that much!)

Likewise, I cannot tell you what to do. What I can do though is shine a light so you can take a look, perhaps see things differently and decide to take action on the new approach. That everyone may see something different is a distinct possibility here as we have different starting points and gaps.

A defining moment for me was to give up the struggle to find a solution. I can't believe how clueless I was for so many years to the principle of immersing myself in ideas and allowing the next step to show up effortlessly!

As an intellectual, I was constantly researching - looking, not walking. When I found a good vehicle, I procrastinated; I may have bought it, sat in it, twiddled with the buttons, even turned on the engine, but for reasons I couldn't fathom, I didn't actually drive off in it.

> ※
> "What do people do when they don't know what the next step is? Most people do nothing. This is not only the wrong choice, it's the exact opposite of the right choice. If you don't know what the next step is, stop looking, start walking." - Jason Leister, Incomparable Expert

How bizarre! I found the knowledge, but lacked the confidence in myself to use it, and my mind remained fearful (of failure) and blocked (to the potential success).

Our thinking is the paradigm we live in, what we believe, what we think business is all about, what we think marketing is.

These things define our attitude and behaviour towards new approaches, understanding distinctions and having the knowledge and language required to operate in a new paradigm successfully. In some cases, certain ways of thinking can be hard-wired into us and take time to shift. Your clients are no different; they see the world through the eyes of their current paradigm.

For example, since evaluation, marketing and operational improvement are my areas of expertise, I'm going to diagnose and "see" more than most other people do. I can judge what's right or wrong with a set up or a system more easily and quickly than someone who is not an expert or is too close to it. I could just "tell" a client what I see, but this is rarely transformative for them; there's no "aha" light bulb moment, because they haven't understood or "seen" it for themselves.

Instead, what I aim to do working with my clients is to focus on what needs to change in someone's perspective (through personal or professional coaching). Not only do they start to see what I'm pointing out to them, but they're also able to understand the distinctions when they look at their business (and maybe even their competitors' businesses).

This is where you can shift from telling & selling to teaching & mentoring, helping people find their own way. And there is a way to greatly accelerate this process by making the linkages.

For instance, if I'm teaching about business website design, I'd want to highlight what are the distinctions about marketing and web design that you should have (but probably don't have) about what makes a good marketing website, i.e. one that works. (Defining success here might concern itself with purpose and profitability.)

※

"This capacity for new thought is known as insight ... [it] is unique to each of us. Other people's ideas can be helpful but they're not tailored for our personal experience in the way our own insights are. They're rarely transformative because one size doesn't fit all. "

"If it's a life-changing insight, it may repeatedly show up in different guises after the initial shift.... I think I've got it [intellectually] and then I see it on a deeper level... in a practical fashion." – Rachel Henke, author of Living Fearlessly

Challenging the hard wiring is essential to transforming practice and what enables a shift in perspective is real education.

There's a key difference between telling someone what to do and having them LEARN why to do it that way. Note that this is NOT about manipulating people; it's about "unsticking" people, and you must *believe* you can help your client - this is paramount. I use this unsticking process a lot in consultancy, asking a series of "what and how" questions to understand the client's context and perspective.

I'll ask "why" questions too to get them deconstructing their rationale about existing business practices and processes they have in place, then pose questions that stretch their thinking, even just simply asking them "had you thought about....?" can yield insights.

Through this process of enlightenment (not me telling them how they should run their business), I can get clients seeing things in a different way, so we can get onto exploring alternative "better" ways of doing things and they can "buy into" the business improvement strategies I'm suggesting to take them from problem to solution.

Having said all that, achieving changes in perspectives and identifying unsticking points and solutions is a little trickier in a book as there's no dialogue! This is why I've added in a lot of questions and points to ponder as you read through, which aim to get you thinking differently and perhaps designing things differently than you otherwise would have. This is similar to the task setting I use in my online courses.

SIMPLIFYING YOUR MARKETING PLAN

When you observe the marketing around us in today's digital age, it looks incredibly time-intensive and complicated – snazzy websites, social media, sponsored ads, sales pages, lead magnets, email marketing, messenger bots, the list is growing. It can make you feel marketing is complex, daunting, difficult and expensive.

Even to those like me with digital capability, marketing prowess and years working in the digital arena, there's now just this massive maze of confusing options and people are flitting about from one shiny thing to the next hoping for a quick result.

Simplification is the "solution" we crave and need to overcome "paralysis by analysis", "fear of failure", procrastination and all the other mindset barriers that keep us from taking action and moving our business success forwards.

And the myth there is some silver bullet that will have clients flooding into your business is perpetuated via LinkedIn, Facebook, Instagram and YouTube by the more prolific marketers and social influencers in the consulting and coaching sphere.

You can easily get brainwashed into thinking that:

1. Digital marketing is complicated and you need some special formula;

2. That you have to be relentlessly singing and dancing on every digital platform the planet has to offer; and/or

3. You could never be "as good as" these other famous leaders.

Poppycock as my grandfather might have said! Let me kick this fallacy to the kerb here right away by saying this is not the case. Leveraged marketing means being laser focused, selective and systematic about what, to whom, when and how you engage and promote things to an audience.

A simple, three-stage process is all that's needed to take people on the journey from problem to solution. Keeping things to three stages certainly goes a long way to making your efforts both manageable and successful, particularly for consulting or coaching.

STEP 1 – CAPTURE INTEREST TO ENGAGE & BUILD AN AUDIENCE.

Share great content via articles, podcasts, videos, social media posts to attract followers; and/or publish an e-book, webinar or free online course with an opt-in or sign-up form to capture people's name and email.

STEP 2 – GIVE VALUE TO NURTURE & EDUCATE YOUR PROSPECTS.

Demonstrate your leadership and build the relationship via your chosen digital platforms by helping and interacting with your community.

STEP 3 – HAVE A PREMIUM OFFER TO INVITE & ENROL YOUR PERFECT PEOPLE.

Invite your subscribers and followers to a free consult or exploratory call. The perfect people will take that next natural step.

That's all I do – all my content feeds into that process. In fact, skipping step 2, I've attracted clients to my consulting business (mostly through LinkedIn, Facebook and word-of-mouth referrals) without even having an email list at all. Go figure!

This is why I urge you to start with the bare basics, make sure your messaging is working and you're getting a good conversion of the right kind of prospects to those free sessions. After that you can turn up the dial and build up something more multi-faceted once you see results coming in.

Nevertheless, it's important to appreciate (and studies continue to show this) that even with the massive rise in social media usage, an email list still yields the highest ROI. Here are some of the advantages.

- Email has the highest interaction of all communications platforms, around ten times compared to social media.

- An email list can be leveraged in many ways and many times over.

- Your email list can be segmented so you can send highly relevant and targeted messages and offers to discrete sub-groups of your audience.

- Emails can be easily sequenced providing structured communication with your audience and prospect group(s) that is easily scalable.

LEVERAGING YOUR TIME WITH SYSTEMS

As a service provider, systematising how you engage, connect with and work with your clients through process automation tools helps you to become more of a *strategic entrepreneur*.

If you want to make more money and serve more people than you currently do, you need to find more ways to engage, follow up and deliver to more people.

For any service to work effectively and efficiently, you need to create a "system" that automates how you attract, cultivate, educate and deliver results for your clients.

Essentially, this means putting in place clear and professional end-to-end processes, primarily to support your marketing and sales, your client onboarding and delivery, and your internal business operations.

Here's a simple (ideal!) customer journey to illustrate what I mean by process mapping. Each step forms part of a structured marketing and sales process, much of which you can choose to automate.

When you map out the flow of work for each stage visually, you can see clearly the sequence of communications, decision points, milestones and actions across your customer journey, from their

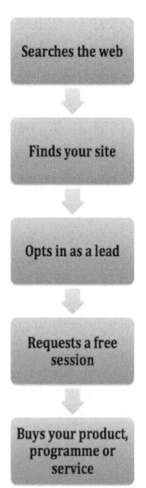

Searches the web

Finds your site

Opts in as a lead

Requests a free session

Buys your product, programme or service

first awareness of you through to being a fully satisfied and loyal client.

This flowchart will be critical for automating your process and generating high-quality leads. You're looking to attract prospective clients (buyers) into your funnel who have a specific desire, problem, pain, struggle or frustration that is of sufficient urgency to create a hunger for what you offer. You feed the system by publishing and sharing relevant content that partially satisfies that hunger.

Your goal is to engage people who want to learn how to do something or get something done and capture them as leads and followers in a time and cost-effective way.

To achieve this authentically and in service to others, your system must start on the front end with marketing that is education-driven and addresses specifically what they want and need. It demonstrates your expert authority, builds your audience and nurture the relationship with them.

At the time of writing, opt-ins that work well for consultants is a "white paper" type of free report, a challenge delivered by email or social media or a webinar.

If you help your prospective client by bringing insights or getting something "done", the problem feels half-resolved, and you've demonstrated you can help them by actually helping them. People are then far more willing to pay you for helping them further, and even better, pay a premium fee for delivering the solutions and results they want faster than they could doing it alone or with your competitors.

On the back end, you would provide a programme or service (digital or otherwise) that delivers the next steps towards a solution and offer high-end services to clients that help them to implement it. It's fully transparent and value-laden.

Once they become a client, you will need a *process* for how you deliver this outcome for them. You may have a client flow process and/or consulting interview structure documented and in operation already or it may just be an intuitive thing you do at this point.

Process mapping how I work with a client is how my own expert system was born, created from the exact step-by-step process I use to diagnose priority areas for business development.

When you can set out the key parts of what you do working one-to-one with a client as a tangible step-by-step process that they can follow, then you have an expert system you can turn into an educational programme.

Because your system (or way of using a standard methodology) is unique to you, you can move toward packaging it as a distinct and branded product or programme, and more importantly, price it accordingly.

Your system needs to be able to deliver the solution (or at least the first one or two steps towards the solution) in a way that is accessible and attractive to your ideal clients without requiring you to be there in person along each step of the process, at least not 100% of the time.

There's a lot of talk now how these kinds of content marketing and webinar strategies have run their course now – because everyone is using them and audiences are tired of seeing the same patterns of engagement. But I have to disagree. I'd always put great stock in using educational material, it's timeless, although we need to keep things fresh and topical to the sentiments of the marketplace.

When you are the advisor/mentor in your spheres of influence and networks, you are serving people's needs. As individuals, we come with "issues" and will always need someone who can share in the big vision of their true potential, and help us overcome fear and doubts so that we can move forward with a plan.

This is why understanding your target market, what they need and their preferences for how they can work with you, is a super important part of how you operate and the effectiveness of what you do.

One of the best ways to do this is by creating an online application process on the back of an online presentation (aka a webinar) that outlines the problem and offers the solution whilst simultaneously positioning you as the expert. The presentation can run live or on replay, can provide a single video training or form a video series you can use later in your marketing. We'll look at the mechanics of all this at a later stage.

WEBINAR REGISTRATIONS

WEBINAR ATTENDEES

APPLICATIONS

CONVERSATIONS

CLIENTS

The main point to grasp right now is that through the webinar your prospective client has the opportunity to learn more about their problem, reflect on some key questions and then pre-qualify themselves by booking a free consult with you.

This is a marketing activity - there's no sales pitch - which reinforces your positioning as a trusted expert. You're simply offering a free strategy session to see if you can help them.

> ※
> "A webinar is critical, because it positions you and it positions your prospect – it involves giving value, generating goodwill and providing context [for the problem you're offering to help them resolve]." – Lee McIntyre, Get More Momentum

It's important to include an application step as part of the registration booking process. This provides an opportunity to see how serious they are, find out more about your prospect, demonstrates you're professional and allows you to pre-qualify who you spend your time speaking with.

In that conversation, you're not selling, you're helping. Your only job in that session is to uncover their pain, need and desire, i.e. to help the prospect to admit their current reality (problem) and what it's costing them, to look at the gap to the desired outcome, and to see the value in how you can help them towards the solution.

High-quality conversations generate clients (and income) and you should be having lots of them. The free session should be a high value exchange for both of you:

- They are able to get to know you, like you and trust you, and you are able to pre-qualify them for your time;

- They get to speak to you privately about their individual challenges, and you get to learn more fully how your target market see their challenges;

- You are *both* able to decide if what you do is a good fit to achieve the result they want.

When there is alignment between what they want to achieve and what your programme delivers, you will find it's straightforward to ask if they would like to learn more about a programme that can help them with the problem they just told you they have. From there, enrolling them as a new client will be a natural conclusion to the conversation.

Although you can advertise your strategy session directly (and I certainly still do this), it's less powerful than when conducted on the back of a webinar or live presentation that's full of great content. This is because you're removing the demonstration of your value, prestige and authority that confirms why you're able to charge premium prices.

When you get this whole process working well and you're enrolling people into your programme or service, you've built the ultimate marketing machine. You can focus on driving more leads into your webinar so you can rinse and repeat, repeatedly.

EVALUATING YOUR MARKETING PLAN

It can be argued that the success of any strategic marketing plan hinges on how well the plan is implemented and controlled rather than the strategy itself. By taking a performance management or evaluative approach to your business improvement action plan, you strengthen your capacity for continuous improvement across every element of it.

The four elements you need in place for increasing success are objectives, metrics, analytics and actions, which are inextricably intertwined in evaluating the effectiveness and ROI (return on investment) of any marketing activity.

 MARKETING OBJECTIVES   METRICS FOR SUCCESS   ANALYTICS   ENHANCEMENT ACTIONS

With each element in place, you are more able to implement a competitive marketing plan and to evaluate and control your marketing activity in terms of time and spend on advertising and promotion.

You've heard the one about the CEO who said "I know 50% of my advertising is wasted but I don't know which 50% it is!" When you understand your ideal target market for what you do, it's way simpler to concentrate your best advertising on your best audience.

The question then becomes what are the best ways to engage with my ideal audience and what are the best media to use to do that.

With digital marketing and web analytics, it's now easier than ever to access robust data across your customer journey from initial contact and enquiry right through to sales and delivery of your product or service.

At its simplest, marketing ROI can be evaluated using metrics such as cost per click, sales revenue and refund rate (as an indicator of customer match and satisfaction). But that doesn't really tell you why your marketing is working well or not so well; it's only looking at the outcomes.

Dive deeper and there's a whole array of beautiful data at your fingertips. If you take the time with web, email and social media tracking and analytics, it can be very revealing. For instance, you can identify definitively:

❖ Which parts of your website visitors are engaging with the most / least

❖ Which offers or opt-in forms and offers are generating the most leads

❖ Where your conversions are good or where you're losing people

❖ How well your leads are engaging with you and your email messages.

Furthermore, embedding analytics tools (such as GoogleAnalytics or Clicktale) in your website means you're able to evaluate your visitor behaviours and customer experience and start to see the story behind the clickthrough rates on your site.

When you know where your *best* customers are coming from or going next, what they are responding to or engaging with most, you can optimise your marketing, remarketing and ad budget drastically. When you can track your web visitors every mouse move, hover, scroll and click, you can literally visualise the customer experience.

The stratification and methodologies of both strategic marketing and evaluation are complex enough to be the topic of a whole other book. The main point to grasp is the importance of clarity in the *objectives* and the need clearly identifiable *metrics* (e.g. brand awareness, leads generated, sales/signups, revenue, customer satisfaction etc).

Evaluating your outcomes allows you to track whether and how marketing objectives are being achieved, where the barriers or bottlenecks are, and where you can improve things further.

But it's important to focus on long term as well as short term outcomes: for example, lifetime customer value in quantitative (financial) terms as well as qualitative (reputational) metrics derived from customer feedback. This gives you an indication of the effectiveness of the strategy overall as well as specific tactics deployed and if the picture alters over time.

While some aspects of marketing may focus on corporate brand awareness, for consulting professionals and small firms, it's more likely your marketing is aimed at connecting with your target market for the purpose of generating sales.

The point of sale provides the next building block to leverage your message, the relationship you've established with prospects, and make an irresistible offer. Take a moment now to write down your ideas and action notes from this chapter, because next we're moving on to look at leveraged sales.

ACTION NOTES

_____

_____

_____

_____

_____

_____

_____

_____

_____

_____

_____

_____

_____

_____

_____

_____

_____

_____

_____

Chapter 5

LEVERAGED SALES

Create a Workable Process

"Sustained success is largely a matter of focusing regularly on the right things and making a lot of uncelebrated little improvements every day."

Theodore Levitt,

Thinking in Management

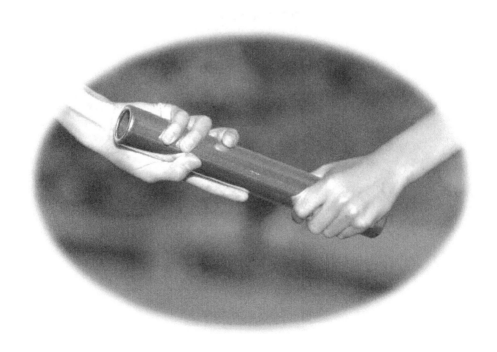

KEY POINTS

❖ Build your audience in the spirit of community so that what you create is not a funnel of prospects but a tribe of like-minded people.

❖ The big goal in leveraged sales is for ideal clients to come to you, not you chase them. You want to be the hunted, not the hunter!

❖ The road to sales is to create a brand offer that is magnetic and irresistible and a consistently executed marketing plan that engages your audience and positions you as a credible and trusted expert.

❖ You attract your ideal client by talking in their language about what they want, why it's important to them, and how they can get it.

❖ Making an offer and adding incentives is simply a service to your clients to help them say "yes" to achieving the outcome you deliver.

❖ A golden rule in sales and marketing is to talk about results and benefits not facts or features of your service or product.

❖ Make it easy, fast, enjoyable and rewarding for people to buy from you.

❖ People trust you and buy into a solution when you clearly explain the problem and the solution, and how one leads to the other.

❖ If you just try to "sell" someone on something, you get resistance, because it doesn't create the strong emotion needed to prompt action, so the logical brain keeps objecting.

❖ Your existing clients are a great source of market intelligence for understanding the concerns, needs and pain points of your target market, and their "problem language" to use in sales copy.

❖ What most clients want is a step-by-step manual, a process for getting from where they are to where they want to be.

❖ Enrolment should be a positive experience for your prospects. Don't focus on making a sale; focus on getting consult bookings.

❖ People who have gone through your education funnel make informed clients and good candidates for your high-end offer.

❖ When you lead with education, people see you giving value first. Teach your unique system and they realise they need YOU to help them.

❖ Building leverage into your sales process will improve your productivity, profitability and overall enjoyment of the winning clients!

MAKING SALES IN A SERVICE BUSINESS

In Chapter 1 – The Power of Leverage – I showed you a simple *Engage-Educate-Enrol* pathway in the form of three different kinds of funnel - our *Offer Funnels*. You really don't need to make things any more complicated than this, at least to start off.

Over the last 5-6 years, I've conducted hundreds of operational improvement reviews both for large institutions and small businesses and one thing is clear to me. As far as lead generation, follow up and enrolment are concerned, there's a conspicuous absence of strategic, dependable, systematic processes for bringing in new business, be it client enrolment or student enrolment.

Honestly, I'm shocked how overly complicated people make a simple customer journey process. Process control seems to start only at the point of onboarding (after enrolment) and prior to that marketing, promotions, sales processes are rather haphazard and frenzied.

After you've decided on the type of platform you will use predominantly for your content and start sharing - blog articles, podcast, video, live presentations, books – you immediately begin to build an audience. Do this in the spirit of *community* and what you create is not a funnel of sales prospects but a tribe of like-minded people who also happen to be engaged and responsive potential buyers.

This is the goal, but I know in reality it's not always as easy as some people online make out, especially for highly competitive niches like business consulting or life coaching. This is why it's very important to get more specific and micro-niche.

What will work though is sharing content that is purposeful and authentic, giving value and being of service to people. So, demonstrate you can help people by actually helping them. People go deeper into your world (and funnel) when they can see for themselves (without any sales pressure) the value of what you do and decide if it's a good fit for what they need.

When you drive sales with marketing content that's engaging and educational, and you take a consultative approach in the enrolment conversations you have with prospective clients, you will tend to always have positive discussions that lead elegantly to sign ups (i.e. sales).

An education-driven consultative sales approach is distinctly opposite to the uncomfortable paradigms of hard selling, pitching and prospecting, which professionals usually loathe. If you take this more leveraged approach, you'll soon be leaving your industry competitors far behind you.

BEING THE HUNTED NOT THE HUNTER

If you want to achieve the kind of business income and freedom you believed is possible working for yourself, and you want to provide consulting or coaching that makes a difference to lots of people's lives, you need a continuous and consistent flow of prospects that turn into ideal clients for your business.

The big goal in leveraged consulting sales is for ideal clients to come to you, not you chase them. You want to be the hunted, not the hunter!

So how do you find and convert those clients or customers without having to resort to pitching, prospecting or selling? The simple answer is this: get really good at marketing yourself and sales become way easier. I'm hoping you understand the difference.

> ※
> "What works is a focus on your buyers and their problems. What fails is an egocentric display of your products and services." David Meerman Scott, The New Rules of Marketing and PR

Yes, there are skills involved in how you communicate your offer to your audience. Whether it's your website, a presentation, a book cover, an advertisement or a conversation, there needs to be good "copywriting", because people buy things based on the words you use.

This is not about manipulative cleverness; it's about learning how to zero in on what your ideal client wants and then explain how your product or service can help them get it, both the logical and emotional arguments.

The road to effective sales is to create a brand offer that is magnetic and irresistible and have a consistently executed marketing plan that engages your audience and positions you as a credible and trusted expert.

I lost count of the number of people with whom I've had a heated debate on the difference between sales and marketing. In fact, I never know why these two functions are so commonly grouped together in an organisation, because they're two very different goals and mindsets. The qualities and skill set of a conventional sales person is totally different to that of a good marketing person.

And just to add fuel to that fire, it's referred to as "sales and marketing" rather than "marketing and sales", when clearly good marketing needs to happen before a sale is made. Perhaps because a sale is the ultimate end goal, and a lot of attention is placed on "sales copy", it's simply been a case of putting that first; but this is an ill-conceived notion.

I'm aware my standard rant on this may seem pedantic, but as a business owner, it's actually a pretty crucial distinction to be clear on. If you do an effective job of marketing, the sales part is easy. When someone approaches you because they like your content rather than you approaching them, the dynamic swings significantly. The conversation becomes a consult not a pitch.

If your marketing fails to attract prospects, your sales team are going to have to pull out all the stops! If your marketing is magnetic, people respond positively, and they pass it on! You become the hunted rather than the hunter and pushy salesperson.

> ※
> "It's far more powerful to have a prospective buyer call you than it is for you to call them." – Alan Weiss, Million Dollar Consulting

GETTING YOUR OFFER INTO THE MARKETPLACE

In business today, the problem is not actually how to get the word out about what you do and what you have to sell; we have a multitude of communications channels and media platforms at our disposal, live and online. No: the problem is that nowadays there's a shortage of attention and a big trust hurdle to overcome.

People are not only inundated by thousands of marketing messages and "special" offers day and night, they're also highly sceptical and resistant to hype and annoyed by anything that seems irrelevant.

Furthermore, everyone has an opinion. Whether it's products or politics, everyone is constantly debating the information we're exposed to. On the streets, in shops, on TV and radio, on social media, everyone tries to influence our thinking and decisions (especially our buying decisions!).

We're now a society where a lot of people have prejudiced judgements and chronic attention deficiency disorder. That's a tricky combination to overcome. Your marketing needs to be laser targeted to penetrate the attention barrier.

When you find a succinct way to combine and communicate two key elements: your ideal client's need and their awareness of your potential to slake that need, you're already ahead of the herd. Success happens when the name hits home, the timing is right and people flock to what you have to offer. Even more success comes when they love your message and tell other people about you.

> ※
> "Your prospects aren't [just] targets... they're the best marketing channels you've got." – Rich Schefren

Before you attempt to sell anything, the challenge for your marketing is to cut through all the other noise, hype and fluff. On top of that, what you really need is to engage people enough to get your target prospects to *ask* you to send them stuff – a state Seth Godin terms "permission marketing".

The problem you need to resolve is this: How can I get my message out on the right frequency so my ideal audience hears it and wants to engage with it and to share it? The ultimate success is not only getting people to want your messages, but getting other people to share it!

The solution lies in the fact that most of these marketing messages are down-and-out disguised sales pitches where they either don't have a clear product or the offer isn't good or relevant to the audience.

However, most businesses don't understand their market well enough to be able to capture their attention or authentically influence their thinking.

> ※
> "Permission marketing is the privilege (not the right) of delivering anticipated, personal and relevant messages to people who actually want to get them." – Seth Godin.

You attract your ideal client by talking in their language about what they want, why it's important to them, and how they can get it.

To capture your ideal audience's attention and engage with them, there are three "musts".

1. First, you must understand your target market's problems and point of view.

2. Second, you must get super clear on what you offer and what you can deliver that addresses their needs specifically.

3. Third, you must ask for permission to enter into the conversation (and community) of what you're all about, inviting them to make a small initial commitment to actively step forward.

As an educator, you're able to use an effective "no selling tactic" to attract and connect with the right audiences. With highly targeted and high value educational content, you naturally market more authentically and more graciously, turning cold or lukewarm prospects to hot and responsive buyers.

> ※
> "Education removes the resistance to new ideas that is inherent in all of us." – Gregory V. Diehl, author of Brand Identity Breakthrough

From a position of permission, you can transition more easily into offering your service or programme without the usual sales pressures or pushy presentations. Although there's merit in adding incentives to take action, like time limited or quantity limited pricing or bonuses, there's absolutely no cunning manipulation techniques required.

Using the approach of giving value through good educational content delivered in an accessible form in order to help your client get a specific result or outcome that they want, you attract your most ideal audience and grow your client base by *not selling*.

This means no uncomfortable sales presentations, no constant worrying about sales pipelines and no stress-inducing target setting. You can make an offer without selling your dignity or your soul by focusing on the deep emotional need that your potential clients have for what you expertly do.

> ※
>
> "It's certainly noticeable that sales paradigms have shifted: it's no longer 'ask and you shall receive', now it's 'give and you shall receive'." - Andy Harrington, Passion into Profits.

In fact, I'd argue that if you have expertise people want and need, it's a total disservice not to make an offer. After you spent all this time helping someone see what lies beneath the problem they want solved, they want to know how to solve it. And most likely, they are super pumped to take that next step to solve it!

So, it's perfectly acceptable to make offers, if done graciously and in service. Imagine all your great efforts to educate your prospect gets reaped by your competitors who do make an offer. That'd really sting right?

Making an offer and adding some incentives is simply a service to your clients to help them say "yes" to achieving the outcome you deliver.

That's not to say you shouldn't work on improving your optimising your communications. Content delivery, lead generation and the quality of your conversations with prospects - whether face-to-face, by phone, email or social media – all depend on delivering the right thing to the right people at the right time.

The ultimate goal is to improve your "conversions" (or to use a sales term, your close rate) once you have a lead of prospect, because this directly affects the return on investment from your marketing or ad spend which impacts your profitability.

> ※
>
> "There is only one way on earth to influence other people: talk about what they want and show them how to get it." - Jay Abraham

What this boils down to is that you most definitely must make an offer, a call to action. It's amazing how many business websites don't clearly say what they do in a simple, easy-to-understand manner and don't ask for the sale with a call to action. You can do this with ease and grace in every piece of marketing you put out there, whether a presentation or a written piece.

After giving them some great content, a natural next step for your ideal client to take with you is to book an exploratory call with you. If you're going to influence a person's decision to work with you, hire you or buy from you through your marketing and your offer, it's essential to first understand them, to appreciate their needs and wants at a really deep level, and that takes skill and effort.

> ※
> "If there is any secret to success [in sales], it lies in the ability to get the other person's point of view, and see things from that person's angle as well as from your own." – Henry Ford

> ※
> "People buy the destination not the plane." – Lisa Sasevich, The Sassy Formula

Focusing on the result people want is a crucial approach taught to me by Lisa Sasevich – the "Queen of Sales Conversions". She advocates talking 90% about the outcome or transformation that you deliver (i.e. the issues, solution, benefits and impact), and spend just 10% on the delivery model (i.e. your service features and format).

An outcomes-focused offer becomes *irresistible* to your audience because it's totally focused on showing people you understand their problem. It's a natural next step to explain how what you do serves their needs and wants.

In other words, after you've provided good educational material, you can give a clear and authentic call to action. From there, you can move more seamlessly to talking about your service or programme as the next step.

When you reach the stage when someone knows, likes and trusts

90%
OUTCOMES
(why & what)

Issues
Solutions
Benefits
Impact

10%
DELIVERY
(how)

Services
Features
Format

you, it's straightforward to transition people to your "irresistible offer". Place it at the end of all of your educational content: articles, web pages, blog posts, on social media, and as the highpoint in your presentations and talks.

Getting the right message to the right audience is a big part of creating an irresistible offer you can drop into all your business activities.

It's widely known in buying psychology that the real reason people buy something is always *emotional*, consciously or subconsciously. Your offer needs to resonate with what people want on an emotional level.

People then usually feel obliged to back up an emotional buying decision with logic, which is the only reason why sales skills handling objections and so forth can be helpful. My belief is that if your marketing does its job, 99% of the sales effort is done.

This is why, on webinars, sales pages and signup calls, you can "help" your ideal client to step forward. Give them a list of everything they'll get with your offer, add in lots of bonuses, and say there's a time limit to create a sense of urgency (or fear of missing out, FOMO: so common it's now an acronym!).

Now I don't recommend all of these approaches, because it can make you look desperate and mess up the value for money balance on your pricing that we talked about in chapter 2). But it's certainly worth bearing in mind that, psychologically, there's an emotional and a logical bridge to cross before someone buys.

Even if they've "bought" into you and "feel" what you offer is right for them – and perhaps even decided they want to buy - it's often an emotional response to your offer (if you've matched with their pain points and desires). People then need some logical arguments to support what's going on in their head before going ahead with a decision.

If you can truly connect with the key issue, problem, struggle or frustration that your ideal client is having or thinking about as they go about their day and provide an authentic message that engages, educates and has the potential to help them, you're almost all of the way there to enrolling them as a client.

CREATING A STRUCTURED SALES PROCESS

As part of your marketing plan, you will have created a lead magnet to capture contacts and follow up with people. You can test out different lead magnets for different audiences to generate more targeted leads and increase your sales conversions.

Since your lead magnet and subsequent follow up should lead seamlessly into your sales process, segmenting your prospects will help to filter out those who are not a good fit for what you do.

You can have the best service ever, but if you don't have a good sales process, the people you engage and educate will fall through the cracks before you can enrol them. Your sales process needs structure and your sales copy needs to speak to the conversation going on in your prospects head – their wants, needs, hopes, fears and so on.

Your sales page is a critical part of the entire end-to-end sales process. As well as the benefits of what you offer, you should articulae who are the best candidates.

It's important to keep your copy concise – I'm not a fan of super long sales letters – but it still needs to be comprehensive and well-structured in order to reiterate your offer, accentuate the benefits and build confidence to move forward and make the buying decision.

Here are three steps to creating a high-converting sales page that I used to help a recent client who was unsure what to include and how to structure it. (There's more help on crafting your sales page in the *iSuccess Business Academy* – go to isuccessbusinessacademy.com to login or join.)

RECIPE FOR A HIGH-CONVERTING SALES PAGE

Step 1 – Identify the key messages and problem language

Before attempting to write the sales page, you need to have a very clear target audience for your offer. Who is likely to benefit the most and the fastest (because of the stage they are at)?

What is the primary need, driver or problem that your service addresses? Why is this an issue for your audience? How do they feel about it? How will things be different when the problem is solved and/or the benefits are seen?

In your copy, you need to speak to your potential client in terms they will understand and resonate with.

Step 2 – Craft your sales page content

There are ten key pieces of content that any sales page needs. The aim is to craft and reiterate these in such a way they flow naturally as a story that leads to a decision to say "yes we need this!" The ten pieces are:

1. Headline / sub-headline
2. Intro video
3. Problem – Solution story
4. Overview of your programme / service

By this point, your ideal customer / service user should be recognising that what you're offering could help them. But next they will want to know exactly what they would be getting, what it costs and whether it would work for them. Thus:

5. Case studies / testimonials
6. Call to action (CTA) button with price / plans – your most wanted response.

Here, you can also show any options such as payment plans, different packages or levels of service. Next, they want to feel confident to say yes to working with you, so we add:

7. A guarantee, conditions and time frame checklist.
8. Team bio – names and headshots which help make personal connections.

Add in a set of further case studies / testimonials here if you have them followed by another call to action.

Next, people will have questions and concerns that need addressing, so we'll add:

9. FAQs – a list of Q&As or a short video.

Time to add a final CTA to create extra urgency like a deadline or special bonus and finally a simple sign-off:

10. Footer – your business name, date, links to terms & conditions, privacy policy etc. and can be helpful to provide a link or button to go back to the Top of the page.

Step 3 – Apply best practices for sales page design

Now you have the appropriate structure and layers of content for your sales page, you need to make sure the design is working for you not against you. Follow proven, best practices in terms of font styles / colours.

Make your sales page easy to scroll and scan read by using lots of big visuals and breaking up heavy chunks of text with sub-headings, bullets, lists and white space. Use images that will resonate with your audience and are relevant to your offer. And use photos of you, your team and your clients (if they agree) to inspire and bring a sense of truth and trust.

The call to action is a critical part of understanding your prospect's next best move towards becoming a client so make sure it stands out throughout your sales page; it doesn't have to be only at the end. Your call to action for a professional services offer is rarely a "buy now" type of transaction that you'd see for retail products. With high-end consulting, selectivity is important because if you're working at the top of the tree as an expert in your field, you don't really want to be a general-admission brand.

Setting high standards for a client signals that you understand your own worth. In the same way that VIP and private clubs work, you build desire in high-end markets by being exclusive. It's what's called a "velvet rope" approach to attracting premium clients - offering limited availability and saying "no" to unqualified prospects.

I've used this in several businesses and find it's not only great for managing my time, it also actually creates more demand and more respect during sign-up calls. Prospects have to sell themselves to me, not the other way around.

(Of course, in a tendering situation when you're asked to give a presentation - it's slightly different, which is why I generally don't tender for work. But on the occasions that I have been selected for interview by the client representative or panel, similar to my enrolment calls, I'd always approach it as a consultative opportunity not a sales pitch.)

In a leveraged consulting sales process, your sales page should be an invitation to take the next step, not an order form. If you're an agency offering a specific "done-for-you" package, I'd still advise you pre-qualify your clients. In this way, your call to action will be to "apply" for a free consult session (your sign-up call).

By adding a "velvet rope" entry into your sign-up process, you create exclusivity, increase your perceived value and make your process stand out to attract better clients. This velvet rope strategy also helps you focus your priorities and protect your limited bandwidth so you can provide the people who decide to hire you or sign up to your programme the service they deserve.

In the spirit of consultative sales, your enrolment call is important for both you and your prospect to find out if what you offer is right for them and is really going to help them achieve the specific outcome they want.

The final leg of the sales process is obviously the sign-up decision, followed often by contract agreement and payment. Because in many cases, the "paperwork" can sometimes take a few days of back and forth or perhaps you invoice after each milestone of a project, I like to add at least the first onboarding steps onto the end of the sales process. This helps your new client to get started with you, adding confidence and trust to the transaction before parting with the actual money.

If what you're offering is a programme or course, then your enrolment and payment will be more cut-and-dry. Nonetheless, taking account of the legal "cooling off" period, I'd recommend you can provide access only to the inception material when you onboard them.

Either way, at the end of your sales process, onboarding should reassure your new client that you mean business and have a structure to what you do, professionalism.

COMMUNICATING VALUE IN YOUR SALES CONVERSATIONS

Clarity, relevance and value for money, as discussed in chapters 3 and 4, are the primers for sales. Most "sales" material for consulting type services just doesn't work, because they tend to focus on the services offered not on what outcome or benefit is delivered specifically as a result of working with you. It's hard to convey value when you're only talking about delivering X number of days or a 30-page analysis.

(As an aside: this is probably why many project teams find evaluation so challenging. While they may be focused on the project's aims and objectives, they tend to write these out as activities and outputs rather than outcomes, i.e. gains, benefits or impact on their key stakeholders, in our case our clients.)

A golden rule in sales and marketing is to talk about results and benefits not facts or features of your service or product.

Your sales copy should be focused on addressing two crucial return on investment questions people will have about your offer: (1) what's the opportunity that will change or improve things for the client; and (2) is that benefit worth the fee? In other words, what's the outcome, benefits and impact from working with you.

Your prospect wants to know how much bang they will get for their buck in terms of outcomes; quality or quantity are secondary concerns. Surprisingly, most consultants aren't too good at articulating the end outcomes they achieve for their clients. Their sales material tends to focus on the *means* to the end – what they do or how they do it, rather than the end result.

At the same time, obviously we know that consultants and coaches tackle complex problems and clients are unlikely to believe there's a single nugget of wisdom or know-how that they are missing that will turn everything around. In fact, suggesting there's some kind of "silver bullet" solution to tackle a complex issue is likely to diminish your credibility as an expert. But they usually like the concept of a collaborative, co-designed process to help them review, analyse and plan the solution.

This is why your consulting or coaching methodology is an important element of how you deliver the intended outcome or result for your client. As we discussed in the previous chapter, when you leverage your expertise through education-driven marketing, what you are doing is showcasing your understanding of the problem and your process to resolving it.

Your education-based marketing content may already have provided a way to help your target clients achieve the first step towards the solution they want. They start to trust you as an expert and solutions provider. In your sales copy, outlining where problems stem from can help someone understand why your offer is a good fit for what they need, as well as agitate the problem and create a sense of urgency to sort it.

Rather than talk about who you are and what you do (which is how most business websites, presentations and sales pages come across), people are more strongly drawn to marketing that focuses on who *your clients* are and what *they* need. Communicating clearly your understanding of their situation and the desired end-result you can achieve for them is key.

A great starting place is to outline the problem, talk about the causes and then the possible solutions, and from there you can more convincingly promote what will change or improve by working with you.

In my consulting process I always start with the question: "what does success look like to you" or "what (change) do you want to see". This encourages (actually forces) them to identify where they are now and where they want to be – closing the "gap" is the tangible result I help deliver. I also ask clients "why is that important to you?" because this moves the conversation to a deeper emotional level and highlights their current pain or dissatisfaction with the situation or problem.

If illuminating emotional benefits is important in consulting, it's doubly important in sales! What you do, how you do it and what outcome you achieve for clients are worth differentiating. Your prospective clients will mostly be thinking about the *means*, because that's what they're used to thinking and hearing about.

From experience, I know that when people feel motivated towards a goal, they are more open to understand the underlying issues in their problem and I've been able to help them take a decision on getting the solution way faster.

The problem is that even your prospects don't always know what the end goal looks like, and therefore they won't immediately be able to articulate why it's important to them. You know, generally speaking, if you ask people what they want, they're not sure. But they can sure give you a whole list of things they don't want! In the psychology of all this, we know that people are more motivated to move away from pain than towards pleasure.

BECOMING A TRUSTED ADVISER

To increase enrolments into your programme or service, or sell a product, it's important to know how to communicate what you offer without coming across as overly salesy. Your aim is not to "make a sale" or "close the deal" in one conversation – it should be far more subtle, graceful and empowering for your client than that.

Through your content marketing, you should have already pre-qualified and filtered those who are a good fit for you (and you for them!) If you have already educated and helped people to understand and start to solve a problem they are having, it provides a trusting relationship to working with you further. This wins new clients by ensuring high integrity for you and high confidence for them.

I'm sure as a buyer, you can easily recognise good customer service. For instance, if a company provides great guidance on their website or excellent advice in their shop, it's easier to make a decision to buy than when a company fails to provide this basic support to potential customers.

The good ones are truly attempting to understand your situation and what you need and help you pick a product that suits. If you get this, it may be easier to see how education works so well as a "sales" tool.

If you make it easier, better, faster, more enjoyable and rewarding for prospective clients to buy from or hire you to achieve the results they want, then you're already demonstrating your value to them.

An education-centric approach circumvents the pushy "always-be-closing" model of sales that many people in professional services hate and instead adopts a "give-to-gain" consulting model that is a far better fit than a sales pitch to how we generally go about our work.

The sales appointment type approach is not well suited to a service-orientated business and the clients you wish to win over. You're going from a standing start. When you generate leads and appointments or sales calls with educational marketing, you'll save at least 80% of the time, effort and money you're currently spending on client acquisition.

A prospective client's decision (to work with you, hire your services or buy your product) is not something you should try to control. Instead, you can design an enlightened path for them as they travel down the buying decision stream. People buy confidence (in how you can help them) more than competence, although obviously you need to underpin your services with professional credibility.

You serve clients best by asking questions, clarifying responses in order to deepen understanding of what their ideal clients want before starting to provide insights, advice, guidance and support that address a specific problem or need.

Educationally, what you are doing is shifting your clients' perspective of the problem and what they think they want, and providing expert input to help them understand what they need to achieve a specific solution or result. This attracts clients because you are "serving not selling" and "teaching not telling".

What this means in practice is this. First, you engage and "consult" with or "coach" the prospective client to understand the thinking behind what they say they want, open up their problem, look at what's behind the pain, stress or frustration they have. Only from this vantage point can you start to indicate a possible solution (or set of solutions), i.e. what can be implemented to resolve or improve the problem they have outlined.

Using a consultative or coaching approach of asking questions and exposing the real underlying problem(s), your prospective client starts to become "educated", to understand their situation better and see possible ways forward more clearly from the expert angle.

Second, your prospective client catches on to the reasoning for how your service or product aligns with their problem and delivers the solution they want and will value.

Educating your clients as they engage with you across the buying process (including after they become clients) brings many benefits, both in financial terms for your business, and in the influence and impact you will achieve. In actual fact, most business owners who implement these strategies are working fewer hours per week on sales and marketing yet earning double or triple their consultancy income.

Leveraged consulting an educational entrepreneur, you're working smarter not harder. Your client engagement process is clear, easy to access, provides valuable insights and flows naturally for your prospects – that's hard for the right client to resist!

As you expand and bring on more and more leads, you can add value beyond your one-to-one time, and support people who haven't even signed up with you as a face-to-face client. And when they approach you, you can charge premium, because they already know, like and trust you to get the outcome they want. Again, this will totally raise your game way above what nearly all of your competitors are doing.

BUILDING THE EDUCATION BRIDGE

When you start the sales process with educating people around the problem or issues they are experiencing, you also help them to understand and resonate with the desired solution and how you will work with them to achieve it. This should lead seamlessly into your post-enrolment onboarding. Make sense?

Your challenge is to engage them in a thinking process or conversation about the *end-result* they want (on an emotional as well as pragmatic level) and teach them why your service or product was designed specifically to help them get that outcome. In presenting your sales offer (what you do), the conversation should be heavily skewed towards emotional triggers associated with the desired outcomes and benefits not towards the features of delivery model.

The problem is most entrepreneurs start their business with only a vague understanding of who their ideal clients are, what they worry about and what they really want. Yet we know that, psychologically, as human beings we tend to make an emotional buying decision then use our logical brain to rationalise our decision!

People trust you more and buy into a solution when you can clearly explain from your own or others' experience of the problem, how the "what" leads to the "so what".

This is why marketing rich in storytelling and insights is so powerful, because it demonstrates empathy and builds trust. In so doing, it helps to bridge the gap between marketing and sales. Russell Brunson (founder of ClickFunnels) aptly calls this the "epiphany bridge" – you take your prospective client on the journey across that bridge with a story. This invokes the kind of emotional experience necessary before any information about features and specifics can excite them. Logic is justification for the emotional end benefit a person has already decided they want!

Let's put that another way:

If you just try to "sell" someone on something, you get resistance, because it doesn't create the strong emotion needed to prompt action, so the logical brain keeps objecting.

However, if instead of just stating the solution, you lead them to it - effectively done by mirroring their situation in a story - the person develops the understanding and has an "aha" moment. When you finally do present your solution, both the emotional and logical brain can say "yes". The decision to buy (or hire you) is then very much theirs and there's no need to "sell" anything.

Getting a clear sight on the emotional end benefit and how your clients express this is a good place to start. Without this, you'll end up wasting a lot of time and money on ineffective marketing messages and hoping something hits the right spot.

Your existing clients are a great source of market intelligence for understanding the concerns, needs and pain points of your target market. Plus the problem language they use to articulate these makes great sales copy.

However, don't assume you always understand the current situation, as we live in rapidly changing times and quite literally "things change". Embrace opportunities to enter into dialogue with your target audience of new prospective clients. In professional practice, this would just be a regular activity for remaining in good standing in your industry: networking, speaking engagements, workshops and free consults work really well to gather data.

One might therefore argue that every conversation with a prospective client is actually also a market research activity not just a sales activity. As you learn how to articulate better the problems they are having, you should notice even casual conversation with your target audience gets easier and you will undoubtedly gain clients from these interactions as people get the sense that you're on their side and understand their challenges.

Bear in mind though that unless you're "educating" your prospects, you'll find, they won't immediately see things from the same perspective as you do even if you're mirroring what people tell you they want. Hearing how they articulate their issues, needs and concerns gives you vital knowledge and understanding that you can build into your marketing messages and sales copy.

Although this upfront market research can seem time-consuming, it's just something to build into your weekly, monthly and annual plan – what you glean is well worth the effort. I appreciate that once you're working on a project with a client, there often doesn't seem the luxury of taking time for reflection, dialogue and deeper consultation so new understandings may never come to light. So how can you use your market research time wisely?

Before you even have that initial "sales" conversation with them (i.e. one that may lead to them working with you, hiring you or buying from you), education-based marketing starts the dialogue much earlier. It provides the structured thought process necessary for a client to understand why what you do can lead to what he (or she) wants, when they probably haven't even articulated it in their own head yet.

You pre-educate them on the nuances of the problem, so they recognise the "gap" we talked about earlier. This makes it far easier to discuss the solution at the point of hiring you or joining one of your programmes.

If you seek to understand what the client wants to achieve as a natural part of an initial consultation, you learn so much about how they express their need or problem. Understanding their emotional end benefit and the psychological stages they need to move through to break through mental barriers and get the results they want (and thus before saying yes to your service or product) helps you to create ever-increasingly powerful marketing messages in the future that resonate with your target audience.

Blending marketing with education for business development purposes is perhaps something I've always done, since at heart I'm a teacher. In every service-based industry I've ever worked (including health & wellness, wealth management, marketing and business support), the direct part of my sales process is a simple consulting conversation.

What most clients want is a step-by-step manual, a process for getting from where they are [the problem] to where they want to be [the outcome].

Using a diagnostic tool or "system" as a basis for this consulting type conversation works really well, because people bring with them all kinds of preconceptions about certain ways of doing things; the information needs to be re-conceptualised in their mind. I found this was very effective in winning new business.

Some might call this "consultative sales", because people who feel they are being listened to and understood, not talked at, while at the same time learning something about the problem they have, are more receptive to working with you.

The educational approach to winning clients uses consulting and coaching type methodologies as a tool for marketing and business development, not just as a single encounter that slides your prospect into a buying decision, but infusing every point of engagement with a prospective client. And one piece of "luck" is that you already possess the consulting and coaching skills that are rather essential to success as an educational entrepreneur.

Educating your prospective client is how you attract and win them over. If what you offer solves a problem they have, notably, starting the process of helping them also demonstrates tangibly that you're someone who can actually help them.

When you lead with education, people see you giving value first. Teach your unique system and they realise they need YOU to help them implement it.

With this mind, maybe you're on a journey of discovery here, just like your clients and customers are with you. Many of my clients and students have said my teachings opened up new ideas to them, they use words like "interesting", "insightful", "educating", "enlightening" and "inspiring", which is great – that's my goal and means I've guided them and helped them move towards a solution to their problem or need ☺.

People often tell me that I got them to "think differently" about the purpose and process of business, communication, marketing and sales, especially online where trust and credibility are becoming scarcities.

STACKING YOUR SALES FUNNEL

Adding leveraged delivery into the mix of your business model, as we'll look at in the next chapter, is a useful transition for customers of your digital products and programmes. They are already fully engaged and educated through your sales and marketing process and so move more readily and confidently into your high-level one-to-one services or high-ticket events.

This is where your *Engage-Educate-Enrol* pathway needs to loop back on itself. With a fully leveraged consulting model, the process is a circular spiral not actually a linear path. Accordingly, in your sales funnel, you do need to stack the deck, as the next figure illustrates.

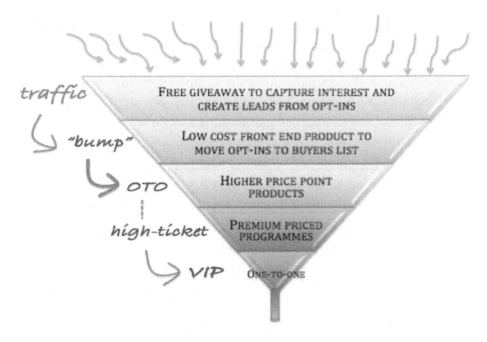

The first block in the "stack" is what you've used in your leveraged marketing already to attract attention, generate leads and engage your audience, such as free reports, blog posts, video series, webinars and so forth. Subsequent blocks are used to continue to give value in ways that move people through an educational experience.

Low to medium priced products, such as a book or pilot course, can provide a "bump" (aka "tripwire") and/or "One-Time-Offer" (OTO) to more high-ticket sales on the back-end as customers move through your funnel. These early experiences of your expertise increase your credibility but importantly they help to identify your most responsive prospects who are willing to buy.

Notably, if you're driving paid traffic to your capture page, earnings from these may help cover off ad spend.

Obviously, you don't build up a sophisticated funnel stack in one step. You start with a simple one-step sign up offer as you build your contact list, and monetise gradually with paid offers. Some argue that the days of the value pyramid are gone, but I'm still an advocate of it from an educational standpoint – you're only asking for a small commitment first, and this builds credibility and trust on both sides.

Here's how to stack your funnel:

- **Sketch out your value ladder** in terms of how your giveaway leads into the products and programmes you will offer and put a rough figure on what you might charge for them.

- **Work out what income you want** from your signature programme, product or service and how many leads, customers and sales that equates to. It's good to know your monthly figures, but it's also essential to know your Lifetime Customer Value. For example: how often do customers buy multiple products, how many upsell conversions do you typically get, or if you have a paid membership site, how long on average does a customer stay for (3-4 months or 2-3 years!).

- **Create** your free giveaway, a compelling heading and sales page for your high value product that captures your aligning, targeting, positioning and branding work to create magnetic marketing messages and irresistible offer.

- **Develop your marketing plan** for how you are going to drive traffic to your website and lead capture page for your giveaway.

- **Avoid the perfectionism trap** - don't procrastinate thinking it has to be exactly right from the start. Digital marketing is simple to test, tweak and make adjustments. These days, with self-publishing and print-on-demand services, even hard copy books can be easily revised and republished.

You can choose to create a simple one-step stack and or a multi-step set of products and programmes. You can gradually move your prospects through this "funnel" or you can decide to create a big launch for a high-ticket offer. I know entrepreneurs who have done both successfully, but most consultants and coaches transitioning to digital programmes tend to feel daunted by the latter and end up not doing anything.

You're definitely leaving money on the table if you don't have any kind of sales funnel mapped out. My advice is: stack your deck, but keep it simple. Even if it's a short stack - a low-end product plus a high-end service - start with the end in mind. Get your audience on the right track engaging with you. Your pricing points will determine what the numbers means for you income wise in terms of the low-end customers and high-end clients you attract and how they convert through your funnel.

Remember, "it's best not to propose marriage on a first date". Start by thinking about how your products and services build value and help move someone forward from the client's perspective. Consider where they are in the buying process and match your message to their level of engagement with you and their confidence in you.

A subscription model is especially effective when there's a sticky online community component as it keeps people engaged and supported. Recurring revenue allows you to build long-term, profitable relationships with your consumers and clients – the perfect solution to the era of digital competition.

SERVING YOUR PERFECT PEOPLE

For your sales process to be effective, your mission, values and beliefs need to be golden-threaded through everything you do, everything you put out into the marketplace, everything you write, say, share. How you deal with people and the impression you give pre-sales (in your marketing) will determine how successfully you convert prospects to clients.

> ※
>
> "[When you're starting out] with a small audience, you actually have an advantage, because you can create more intimate relationships with people, which means you will experience way higher [sales] conversions."
> – Stu McClaren, TRIBE

I can't stress enough (so I'm doing it again) that building your brand message and a compelling sales offer starts with a crystal-clear vision about what your target clientele need and want. Before anything, you must get this sorted and align it with your value and business brand.

Without this "brand standing", your potential customers won't know what you're about, what your core service is, what quality and results you're committed to, and how selective you are about who you work with.

Hint 1: Not being readily available for everyone and everything actually makes you more attractive to your ideal client! Identify clearly your "tribes and territories", those people you can most help and therefore best serve.

Hint 2: You don't need to build a massive audience or list to start creating momentum with your message and making some early sales.

And for yourself, when you tune into what gives you personal satisfaction (when you're working with a client or deliver results you promised), you'll get clear on the reasons for doing what you do and helping who you help. This really helps your sales conversations.

Let your vision of what you want to achieve with a sale go beyond any money goals, at least initially. If you're giving people what they want, the money flows. The aim is to engage with your prospect in a way that makes you an invited and welcomed guest (rather than a noise or a nuisance).

To do this, we build on all the work done in leveraging you and leveraged marketing - you need to be positioned as an expert – develop your authority status and brand – and decide how you want to work with and interact with your digital clients.

Working out exactly how you make a difference to your clients, in terms of a specific problem you solve or result you deliver, can take some head-scratching effort but pays back dividends in the ease of your enrolments. It's time well spent, because that clarity is going to be your biggest asset in terms of positioning, branding, pricing and sales.

Building leverage into your sales process will improve your productivity, profitability and overall enjoyment of the winning clients!

CREATING AN ENROLMENT EXPERIENCE

Strategy or discovery calls – consult sessions - are a great way to complete the *Engage-Educate-Enrol* process. The call should be structured and by appointment so you can gather some background information from your prospect and pre-qualify them.

A good enrolment conversation gives relief, hope and incentive that the full solution is within reach. You need to provide the prospect with a lot of value without giving away too much. It's most definitely not about delivering one big sales pitch.

We've already looked at the role of education in the sales process. Creating relevant, targeted, education-rich content helps you engage the right audience and build a trusting relationship with your most ideal prospects. The next natural step is for them to enrol in one of your programmes or sign up for a service. But we still can use the enrolment call to give further value as well as sign them up if appropriate.

Enrolment should be a positive experience for your prospects. Don't focus on making a sale and getting clients signed up; focus on getting consult sessions booked in.

In the free consult session, when we come to the actual point of sale, all this upfront investment helps ease the sale because the material and support you've provided fast tracks the buyer's decision-making journey. Their education of what you can deliver is helped along in terms and concepts that they already understand, and is indeed a demonstration of how you are assisting them. (Whether you deliver your solution directly via one-on-one, in-person services or via group programmes or online courses becomes irrelevant.)

Most people will hire you when their need is felt to be urgent or pressing, but they also want to believe what you offer will help them move in the right direction. Your products, programmes and strategy sessions are all ways you can demonstrate you understand and can help them. It creates a connection and builds the trust required for them to make the decision that they need you.

Your initial education-focused materials are all intended as a lead-in to inviting the prospective client to the free consult. Some call this a strategy session, a discovery call or an exploratory call; others label it an enrolment call, a sign-up call or even blatantly a sales call. Whatever you call it, make it an attractive offer where you clearly want to help them, not a thinly disguised sales pitch. Give it a purposeful name and make sure the focus is what they want (a solution), not on what you want (a sale).

When you avoid looking at business development as "sales" – and you focus on booking enrolment calls in the first instance — your mind gets into gear with what you do naturally as a consultant or coach, which is inspiring and helping people to commit to a desired result.

A good consult is where you help the person see what's been holding them back. The gift is one of clarity; they no longer feel stuck, and have been given the next steps to take. The call should make the solution feel within their reach and your only pitch is to ask "do you want some help implementing that?"

At the end of the enrolment call, you will either have a new client or you won't. Perhaps it's a no but not a never. It may well be that the timing is not quite right for them or maybe just that you don't feel your programme is the right solution for them. In this case, they will stay a subscriber and/or follower and go through another cycle of the engage-educate-enrol process, perhaps in a different segment if the call revealed your programme isn't quite right for them.

The good news is, when you create a sales funnel, alongside good follow up (by email or phone), education-based marketing does much of the trust building and selling for you. This means when you get on a call with the prospect, they're already half on board with you. Go into the call with the mindset of seeing if you can help the person, and if you can, tell them about your programme, product or service as the vehicle for them getting the help they need.

To reiterate: when creating an effective funnel, you need to be clear on what you offer and what problems it solves. You need to be able to articulate the benefits and results that your service or programme delivers.

Most of us aren't too good at that, to be fair. Without the right guidance, it can take a lot of trial and error to make that sales page, video or presentation convert into excited buyers! But if you learn how to make your material really aligned with your target audience's needs – the thing that's keeping them awake at night - it's compelling.

The "trick" is to help them get clarity on exactly how they can achieve a specific result they desperately desire. You can let your material do most of the problem explanation and trust building work for you, which means you end up only doing one-to-one calls with highly engaged applicants. You shift from selling to helping so they get value and see you as the way to procure the solution to their problem.

People who have gone through an inceptive education with you make ideal clients and good candidates for your high-end products, programmes and services.

ENROLLING & ONBOARDING YOUR NEW CLIENT

In your business, I'm pretty certain you will have some kind of workflow for how you bring clients in and start working with them. Even if it isn't forcefully "managed", do you have a process?

- ❖ *What do you do to generate initial enquiries?*
- ❖ *What do you do next to follow up with a new contact or lead?*
- ❖ *Do you have an application form for your consult sessions?*
- ❖ *Do you use an electronic appointment system or book by phone? (Who handles all that, you or an assistant?)*
- ❖ *Do your confirm receipt after someone submits an application or makes a booking? Is it email, phone or letter? What happens next?*

At the very least, you should have in place some kind follow-up, a confirmation email or call-back, possibly asking them to submit a pre-consult survey and sending them some nurturing (email or phone) communication to ensure they turn up and have a productive session with you.

What exactly happens during a consult enrolment call with you? Do you have a structure for the call? Towards the end of the consult session, do you have a process to enrol the prospect over the phone or do you send them to a "signup" page? Try setting it out what you do as a process map.

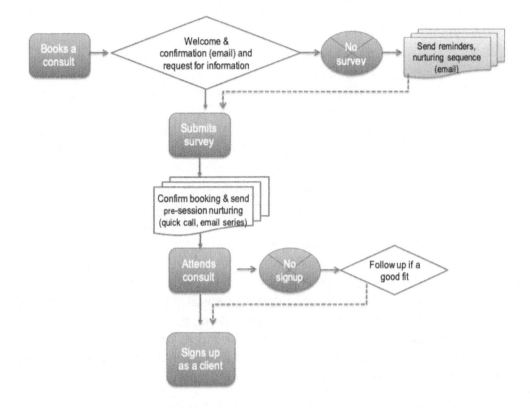

Similarly, let's say someone watches one of your webinars and signs up for your product or service, how will they pay you? Is there a contract to sign or terms and conditions to agree to?

If they don't sign up right away, what kind of re-engagement communication will you have to help deal with objections and encourage them to take action? Could you perhaps offer a payment plan or a different lower cost option?

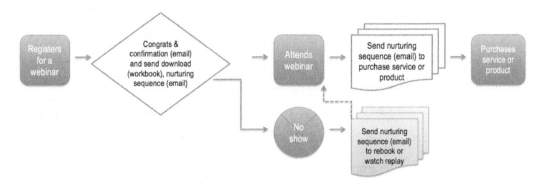

Once someone is a client, what happens next? How do you get the new client on board? What contract, letter of engagement, documentation, login access or induction do you need to provide?

As you start working with them, how do you manage milestones, issue invoices or handle payments? Here's an illustration from my consulting client project process, simplified version.

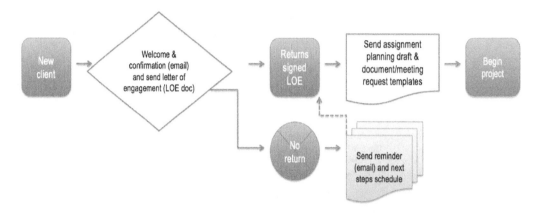

While we've focused here on leveraged sales, you can, of course, create process maps to systematise any or every internal manual process in your business. Indeed, it's a good idea to produce a process map and document your key business processes: for instance, how you respond to prospect or client emails, manage events, schedule social media posts, create invoices, chase payments. Think of repetitive tasks you can outsource or automate.

Now you have your client onboard, how you work with them is where we move to leverage your expert system – next up is leveraged delivery.

ACTION NOTES

_____

_____

_____

_____

_____

_____

_____

_____

_____

Chapter 6

LEVERAGED DELIVERY

Vital Tactics in the Digital Marketplace

"The secret of change is to focus all of your energy not on fighting the old but on building the new."

Dan Milligan,

Way of the Peaceful Warrior

KEY POINTS

❖ When you position and brand yourself around a distinctive problem your target market has, they realise they need *you* to help them implement the solution.

❖ Having your own system in place for how you work with a client means you can easily design a programme - workshop or a whole course, either face-to-face or online - that mirrors your step-by-step process.

❖ Your perfect client is one for whom you can deliver their desired result in the shortest possible time.

❖ If you want to make more money, serve more people and have a bigger impact, you need to find a way to leverage your expertise and create more value in the marketplace.

❖ High-quality online education remains a tremendous growth industry, and the global market is huge. As the market keeps evolving, successful businesses lead rather than follow the herd.

❖ One high-value signature programme promoted through one great webinar is a simple strategy that can turn your business success around, overnight.

❖ No matter how great your content is, people will not automatically buy a high-end product without you making a convincing case for it.

❖ Validate a new idea by creating an introductory product or the first "module" of your full signature system as a short course and pilot it with your target market.

❖ Dialogue is the cornerstone of effective learning and can make your programme more engaging, experiential & outcomes-focused, and thus increasingly high value & premium.

❖ Don't waste time trying to get clients to sign up to what you think they should have. Instead, listen to what they tell you they want, and then create it for them.

❖ Being an educational entrepreneur is about making yourself and your expertise available to big audiences and providing people with a learning experience that delivers the intended outcome and a lasting benefit.

LEVERAGING YOUR EXPERT SYSTEM

In the preceding chapters, we've laid down foundations for leveraging you, your expertise and your expert system in terms of the unique methodology you use for getting results for your clients. We've explored ways to create and promote a distinctive core concept and magnetic brand to wrap around this, so your target market sees what you do and why you do it as the solution they're looking for.

When you position and brand yourself around a distinctive problem your target market has, they realise they need *you* to help them implement the solution. We can build on our leveraged marketing and leveraged sales approaches to find ways of leveraging your expert system beyond your face-to-face consulting, coaching or "done-for-you" agency types of work.

Having your own system in place for how you work with a client means you can easily design a programme - workshop or a whole course, either face-to-face or online - that mirrors your step-by-step process.

The art of standing still in your business is to continue to market like crazy to bring in more sales of one-to-one clients until you're maxed out. Sadly, that's the frequent "burnout" I see with small business owners and freelancers. If you cannot deliver in other ways than face-to-face, one-to-one or "done-for-you" services, you will quickly hit a ceiling and run out of time, energy and sanity!

To grow your business, this is the point where you need to move towards leveraged delivery in our *SCALE* model. If you started the business based on your prior career and skill set and you just think the one-to-one consulting services work that you're doing is the only way you can earn a living, take your head out of that sandpit. (Sorry, I'm being cruel to be kind if you still haven't sussed out the power of leveraging your expertise.)

Once you have secured and satisfied a few clients, and you take them through your expert system, you demonstrate that your expert system works well to solve the problem they came to you for. The next important part of the reformation is therefore to process map what you do working on a typical client project and find delivery models that allow you to help more people than working one-on-one with a client.

Your perfect client is one for whom you can deliver their desired result in the shortest possible time.

Remember if you don't have a leveraged consulting delivery model, if you are only trading your time for an hourly or daily rate, you limit how many people you can serve and how much money you can earn in any given period.

Even if you have leveraged you, your marketing and your sales process, and you're prepared to work 24/7, as a solo professional or small team there's ultimately a cap on your income potential. If you work on a project billing basis rather than hourly or daily rates, there's a ceiling on how many projects you can undertake, as an individual or as a firm unless you hire more consultants.

Unless you can clone yourself, (and if you've watched Michael Keaton in the movie "Multiplicity", it all ended in mayhem anyhow!) you need to stop doing everything yourself and implement systems (and in time, a team) around you and create products and services that don't require your personal time, attention and energy in order to generate income.

You'll probably find the same issues keeps coming up for them and by creating guides and templates, there's probably a lot you could do to support them remotely. (If you already do this then you're already part-way towards leveraged delivery!)

Rather than keep filling your schedule with more clients with supposedly all different needs you need to pander to, which is stressing you out, think how you can leverage that issue as a product.

From working with hundreds of professionals, I know every consultant is able to extract one unique proposition that their clients continually struggle with. You can use this to attract a specific and highly profitable segment of your target audience and offer an alternative way of working with you.

UNDERSTANDING HOW VALUE IS CREATED IN BUSINESS

The financial folks will tell you that value is created when a business earns revenue that exceeds expenses. But as I've talked about earlier in relation to "value for money", I believe that for a service-based business we need a broader definition of value creation that can be considered separate from monetary measures.

If you want to make more money, serve more people and have a bigger impact, you need to find a way to leverage your expertise and create more value in the marketplace.

Savvy business owners are catching on to the significantly higher degrees of leverage that can be achieved by embracing an education-driven, online and one-to-many business model, so they can reach and serve a bigger audience and at the same time generate multiple and passive streams of income. (Here I mean "passive" in the sense you're not trading time for money, and once built you can deliver many times with little or no need to be physically present. More on that later.)

Building a consulting business as an educational entrepreneur to achieve a fully leveraged strategy may require a shift in mindset about how you market and deliver your services and products, how you reach and engage with the people you serve through efficient marketing systems. Done carefully, however, you can substantially leverage your time and expertise to increase your influence, productivity and income by reaching and impacting more people.

And I hope from the previous chapters you now appreciate that building education into your sales and marketing process goes further and deeper than just giving people information. The same is true for leveraged delivery. Educational products and programmes are an obvious add-on to what you already do as an expert and service provider and create value to your consulting and coaching clients.

It has to be said that a lot of business owners invest time and money creating products or courses no-one wants to buy. This is usually because they didn't do their market research homework or test out the idea before going full steam ahead. Either their price point doesn't fit their target market and they can't charge the prices they expected or they aren't communicating the value effectively in their marketing and sales calls.

The consequence is they don't achieve either the reach or revenue the endeavour intended and feel it's a total flop and they failed. I don't want that to be your experience. Everything we've covered so far is to help you build the whole customer track on solid foundations - from the inside out and right side up!

The value of the educational entrepreneur is measured through the results you deliver and the satisfaction of your clients - influence and impact precede income - always.

Many people build information products into their business thinking they will offer a free guide to generate leads or make a quick buck selling an e-book or two. This is also not what educational entrepreneurship is about – it's a holistic business model not just a set of tactics or an "add-on". It's critical that you're prepared to raise your internal bar for what's possible here with an education-based strategy for business growth.

You need to know that what you deliver fits your target audiences biggest wants and needs. If you set a goal to deliver a positive outcome from the get-go, you're on the right track. If you build education into your content marketing and consulting work, it's a seamless and authentic transition into sales to win new clients and customers and improve your retention of existing ones.

Education-driven marketing is more successful for winning clients than any sales strategy or technique I've ever come across. There's not a more authentic way to achieve a "sale" than by providing your target audience with valuable, educational material and helping them in a tangible way towards the outcome they desire. As we established back in earlier chapters, people buy services and products from people they *know, like and trust* and, remember there's no better way to demonstrate you can help people than by actually helping them!

While sales-based marketing is about telling people how great you are at helping people solve a problem, education-based marketing can show them how valuable you are by actually helping them.

Real education requires a more thoughtful design than just providing information - a "read-this, do-that" type training model. You can easily search and find plenty of good information and keep up to date with the latest marketing or sales techniques, but often you don't fully understand why they work or how to make it work, so you never end up fully embracing or implementing something.

If you build value into everything that you create for your clients, that's when the money comes.

Achieving learning outcomes is what education is (or should be) all about: it's about supporting people, to not just know more but to implement and achieve the results they want. That's the value they are paying you for.

DELIVERING YOUR EXPERTISE DIFFERENTLY

Beyond your consulting or coaching work, there are many different ways you could share your knowledge and experience through digital products and programmes. Digital content provides a means to create value by leveraging your expertise in a different way to your one-to-one consulting work. Rather than see a product or course as something else you have to "sell", I want you to view these as delivery model choices.

As Steve Jobs famously remarked "You've got to have a problem that you want to solve, the wrong that you want to right and it's got to be something that you're passionate about because otherwise you won't have the perseverance to see it through."

High-quality online education remains a tremendous growth industry, and the global market is huge.

Other than giving advice and working with clients face-to-face and one-to-one, or delivering "done-for-you" services", how else could you serve your audience? For instance, in leveraged marketing we mentioned

> ※
> "We can't look at the competition and say we're going to do it better. We have to look at the competition and say we're going to do it differently." – Steve Jobs, CEO Apple Inc.

creating articles, reports, videos, podcasts, e-books, e-courses, webinars, tools, templates and so forth to attract your target audience to you. These are all very popular for people looking for help and guidance. You don't have to give them all away for free; some can become low-cost products in your value ladder.

Note that these are also the kinds of resources you can use in face-to-face situations too, such as in presentations as giveaways for capturing leads or offer as added value or an add-on purchase to your consulting and coaching clients.

Of the various types of educational content that you can produce, pick one that you're most comfortable with and proficient in and can work your magic with. Think about how your materials can be structured into a programme or course that helps someone learn something and achieve a tangible outcome.

Creating a series of low-cost to high-end products within a membership site helps you generate both regular cash flow and recurring income.

Look at how you can best achieve your business vision through the lens of a leveraged strategy. Digital products and programmes can generate highly lucrative streams of income for your business if marketed effectively. Although an education product can work as both an on-line and in-person mode of delivery, digital delivery certainly appears to offer the more leveraged strategy, for marketing purposes and client reach, but also in terms of leveraged profits.

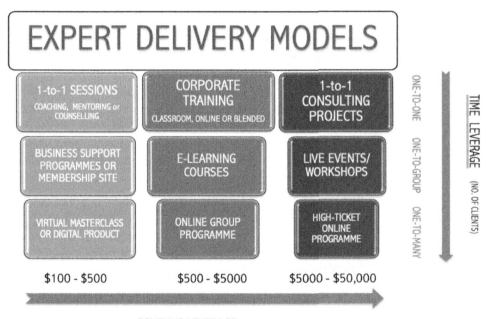

The diagram here shows a few examples of how different expert delivery models leverage your time (in relation to the number of clients you can support), and your revenue (in relation to what you might earn per client).

PRODUCING EDUCATION NOT INFORMATION

If you're already sold on the idea of offering digital products and programmes, you can rest assured you're on your way to building a fully leveraged consulting business. But as far as what it takes to succeed in the online education business, let's just make sure we're starting out on the right foot!

Now, let's first get super clear on one important point: information and education are not the same thing, albeit often intertwined in marketing and sales terms. Because information is now so readily accessible via the internet in easy-to-consume formats, and searches conjure up hundreds of results, you can get lost in an ocean of content. Your clients will too and you'll lose sales.

Let me illustrate. Education will help people understand concepts behind a given piece or set of information. A course can do this by delivering a dedicated curriculum (a kind of "formula") in a specific order, whereas a membership (where ongoing content is provided on a regular basis) is great for mastery of those concepts and ongoing support and mentorship.

Your "best" delivery method will be the one that helps your client achieve the result they want in the fastest timeframe. But it needs also to provide an enjoyable and motivating experience for them as they work with you. That's true whether you use face-to-face, online or a blended approach. This is a fine balance between how many people you can support and the level of interaction they have with you.

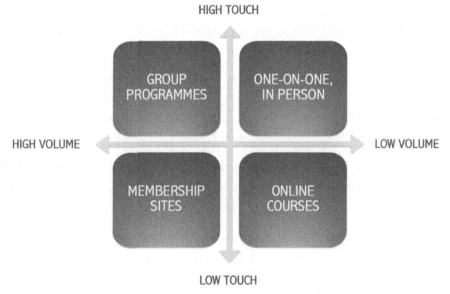

As the diagram here shows, certain delivery models enable you to work with a *high volume* of participants in a *high touch* manner; others less so. Some will require more up-front time and effort to create than others.

Pick what's needed (pedagogically), mix it up so you "design for learning" and price according to the level of input you personally need to put into the programme and each participant, with a view to appealing to the perceived (and real) "value for money" to your client.

Overwhelm is probably the main reason why information doesn't help people to do things better. Even if it feels like you want to do one simple thing in your business, you know like "get more clients"; information is generally not the answer. Because the solution is more complicated than that silver bullet idea.

If you're like me and have a love of knowledge and learning, it's easy to get sucked into avidly consuming content. The internet is like TV channel hopping for professionals. Personally, I still fall into the internet abyss when I'm trying to get clear on a plan. On at least two occasions, I've wasted days, weeks, months trying to fathom out how the pieces of information I've garnered fit together to give me the clear path I'm desperate for. Then I give up and buy a course, only to be left high and dry with a high-ticket version of the same information. And I'm still none the wiser what's right for where I'm at.

I don't want that experience for my clients. I want to drastically shorten their learning curve and avoid them making expensive mistakes. And I also want them to benefit and for what I do to have a significant positive impact on what they do.

The educational entrepreneur aims to serve his/her clients by bringing out new perspectives and distinctions, by opening up ideas and creating new possibilities in your clients' minds, expanding their horizons and potential.

As the market for online learning keeps evolving, successful businesses lead rather than follow the herd.

It's a two-way process because of what your client also brings to the table – their unique business, personality, situation or challenge. This makes things interesting for you, because this "co-generation" of a solution or plan of action is just the kind of activity you're used to doing as a consultant or coach, therapist or designer.

Most information products flooding the market this decade only deliver results to a fraction of their audience, because the learning design is one of publishing not education.

Packaging your expert system into an effective educational design is paramount.

In turning your expertise into education, you will need to think carefully about how you design the learning for your consumers. You can't just pour a load of information onto a page and call it a course. Educational content needs purpose, structure, engagement and support, including:

✓ *A meaningful topic and core concept*

✓ *Clear objectives, outcomes and measurable results*

✓ *Purposeful tasks and resources*

✓ *Some kind of interaction or dialogue*

✓ *Progress tracking.*

Here's why. There's a tonne of techniques you can learn about to get more clients and another tonne of reasons why some things will work for you and some things won't; it depends on what else you have going on. So, it feels like you need the "secrets" to "crack the code". (Yes, I've fallen for that hype for sure – useful info, but just didn't move me forward.)

Have you ever felt like the more knowledge of the problem and possible solutions you gather, the more overwhelmed, confused and stressed you feel? Well, you can bet your clients feel the exact same way too. What they need most is to understand how the information you give them fits into the overall objective of what they want to achieve. They want to see how to progress from step 1 to step 2 to step 3 etc to achieve the end goal.

So as an expert, your best strategy to help your clients get the outcome they really want is by adding *value* to the knowledge base. This is how you get noticed. Find your voice, give people a clear deliverable: a new perspective, a set of principles, a process, worksheets or a system for thinking through, planning and implementing the thing they want to do. And make sure you deliver on your promises!

DEVELOPING PREMIUM PACKAGES

If you're currently trading time for money as a consultant or service provider and not offering high-end educational products or programmes, you are hiding your light under a bushel and not fully serving a potentially massive additional client base.

Creating a packaged product or programme is one of the best ways to acquire clients who otherwise couldn't work with you. If you only offer face-to-face and one-on-one, they may not be in a position geographically or financially to use your consulting or coaching services.

In brief, a package is a something you offer that is not based on how many hours or days you provide. It could be a bundle of resources and tools, a structured set of sessions or a 6-month group programme. It could be a purely digital product or course. Or it could blend digital resources, virtual sessions and one-to-one time.

Until you embrace specialism and niche specificity, you'll waste a load of time and money trying to be all things to all people!

What you choose depends on your business, your niche, your skillset, and your preferences. However, what is critical to creating a great package that people actually want to buy is that it's based on *value* not hours. It focuses on solving a specific problem, delivering a tangible result and has a defined start and end.

Even a premium package that ends up being the same cost to your client as your high-end consulting or coaching services can feel like a more attractive proposition. If your only offer is a consulting or coaching arrangement, people can be put off because it's hard to budget for something that is, to all intents and purposes, open-ended and vague. They may feel like there's no guarantee how long it will take to achieve your intended goal.

The thing to keep in mind is this: people are most decisive and confident to invest in you, your products and your services, if *you* are decisive and confident about how exactly you can help them and what the outcomes of success are. Your pricing is all about positioning and posture. Being specific – a specialist or micro-niche - actually broadens your potential to attract business rather than limits it!

I'd define success of a premium brand as working at the top of tree on solving complex problems, as we've said from the start, and ensuring your client's desired result is fulfilled. The objective is to utilise your expertise in a way that achieves the level of revenue you desire whilst fully serving your clients' needs. Your marketing strategy, educational content, products and services should all reflect this end-goal.

If you do work that you're passionate about, good at, and love spending time doing, and align it with the most pressing problems potential clients in your industry are facing – that becomes your "genius zone". In the premium marketplace, this is where your specific set of knowledge, skills and qualities are perfectly matched to what your audience needs. At the same time, when you're in this zone you are able to use your talents to achieve your own vision of success and sense of fulfilment.

> ❊
>
> "An organisation's ability to learn, and to translate that learning into action rapidly, is the ultimate competitive advantage." – Jack Welch

If you consider your own journey and experiences, the people who are likely to be most wildly and magnetically attracted to you are those on that same journey. To them, you are someone who has the knowledge they need, who's been there, understands their problems, gets what they want, and are therefore best equipped to help them.

This is why often our business needs the personal touch, as you empathise, knowing first-hand and intimately what people need and want; you know how they express their frustrations, concerns and issues when searching for answers, and how you can reflect this back in how you talk about your premium product or service.

DESIGNING A LUCRATIVE SIGNATURE PROGRAMME

Signature programmes – that is, branded packages of unique, ownable and results-driven education that delivers on your audience's needs and goals – have been coming of age for quite some time.

Essentially, what you're doing is shifting the selling of your one-on-one time (consultancy, advisory, coaching etc) from the front end to the back end as "premium" service. A signature programme can offer a great halfway house for you and your clients; you can deliver it face-to-face to test it out, you can deliver it in blended mode (partly online), it can be group based and include some one-to-one individual support. It really depends on the model you choose that works for you.

Obviously, a key driver to selling your programme is creating a magnetic, catchy name, as we talked about in earlier chapters. But as with all your branding and marketing materials around your chosen niche or core concept, the emphasis in delivering it especially should be on "results". People buy high-end courses because they want to learn how to achieve a specific outcome that the course promises to deliver.

This process starts with your marketing and your sales page. When structured and written correctly, your promotional material is all part of the learning experience for your audience. As you take your visitors on a journey to learn more and more about your programme or course, your ideal participant is drawn in and able to make an informed decision to sign up.

With reference back to the seven growth industries declared at the book's inception, let's scrutinise the enormity of the opportunity for massively increasing your reach and revenue through a high-end e-learning programme.

The Internet has created a whole new set of opportunities for providing online learning services. Over the course of my early career using technology in teaching and learning, I've experienced many revolutions in digital education, but also a kind of evolution. There has been rapid development from teachers making small innovations within the traditional curriculum to creating sophisticated blended learning programmes (that combine online and classroom-based approaches). We've experienced a bull market in open educational resources (OERs) and massive open online courses (MOOCs). And now the growth of online, interactive, personalised programmes is on the rise.

Furthermore, with all the hundreds of information marketers on the web now offering "how-to" products, between the pages and pages of search results for any given niche is ever-growing public scepticism about the value of these products to the consumer.

When you move into the educational entrepreneurs' space, you are differentiating yourself from the information marketers who are constantly reinventing the next shiny method to "sell" you on their products, as well as from legitimate network marketers who are tied to specific products and companies and "biz opps".

One high-value signature programme promoted through one great webinar is a simple strategy that can turn your business success around, overnight.

As an educational entrepreneur, you are also differentiating yourself from the formal, qualification-led programmes that give you a piece of paper and rubber stamp your knowledge, but don't necessary guarantee your success as a graduate.

When you map out a way to take someone through a learning and development process based on your "in the field" expert system that delivers *results* for them, then you're able to command, charge and get paid premium prices. Your competitive advantage here is not actually in providing good information or conveying useful knowledge, but in generating tangible, measurable outcomes for that individual or organisation.

So, when you focus on your ideal clients, identify, understand and empathise with their most pressing issues and in your unique style help them to produce a solution, this builds your attractiveness in the marketplace.

Next, let's ask whether going digital worth it from a business growth point of view. Consider this: by creating systems and processes representative of what you already do as an expert consultant working with your top clients and by marketing and delivering educational products and programmes in digital formats, you can expand your reach and help more people. Agreed?

It follows that this naturally increases your capacity, your client or customer base and your revenue. From one signature or membership programme, you can serve a much wider audience and create multiple and consistent streams of income. It's win-win for both you and your clients.

Don't just look at high-ticket and subscription programmes as a revenue model decision – in origin, these should be value and delivery model decisions.

Together, the world of education and online business, web publishing, learning technology and global reach are driving a lot of professional services to create new ways of serving clients (and making money). By packaging your expertise into easy to consume products and programmes, you can work with people in both face-to-face and digital environments, but you're no longer restricted to local – your clients can be worldwide.

That's not to say there isn't still a place for working face-to-face and running live events / workshops. I continue to do both in fact, because I enjoy both and serve people in different ways and at different levels doing both. Your expert status, venue and price point are key factors for who you attract and it's important that you can offer your participants progressively rich ways to work with you.

CREATING AN AUDIENCE REVOLUTION

The Internet makes it possible for local players like solo professionals and small service firms to make as big an impact in the world as the big global enterprises. There's no need to go down the risky start-up route; you can share your expertise with a worldwide audience across a multitude of media platforms from a simple blog or podcast to a video channel or mobile app. The "Internet of Things" is already here and by 2020 over 30 million devices will be connected and reachable.

However, there's little point developing a full-scale signature programme if you don't yet have a hungry audience and don't know for sure if it's a fit for what your target market wants. But when you put yourself out there - writing, speaking, teaching, as we've covered – you can test the waters of your ideas and content.

If your message comes through with authority, authenticity and integrity, your voice will be more cogently heard, confirmed or progressively refined as your following grows. If you are seen to be serving their needs, your expert status stands out as a beacon that can swiftly amplify a unique and compelling message.

> ✳
> "Being in perfect alignment with the needs of your audience is the most powerful tool in a marketer's arsenal." - Danny Iny

Couple this with real strategic data on what you audience is looking for and how they wish to engage with you, and you can proactively seek to connect and share as an influencer.

In the technology revolution, we see new market research software and tools harnessing the merger between "Big Data" and social content to enable the prediction of buying attitudes, across your target demographics. Tracking real-time opinions and behaviours means you can deliver a honed engagement and customer experiences.

Knowing who your target audience is, what you want to sell that suits their needs, and how you want to deliver it is something you need to work out first. It does take a fair bit of time and effort, but it's worthwhile.

But it's little use being great at what you do and in perfect alignment with what you client needs if no-one has heard of you or can connect with you. Obviously, you do need a good marketing plan to start the ball rolling, so creating a "platform" and growing your audience is an important early action to take.

There are plenty to choose from: blogging, a Facebook or Linkedin group, a video channel (e.g. on Youtube), podcast (e.g. on iTunes), Instagram. Focus on one platform at a time, one that suits both you and your audience demographic. Pick on that you both enjoy and will do consistently. When you put all your efforts into that one thing and show up consistently, you will get good at using that channel, and your following and email list will grow from there.

It's a fact that the size of your email list will determine your income. This is very sobering and food for thought, especially if currently your network is fairly limited. But attracting the right audience for your list building is equally critical – quality over quantity.

Building a *targeted* list should be your priority income-producing activity. What you share and the lead magnets you link to need to be laser targeted, as we've covered in the previous parts of the book.

The more of your key audience you engage with, the more attention you will gather from people who are interested in what you share, what you do and how you can help them.

Your goal is to put enough of a taste out there in your spheres of influence to generate contacts or leads, whether initially that's by networking, speaking at events and collecting business cards or by content you publish and lead magnets on your website. It doesn't matter how you do it, you just need to do it.

Since ultimately you want to give your target audience a great reason to leave you their contact details, your first offer should be something valuable that you give away for free. An educational product is one of the fastest ways to build a contact list or database of your ideal, prospective clients, especially if it is laser targeted and highly valuable to them.

In a face-to-face environment, consultants have been using a similar strategy for decades … it works! For instance, if I'm doing a presentation, I'll throw out a "hey here's something great", and show them a valuable free report or special introductory offer voucher for our course, explaining what it is and what it can do for them. Then I'll say "anyone who wants this" and invite them to leave their details. You can just pass a sheet round the group or provide a business card bowl. I like this approach because it's really informal and non-pushy. Then as a follow up you can post/email it straight out to them soon after the event with a nurture series of further emails.

The challenge nowadays though is that "landing pages" and "lead magnets" are becoming increasingly common, such that you really have to "wow" your visitors, who are possibly somewhat jaded from yet another e-book or webinar. Your content must be highly specific, compelling and easy to consume.

From what we covered in the previous chapter, it's hardly a leap of faith to understand that video (including webinars) is very much a winning "all-in-one" platform for the educational entrepreneur to build an engaged audience, even from scratch. Producing video allows you to unite multi-media (i.e. text, audio, images, diagrams, flow charts, mind maps etc), interactivity (e.g. animation, quizzes, games, autobots etc) and your unique personality, into an engaging and educational design.

Video provides a seamless medium to bring your different material together into a coherent whole piece of educational content and to bring your personal brand to life in the eyes and ears of your audience.

DELIVERING RESULTS PEOPLE LOVE TO PAY FOR

In the digital economy, the best metrics to indicate you have a winning product concern enrolment, engagement, attrition and completion. Depending on how you set up the programme and your refund policy, how much people like your programme, how they engage with it, and how long people stay on the course, can be way more critical than how many people walk through the front door.

As a consultant-teacher, I like to think I give great insights, service and value to my target audience. I love it when people share and comment on my free stuff, because it shows me it's valuable and enjoyable. However, like you I'm sure, what I'm after is paying clients - people willing to *pay* for my expertise.

Strategically, you need to be assertive in this regard.

No matter how great your content is, people will not automatically buy a high-end product without you making a convincing case for it.

The goal is for a proportion of people who engage with your content and download your free or low cost offers on the front end, buy what you offer on the back end - your products, programmes, memberships, services and event tickets. This is why it's essential to work out your conversions and lifetime customer value (LCV). When you know how much profit you're making across the entire funnel, you know what you can afford to pay for your clicks and leads.

On the front end, you are looking for people who want to achieve a particular outcome that you can help with and deliver something that actually makes the time and energy they spend researching, web surfing worthwhile!

On the back end, you want to engage the *hyper-responsive* people who you want to invest your time and energy in, because they are the most likely to continue their journey with you and get great results, and so they will buy from you at the more profitable, juicier ends of your marketing funnel.

Don't get me wrong on this though. I am not saying that you shouldn't want people on your website browsing around, reading your articles, watching your videos, downloading free resources or sharing your content, since this is key to attraction marketing.

I definitely recommend you take time to produce some good quality, free education-based content as vital marketing collateral. It's how your target visitor becomes acquainted with you and starts to trust you.

BUILD ONCE, DELIVER MANY TIMES

I've introduced the "build once, delivery many" concept already – it's the short-term effort of creating a signature programme to make long term gains of delivering to more clients, over and over.

When you reach the point of having booked yourself solid, you can raise your prices and reduce your hours in order to free up time for design and development of a more leveraged model as an educational entrepreneur.

Packaging your unique expertise into branded digital products that your ideal audience wants, wherever in the world they are, benefits you in three brilliant ways:

1. You create **sustained leverage for your time and expertise**, as your content, courses and programmes give your consumers a first taste, an opportunity to experience the value of what you offer in your high-end services.

2. You **create multiple streams of income**, many of which are "passive", i.e. you no longer trade time for money delivering to every single customer-client.

Understandably, you'll need to spend time marketing or have a budget for outsourcing this, and from time to time, you'll need to do a little tweaking of materials. Depending on your field and how "evergreen" your topic is, you may find you need to create and launch new products from time to time.

3. You need only spend your individual time with **highly qualified, top-paying clients**. Nonetheless, this one-to-one time to enrol someone into your programme is another skill you can hone over time. In my own business, I use either an application-only model or a consult session to qualify that my prospective client is a good fit and that I can genuinely help them before I agree to a project or enrol them on a programme.

What's great in today's technological environment for e-learning, is you don't have to have a fully-fledged, polished course all created before you can start marketing it or even delivering it! Seriously, this is gold. It's actually best when you don't, because your clients/students will help you shape the content to deliver what they really want and need. In my experience, your course satisfaction will be way higher when you don't give them only what you *think* they need.

Even if you've done your homework, new issues and sticking points will come up along the way, which means you'll want to refine or redesign the course a fair bit before it's "perfect" (if there is ever such a thing).

If you first design a pilot and develop the full programme "on the fly", it means you don't need to invest time and effort up front or risk it not quite hitting the mark.

By gauging interest during the early stages talking about, promoting and "soft" marketing your course, you can understand more how well what you're producing fits with your audience's problems and desires and identify the right problem language for a bigger launch.

> ※
> "Selling your online courses through paid advertising can be effective, but when it comes to building trust and rapport with your audience, nothing beats high-quality content." – Dorie Clark

Validate a new idea by creating an introductory product or the first "module" of your full signature system as a short course and pilot it with your target market.

Another way is to *co-design* the materials on the programme, so you are tapping into the needs of your participants through live interaction, module by module. This way when you've completed the first pilot run, you will have lots of useful feedback (some of which you can use in future marketing), and importantly you'll know what worked well and less well and will have improved things along the way for the next time.

Lisa Sasevich talks about *"building the plane as you fly it"*. At first, this seemed a scary prospect to me, because I usually like to feel fully prepared and have everything in place before I launch. But actually, co-designing your course with your participants in a group environment is highly interactive and enjoyable. And it results in a much tighter fit of the teaching to their needs and a better learning experience for you and them.

It's ok if an initiative you take isn't perfect on the first run; it's not a failure, it's an opportunity to learn!

CREATING AN ENGAGING & SUPPORTIVE EXPERIENCE

As we've discussed, content marketing enables you to build up a natural and authentic brand presence. But a lot of course content fails to deliver as far as consumer engagement, satisfaction or completion are concerned.

In consulting terms, complex problems are not easily solved by working through information or a static course - they require some kind of *dynamic*: dialogue, feedback, experience, visible progression and real results. In today's marketplace, it's clear we are past the peak of growth in online information products and skills trainings. Aside from certified qualification courses, people are increasingly sceptical of investing in high-ticket programmes, and those who do rarely complete the programme.

What people want is not more info that doesn't *change* anything for them; they want to get their problems solved - a tangible return on investment. Your client (aka customer or learner) needs to be guided, but also motivated, challenged, and understood.

This shift in consumer perception is driving a shift in the design of online products towards more interactive forms of delivery. People are placing increasing value on the supportive and social environment of group programmes and membership sites. This brings further expectations from our clients and places pressure on us to create something that works.

> ※
>
> "The reason most business owners buy courses and then don't complete them isn't because they are lazy or lack discipline – it's because MOST of those courses hinge on that person always knowing their foundations." - Rebecca Tracey, The Uncaged Life

There is plenty in the literature to support the premise that good education should provide interaction and dialogue – a reciprocal teaching and learning experience that supports a person to comprehend and learn key concepts, to develop and practise skills, and/or to get something done. Together this is what leads them to achieving the outcomes your course or programme promises.

There are certain types of content that really help to maintain our interest, whether used for marketing or in a course. And that's visual, interactive and experience-focused content. Course designs based around video/animation, interaction and "gamification" means participants are far more likely to stay engaged and motivated, do the work, complete the programme, and so get the results they want. Their success is crucial for *your* success.

The renowned educational psychologist, Vygotsky calls this the "Zone of Proximal Development". Operating in this dialogic zone, i.e. with the right level of discussion, feedback and support, people are more likely to complete your course successfully: they learn, take action and achieve the intended results.

Today's digital tools can provide these "experience" elements as well as important accountability. With some course delivery platforms (and by no means all), you can use psychological triggers that help maintain interest and motivation. Notably, AccessAlly (a Wordpress plug-in) and Xperiencify (a brand-new learning management software coming on the market at the time of writing), incorporate progress trackers, quizzes, games, competitions, leader boards and achievement badges you can add into in your programmes.

You can also set up online social spaces for peer support (e.g. discussion groups within your course site or created in LinkedIn, Facebook or workspace apps like Slack) so that your contacts, students or clients can ask questions and get feedback, either from you and/or from others in the community you create.

In other words, you can build into your programmes whatever type of

> ※
>
> "When you consider the staggering failure rate of online courses these days, it's easy to see why the self-paced learning industry is dropping year on year... Meanwhile, the gaming industry is surging. That's bad news for creators of traditional info products, courses and trainings... but great news for anyone who's ready to dip in to the exciting new realm of experience products."
>
> – Marisa Murgatroyd, Xperiencify

engagement you enjoy most and your clients will get the best results from. In terms of the level of low touch to high touch, you choose the blend and the number of participants, then price the programme accordingly.

Dialogue is the cornerstone of effective learning and can make your programme more engaging, experiential and outcomes-focused, and thus increasingly high value and premium.

As I've found from both my teaching and coaching experience, I know that dialogue is what helps people with the challenge of moving out of their current thinking and comfort zone to accomplish something new and improve performance.

What's interesting is how interactive tools used in education are now being integrated into front-end marketing. According to new research by Kaizen, a content marketing, PR and SEO agency based in London, future success will lie with the use of video content, immersive content (e.g. virtual reality) and added value content (i.e. no product offer attached).

With the advent of live video streaming, customised messaging, interactive quizzes, retargeting and segmentation tools, online communication with our leads and followers has becoming increasingly personalised and responsive. Interactive video, where comments or reactions to the video can be used to guide its content, adds a personal layer to everyday YouTube videos, making it much more engaging and relevant to users.

Conversational tools like artificial intelligence (AI) and machine learning (ML) are proving game changers for nurturing leads and dealing with customer queries on a large scale.

Instructional design and use of advanced tools are beyond the scope of this book, but worthy of attention when you're ready to up your game. However, there are some quite simple-to-use tools around today that allow you to:

- Find out more about your target market's needs via the use of online surveys.

- Interact with your audience (be it prospects, participants or clients) via live virtual presentations.

- Engage a specific segment of your audience using responsive quizzes.

- Create an online community of practice.

- Provide real-time responses in response to trigger words via "messenger autobots".

- Pre-qualify your prospects for a one-to-one session with you via application and scheduling tools.

In other words, you can take advantage of interacting with your audience across your entire engagement, education and enrolment process.

USING CLIENT FEEDBACK FOR YOUR NEXT BIG IDEA

Developing any new business opportunity carries an element of risk, given the time, money and effort you have to invest and no more so than when you're putting yourself out there into the world with an educational product.

Rather than second guessing what you think your potential clients or existing clients might want or need (or running around trying to please everyone), instead listen to what your prospects and clients tell you they want when you're talking to them or working with them.

You can pick out key phrases they commonly use to state the nature of their challenge or problem or the solution they are looking for. Testimonials you receive afterwards may also give you a clear steer for how to develop new material and courses and a "voice" that highlights in their words the key benefits they have experienced of working with you, which you can also use in your marketing.

A key thing I learned that now serves all of my product development is this:

Don't waste time trying to get clients to sign up to what you think they should have. Instead, listen to what they tell you they want, and then create it for them.

For instance, in my network marketing days, people saw what I was doing marketing the products on the internet and kept asking me for help with "how to be successful online". It's how my original *Success Blueprint* came to life, titled (no surprise but unoriginally by today's standards) "How to Build a Successful Online Business".

You can use internet marketing tools, systems and resources to support the principles of leverage and automation discussed earlier in the book, but if you've got the wrong thing in the wrong place with the wrong message, you just wasted a lot of time, money and effort shooting yourself in the foot.

BRINGING YOUR PRODUCT TO MARKET

No matter how many times you have heard the phrase "this sells itself", no product or service ever sells itself without bringing it to the market effectively. Remember you're building a business – not doing a job or a hobby. Finding new clients and customers requires market research to be done first, and marketing to be planned, organised and executed.

Effective content-driven, education-based marketing that pulls customers towards you, i.e. "inbound" marketing (also known as "attraction marketing"), is preferable to "outbound" marketing (also known as "interruption" marketing, i.e. mostly paid adverts that aim to get your message out and hope for a response: print, television, radio, direct mail).

Advertising, pitching and prospecting is rarely effective for high-ticket services, because it doesn't have the full interest or permission of the audience and it fails to build the kind of trust relationship necessary to win your client over.

The exceptions are probably LinkedIn, Facebook and YouTube, which are perfect environments for small, low cost adverts that can be easily targeted (and re-targeted) to specific interests and groups as well as general demographics. These platforms are also great social places to keep the engagement and relationship building process going by channelling people already on those sites to your branded content and community groups, within the very same environment.

If you're already networking with your target audience, in person or online, then doing free talks, joint ventures and affiliate schemes are also great ways to promote your courses or other educational programmes without having to spend a lot of money up front on advertising.

Being an educational entrepreneur is about making yourself and your expertise available to big audiences and providing people with a learning experience that delivers the intended outcome and a lasting benefit.

Your aim is to inspire your ideal clients to say "yes" to investing in themselves and their business and to take the high value education you provide on the front end to a deeper level with you through your back-end offer. A high-ticket offer can be a training course, a signature programme or your premium service, an opportunity to work with you as a consultant or coach. You fill in the specific thing for what your next step is going to be for them.

TACKLING ROAD BLOCKS TO TRANSFORMATION

Adapting your knowledge and expertise from a consulting process and service to an educational curriculum and product comes with its own challenges. There are many different modalities to choose from: learning designs and content formats (text, audio, video, interactive, social) as well as an array of online delivery platforms, learning management systems and course creation sites you could use.

Knowing how to bridge the performance gap using your expert system should help you identify what types of content are most fit-for-purpose and an effective and efficient way to work with your clients through the programme.

You're creating a "design-once, deliver-to-many" model supported by a client-driven action plan, i.e. the activity-led way you would normally work with a client. They can choose to work through the steps with or without your support – either way, they *learn from doing*. This is the "done-with-you" or "do-it-yourself" approach to pricing your products and services (which I learned off legendary internet marketers like Perry Marshall, Frank Kern and Russell Brunson).

For me personally, but also my clients – and see if this rings true for you and yours too - I noticed that as you go about implementing what you're learning, you hit a barrier, be it a mental or technical block. (This is why information products rarely deliver a full solution for the results people want.)

For example, say I'm helping my client with setting up their business, pinpointing their ideal audience and developing their marketing and sales processes, they have a lot of questions along the way. I tend to know a lot of these "FAQs" (frequently asked questions) now, because I've done enough client work face-to-face to know what comes up for people. But in the beginning, and in any one group, there are always new stumbling blocks you didn't anticipate they'd have.

If you want to offer increasingly premium services as part of your leveraged consulting strategy for business growth, as we've said, developing a signature programme is very efficient use of your time.

As clients work through your programme and get results, they get to know, like and trust you on a deeper level and are happy to pay for greater access to you as a consultant. Clients who are "primed" are also far more committed and get results faster!

Your client has two options: they can go through a programme or course, learning and taking action in "do-it-yourself" mode or they can go through in "done-with-you" mode as a VIP client.

In the latter case, the extra premium price they pay is to get you, the expert and teacher, as a mentor by their side, giving them feedback, getting them unstuck and moving them forward.

Your client-participant is more likely to stay focused and productive when you can address practical "how-do-I-DO-that" questions as they emerge, as well as the accountability to progress through the programme. This is when you can hop on a live call or create a quick template to help them, that can then be added into the programme. It creates a kind of "just in time" learning.

This is an immensely valuable benefit that you can promote in your marketing and sales copy, that they're going to get much better results in a shorter time, and that is worth a lot to a client.

The "done-with-you" model obviously requires you to "run" the course rather than enrol people and leave them to it. So, it's worth thinking about the cost-benefits to both you and your customer when you set your pricing – whether it's primarily a mentoring type programme, a self-study course, a content site or a blended model.

If you want an example of this, take a look at the *iSuccess Business Academy* membership model as outlined on my website at jayallyson.com/isuccess. It's an innovative mix of front-to-back and back-to-front – a kind of "push-me-pull-me" design. Let me explain!

You can take an all-in-one 8-week intensive "Done-With-You" programme that includes membership on the back-end to provide ongoing support for implementation. Or you can just opt-in for stand-alone membership with access to resources and courses to support "Do-It-Yourself" and choose to add on a mentoring programme (at three levels to support your preferred time, pace and budget, but provides the same accountability and "done-with-you" support as the intensive programme).

In the next step, we're moving on to creating an actionable roadmap for implementing your selected leverage strategies. But first, I encourage you to jot down in the companion workbook any inspired ideas and actions for how you will lay the foundations for your success in your service delivery model.

ACTION NOTES

_____

_____

_____

_____

_____

_____

_____

_____

_____

_____

_____

_____

_____

_____

Chapter 7

YOUR LEVERAGED ROADMAP

Make It Happen for Yourself

"A good plan focuses your time, energy & resources on the "right" projects that GROW you, rather than just keep you busy."

Karen Skidmore,

True Profit Business

KEY POINTS

❖ Carving out products or programmes from your expert services that you can deliver digitally enables you to reach a massive global market, and there's room for all of us.

❖ Align your digital strategy with both your personal and your financial goals.

❖ The more you put the building blocks into your business architecture, the more you build capacity to scale things up.

❖ The way people search for and consume information has changed significantly over the past decade. Nowadays businesses have to get smart about content and connections.

❖ If we just learn and brainstorm but don't implement and test anything out, then we're just pandering to our own worst enemies, namely procrastination and perfectionism.

❖ When you help someone do something better, the value you deliver takes you from anonymous seller that people ignore to trustworthy teacher your ideal audience wants to hear from.

❖ Very few people want to know exactly what you do or how you do it; they're interested in feeling good about what you do and engaging in conversation about the desired outcome or solution to a problem that you provide.

❖ The power of education in client acquisition is partly "indoctrination" and partly "demonstration" of how you can help them.

❖ Online education membership sites provide a very natural digital upsell.

❖ Believing a strategy can double or triple your income is not easy. Even though an approach may appear very feasible, most of us are intrinsically risk averse and our cynical brain may dismiss it entirely.

❖ When revenue is down or growth is slow, consider whether the problem is an operational one or a strategic one.

RIDING THE BIG GROWTH WAVES

Professional services providers are in the midst of a radical transformation in what they can offer their target market, how they use their expertise to deliver results to clients, and how they generate revenue.

Increasingly, innovative and entrepreneurial competitors are introducing non-traditional business models and setting up training and publishing divisions, which are rapidly gaining acceptance and pushing many other firms to re-think how they attract and serve clients.

This is why, after our journey together (at least as a reader of this book), in this final word I want to impress upon you the big growth waves you can ride with leveraged consulting as your business development strategy.

Let me get super clear and emphatic. The opportunity is more than just "big", it's HUGE. When you combine consulting and/or coaching as an industry with the increasingly mainstream market for online publishing and e-learning, the opportunity to take your influence, impact and income to a whole new level is gigantic!

Carving out products from your expert services that you can deliver digitally enables you to reach a massive global market, and there's room for all of us.

However, without differentiated brand positioning and building authentic relationships with your audience, what you offer faces commoditisation.

You need to claim your unique idea and way of doing things: stake out your territory and build out your tribe, so that you can slice out market share – a piece of the pie, so to speak - from the big players in your industry.

Let's look at the research for a moment just to see the magnitude of the growth potential and major trends. According to the Professional Services Market Global Report 2017 published by The Business Research Company, the global market is forecast to register a 5.4% growth rate from 2016 to 2020, reaching almost $5 trillion. Statistics show the USA accounting for around 40% of the market, worth about $1100 billion in 2016, the UK 10%, China 10% of the global market.

Within the professional services industry, the consulting sector is one of the largest and most mature markets worldwide, from big established international firms to self-employed freelancers. The global management consulting market alone is worth an estimated $130 billion with Operations Consulting holds the lion's share of the market, at an estimated $70 billion, followed by HR Consulting and Strategy Consulting, which each have $30 billion markets.

While the industry has continued a steady rise over the past few years, slowing growth suggests global macro, technology and sector regulatory trends are due to impact on future expansion.

The shifting challenges and changing make-up of the global consulting industry are summed up in the 2017 Professional Services Maturity Benchmark" report commissioned by Deltrek, based on an analysis of over 400 professional services firms. This stated that: "While the backdrop for [growth in] the professional services industry is quite bright, the challenges associated with sustaining and managing growth have never been more daunting."

The market for professional services is shifting as clients face new business challenges. Now more than ever, service-centric businesses need to re-evaluate their niche specialisms, sales process and marketing systems to ensure they are well-positioned in expanding marketplaces and bring in enough clients to sustain growth.

Reading across the major trends that are transforming the professional services industry, there are several significant shifts that impact our ability to survive and thrive as independents in a competitive marketplace.

1. **Tailored, individualised and practical consulting** as the new norm with closer ties between consultant and client, whereby specialised expertise, delivery of sustainable improvement and knowledge transfer back to the business are key desirable trades for clients.

2. **Modularising and combining services**, such that clients can pick and choose specialist consultants, training or outsourcing services to fill internal gaps or bring several consultants together to work on a project. This means segmentation of expertise and partnership working will become more important than ever. Firms that both differentiate and collaborate are more likely to win clients who require a mix of specialist advice.

3. **Value-based pricing,** with consultants acting as advisors rather than just being service providers paid by the hour. This value-orientated revenue model can help professional service businesses to increase their revenues and profitability through education programmes.

4. **Online publications** on independent websites, general consulting sites or specialist sites. This provides a way to communicate and promote your expertise and thought leadership and build reputation, prestige and trust, and is increasingly the way clients are finding and selecting consultants.

5. **Social media** for finding and engaging clients online, marketing and monitoring competitors. A solid social media presence helps a business

improve brand awareness, deepen relationships, increase their client base and boost client satisfaction.

6. **Automation** of back-end functions to improve "value for money" using technology to reduce operational costs and time to respond to customer requests. With limited time available, consultants need to know where their direct client-facing time can be spent most valuably.

7. **Virtual / online services** to cut business costs and help increase revenue. Professional services businesses need to adapt to technology changes and should be ready to take major steps in this direction to take on new business challenges and maximise growth.

These trends and many other factors at play are forcing a significant shift in how and where consultants, coaches and other expert service providers can add value to their clients in the future. The most successful are embedding their expertise within digital materials and software solutions that are tailored to the specific and ideal clients whom they wish to serve. They are developing their digital and educational know-how to create high-value educational products delivered one-to-many rather than one-to-one.

In today's connected world, development of new products and programmes that embrace and leverage digital technology are a core part of the most market-savvy business models. Digital education is not only a vehicle for generating additional streams of revenue. It is also a means for consultants and coaches to connect with a wider community and serve clients' needs in ways that are both flexible and impactful.

MAKING THE DIGITAL SHIFT

While we can have lovely, lofty goals of building a leveraged lifestyle business totally aligned with our professional and personal goals, serving people we feel called and able to help, business is business and you're here to make money too.

It's important to:

Align your digital strategy with both your personal and your financial goals.

A key question in your mind about any of this is undoubtedly whether digital transformation is going to yield a satisfactory return on your investment of time, effort and money. Will it yield a personally satisfying way to work, as well as be financially profitable for you?

As a service provider – whether self-employed, freelance, or a small firm - if you're currently delivering only face-to-face services and doing "ok for now", what you'll really want to know: is *"going digital" worth it?*

Ultimately, digital transformation is what enables you to shift from:

- Advertising & selling to filtering & harvesting
- Active income to passive income
- Low-end clients to high-end clients
- One-to-one services to group support
- Local clients to global markets.

Success leaves clues. Think about how you can adjust what you are currently doing based on what insights you glean from others' success. Be observant and listen selectively to those doing well or who are ahead of the curve you want to be on. Be innovative to ride the wave while managing risk. Stability comes in many forms – but standing still isn't usually a good choice.

The more you put the building blocks into your business architecture, the more you build capacity to scale things up.

Your strategy doesn't have to be crazy ambitious "all-or-nothing" to make inroads. You can integrate stepwise leveraged approaches into your business strategy with two main areas of digital development:

1. Implement online systems to manage your marketing, relationships, sales, customers and delivery; and

2. Package your expertise into different kinds of digital products and online programmes.

Let's look first at the digital marketing side – because that's relevant for attracting clients whether you deliver a face-to-face consulting service or a virtual programme.

In today's digital world, where the content we all consume every day is multi-media, multi-channel and multi-device, in order to maximise both reach and engagement with potential clientele, your business strategy must address how the market now accesses (and prefers to access) information. This means understanding where your ideal audience hangs out and their preferred media formats as marketing "touch points".

The way people search for and consume information has changed significantly over the past decade. Nowadays businesses have to get smart about content and connections.

The way people search for and consume information has changed significantly over the past decade. While there's still a role for direct marketing in traditional forms - brochures, sales letters, presentations - these rely heavily on getting in front of the right audience.

Certainly, unless you're in a highly specialised field, the return on investment (ROI) of time, money and effort with direct mail and face-to-face networking can be rather hit and miss in terms of generating a fruitful business pipeline and consistent flow of clients.

Just think about this: the most popular internet sites in the world – Google, YouTube, Facebook, Instagram – are all about content and connections. Couple these platforms with your commitment, as a service provider to give value and help people in your chosen niche, and you have a powerful competitive advantage.

In the past few years, we have seen social media become vital components of successful businesses. People favour a real open and honest connection over impersonal and generic marketing. And this is probably why live video in particular is the biggest trend. It allows you to engage you with your target audience quickly and effectively. Live video can give a face and soul to your business, allowing you to stand out and distinguish yourself from your competitors.

Social media platforms certainly provide us with a ready-made and massive distribution channel straight to a highly targeted audience. But it's probably a universal truth that video is the media of our era. With the growth of smartphones, video is one of the easiest ways to build your brand. If you're not distributing videos to market your business, you're putting yourself at a major disadvantage.

Well, even knowing this, for me I felt stumped, because I hate being on photos let alone video. As an introvert, I'm pretty sure I'm not the odd one out here and many of you can relate! I can talk, write and consult on my subject fluently and eloquently with passion and proficiency, but point a camera at me and I freeze. If you're the same, you know how frustrating that is.

Still, I knew video would bring my content alive, so rather than point the camera at myself and cringe. I started creating videos using powerpoint presentations and animation - simply doing a voiceover for my slides. This meant I could at least move forward using video in my marketing. I still haven't quite overcome my reluctance and discomfort being on camera myself or doing live video – but I'm getting there and it's definitely on the cards!

Educationally, video is certainly one of the best ways to engage an audience these days, because that's generally how people prefer to consume information and learn. This is an increasing preference too, since more often than not these days we are accessing content on a mobile device and it's way easier to watch and listen than it is to read and scroll.

One research study I read showed that 80% of audiences find it more convenient to watch videos rather than reading long blogs and articles. While many futurists predict that the cross-channel strategic advertising used successfully by large corporate brands can deliver competitive advantage to small businesses that utilise integrated marketing strategies, others suggest that businesses that devote resources to live streaming videos will dominate their industries.

Now if you are thinking you don't have the skills, time, money etc. to produce flashy digital material and therefore can't do digital marketing, create videos or build online courses, think again.

Thinking like that meant I stalled my own business growth for several years. I had such a sense that my "stuff" wasn't going to be as good, as polished as others I see out there strutting their stuff, and my ego wasn't going to do anything that wasn't top notch. So, I kept learning more and more, buying this tool and that, trying things out, changing my mind about what to focus on, spinning my wheels and generally getting my knickers in the proverbial twist.

While I knew having a signature programme really was the only way for me to play a bigger game and get my "stuff" into the world, not pulling the trigger on creating video content was a key activity holding me back from creating it.

If we just learn and brainstorm but don't implement and test anything out, then we're just pandering to our own worse enemies, namely procrastination and perfectionism.

On realising these two personal traits were my biggest barriers, I finally got out of my own way. Because taking some kind of action – fearlessly imperfect - is what finally moved me forward.

BECOMING DISTINCTLY VALUABLE & SLIGHTLY FAMOUS

In hindsight, it's easy to see that my reputation, value and visibility are what attracted clients and kept me financially afloat rather than any direct selling per se. It finally hit me that standing out, as an expert authority on a specific subject and being seen as a service provider to offer something clearly defined and of clear value, is the one of the most critical aspects of a leveraged consulting strategy.

> ✳
> "In your business, as you grow in desire, your income and your impact on others grows as well." – Rob Kosberg, Best Seller Publishing

Showcasing your qualifications does little to persuade prospective clients to buy your services – they expect you to have credentials. The question in a potential client's mind is whether you can help them achieve the specific result they want.

In the early days of establishing yourself, you first have to earn the attention of your market as someone who delivers. You can pull people in fast and get them in a funnel with paid advertising - and you'll see tonnes of sponsored ads on social media and google like this. But you prove yourself and build trust when you actually help someone make *progress*, such as with one or more of the following:

- ✓ A goal - something that the ideal client absolutely must achieve
- ✓ An opportunity - what they'd like to do better or faster
- ✓ A challenge - something that blocks them from achieving goals.

When you help someone do something better, the value you deliver takes you from anonymous seller that people ignore to trustworthy teacher your ideal audience wants to hear from.

Taking this approach to building a brand is what Rich Schefren terms "mavenship". It requires a fundamental shift in mindset, one that embraces generosity to put your ideas out there, rather than secrecy to protect your intellectual property. It builds your brand equity.

There are huge dividends to such openness. (In fact, in the education sector there's been a movement over recent years towards OERs (open educational resources) and MOOCs (massive open online courses) as a strategy to showcase what they do and drive enrolment onto paid programmes.)

It's equally important to specialise and become the go-to person for that one thing. Many consultants and coaches just market themselves as generalists, that gives you a huge hurdle to convince someone why you and not someone else. When you rise above the parapet, and specialise, magic starts to happen. This is the expert value pyramid.

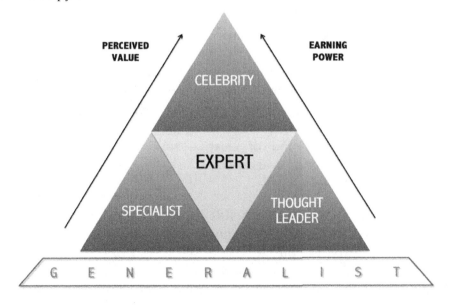

However, even when you specialise, you may find you're not yet truly unique. Maybe you're a fitness coach who specialises in nutrition; that's pretty broad. What makes you unique might be who you work with and what their particular desires are: for example, menopausal women who struggle with tiredness and weight loss.

When you add in some thought leadership and promote yourself through education rich content, you claim expert status in that specific niche area - X, Y or Z not X, Y and Z. With the digital channels at our disposal today, especially video and other social media, you can quickly start attract a following and gain meaningful celebrity status in your field. This heightens your perceived value and desirability in your prospect's eyes.

> ※
> "If you're willing to expend the effort to create well-crafted content, you'll distinguish yourself in a crowded market-place where many people are serving up tasty morsels, and you're taking the time to create something of substance." – Dorie Clark

When people desire a very specific thing and can clearly see what you offer is "just the thing they need", they want it – now! And, they're willing to pay more than the going rate to get it.

Once you start to earn the "maven" expert status, and have standardised channels to engage with your audience that you become known for, this also means you don't get too distracted by other ideas and shiny new marketing tools. You'll have much more time and freedom to focus on research, strategy, planning and serving, so creating increasingly greater influence and impact, as well as higher levels of income.

Ask yourself persistently: how can I leverage my content and reach more people? If you're wondering what integrating your authority brand with content marketing do for your business, here's the argument for why this is a game changer.

Your best prospects are essentially in the market for a solution to a problem they have and actively searching for answers and researching their options.

Top performing service providers, agencies and firms can demonstrate their value by educating their audience and building an authority platform: a digital presence such as a website or media channel. When people search for a specific issue, need or problem, your branded sites and content should come up in the results.

Implementing an effective brand plan is not massively different to your usual business as a consultant, coach, trainer etc. First, clarify the expertise and distinctiveness that is uniquely yours. Next, package the problem and your point

> ※
>
> "Never before have we had the chance to build a brand like you can today, then leverage it to expand your business, increase your sales, and enhance your credibility and your bottom line."
> – Areva Martin, Guest Writer for Entrepreneur.com

of view on it into valuable educational content to satisfy the questions in the mind of your target audience and build trust.

Make sure you give time to study and research and to strategic and creative deliberation. As a professional and an expert, you need space to recharge and think, so you can consistently come up with new insights and communicate them effectively.

When you couple this model with systematised processes and content marketing, you can quickly grow your fan base. Having more influence and making an impact on people is a sure-fire way to grow your income. People who know, like and trust you, tell their peers – word-of-mouth is powerful, especially on the internet and via social media networks.

This is perhaps easier said than done if you're not totally clear on what you uniquely do and that's where most people hit their first barrier. It's why aligning with your purpose is the starting point for how I work with clients to help develop their growth potential. Likewise, if your content lacks a distinct style, voice and tone, it won't stand out.

While we're not expecting you to create world famous brands or personalities the likes of Coca Cola, Nike, Virgin etc, what works specifically for service-focused professionals like us, is really communicating the "heart" of your purpose, ideal audience and expertise. This is the centrepiece for what you do, the results you deliver to clients, and importantly why you do it.

> ※
>
> "The saying it's not what you know, it's who you know ... should really be 'it's not who you know, it's who knows you (and respects you). You can know people but it doesn't matter if they don't vouch for you." – Mark Hoverson

Very few people want to know exactly what you do or how you do it; they're interested in feeling good about what you do and engaging in conversation about the desired outcome or solution to a problem that you provide.

Despite the tremendous opportunities of the internet and social media for communicating our value and what we stand for, many are blind to the benefits of this global reach. A business stuck in the old paradigm clings to marketing approaches focused on advertising what they do and not engagement in why they do it.

The solution is to transform your sales and marketing paradigm from simple communication to a deeper dialogue with your ideal tribe that touches the emotional reasons they need your help. You become valuable, and people remember you, when you care as much or more about it as they do and can deliver the desired outcome.

EDUCATION AS A TOOL FOR GROWTH

Education as a tool for greater engagement that leads to business growth stemmed from a significant "aha" moment I had during the

> ※
> "People attach value to things that affect them emotionally. If there's no way for them to place your work into their understanding of the world, it won't resonate with them, which means they won't value it." – Derek Murphy, Guerilla Publishing

rebranding of my consulting practice. I wanted more cohesion in the work I was doing. When I looked at the intersection of my expertise and experience in educational, professional and business development, the role of education in entrepreneurship became suddenly apparent as the big cohering. I started writing about it, running workshops and from one presentation, I created an online course around it.

Many years of supporting, training and mentoring independent professionals, entrepreneurs and business owners led me to piece together the issues facing service providers in how to market and deliver what they do. I'd found myself instinctively using the same "education" working with my clients on projects concerning operational improvement, strategic marketing and business growth.

Whether I was working with independent consultants, small businesses or large "not-for-profit" organisations, I was intuitively using a "secret" diagnostic process behind-the-scenes that was proving to be a valuable change tool. And what I find is it mostly comes down to a lack or limitation in certain dimensions of their business development.

At this point, my expertise stopped being tacit knowledge that I was using with each client and evolved into a proven framework, which I called *iSuccess* - and a methodology I've since branded as the "Digital Roadmap". I found myself using the same structure and set of criteria time and time again to understand the business, diagnose the barriers to growth and offer recommendations for improvement.

Whether my clients were starting out, struggling to gain momentum or looking to make some change or transformation in their business, this step-by-step review process was helping them to think differently about their market and brand messaging, and their customer engagement and sales processes: conceptually, strategically and operationally.

For me, the educational aspect of working with clients is about enlightening and empowering people to discover solutions for themselves, to think intuitively as well as logically, to see into their blind spots – personal and operational; and then agree on the best course of action for implementing the necessary changes. Just sharing articles or videos cannot achieve this; because it requires a higher level of engagement on the part of your audience.

The power of education in client acquisition is partly "indoctrination" and partly "demonstration" of how you can help them.

Using frameworks, tools, models and exercises supports your client work in a more powerful way by providing the necessary vehicle for active learning and reflection. With an education-constructed delivery, I feel far better equipped to help people stop wrestling in the dark with all the different components of their business; to bring things into the light and provide structure, solutions and plans. And they can move forwards at their own pace whilst running the business too.

For your client, whether or not they signed up for a course, a membership or mentoring programme, working with you should be a positive and productive journey – a process of stepwise progress. It should not overpower or overwhelm them. When you take somebody one step at a time towards the promised outcome using your expert system - what Stu McClaren terms a Success Path™ - they are most likely to want to continue all the rest of the way with you.

The need to see the big picture and do some kind of diagnostic is important – and it's what you as a consultant or coach uniquely bring to high-end client work. We live in an age when email list building is getting tougher and tougher.

> ※
> "Just tossing out a free gift isn't enough to attract the right subscribers… nor is it powerful enough to keep their attention long enough to build a relationship with them." - Nathalie Lussier, AccessAlly

Lead capture pages and free opt-in boxes are now so commonplace, our audiences are starting to ignore them completely! This means your opt-in offer really needs to stand out to gazump your competition.

At the same time, high-end clients of consulting services are likely to be pretty savvy about internet marketing tactics – this isn't their first rodeo – they opt-out just as readily as they opt-in once they have the goodies and a boring email series begins.

If we are to move towards leveraged consulting and be effective in the digital marketplace, it's time to turn to more eye-catching, impactful and influential ideas. We need to give our valuable high-end clients an action-provoking experience so they hit some kind of milestone in where they're trying to get to. This demonstrates we can really help them "move the needle" so to speak.

In today's crowded marketplace where consultants and coaches are abundant commodities, there are three principles that make sharing high value educational content a powerful strategy to stand out and get noticed.

First principle: Education trumps information.
Research shows that that information alone does not help someone learn, understand or foster the kind of shift in beliefs or behaviours necessary for transformational change to happen. Blasting out "expert" content alone will not lead automatically to enrolling clients; in fact, it's making us all feel rather overwhelmed. But a well-structured, guided path offers an excellent and refreshing solution for your prospects and a first step for building a relationship.

Second principle: Dialogue is empowering.
It's crucial you understand your potential clients (or customers); that you vary your message and approach to suit their preferences and experiences; and you make yourself available to support them through any questions that come up. This requires *dialogue* that is an inherent part of any good educational programme.

And third principle: Needless complexity is a repellent.
Having a single digital platform as entry point into your high-end programmes and services means you can focus your marketing on one channel, grow your audience and build trusting relationships.

For example, on my website (jayallyson.com), I have only one core offer (aside from my book) - an invitation to join the Academy (or wait list, if not currently open to new members). What this means is I can focus all my efforts on just one marketing funnel and drive my audience to one landing page to sign up. (I do have other offers on my website, such as a free "discovery" session and free "downloadables" that help build my email list, but ultimately, I'm channelling everyone into one process.)

When someone joins the Academy (or the Wait List), I'll follow up with a series of automated emails, one of which reminds them that they can book a free personal consult with me by phone or video call – deepening the interaction from one-way communication to two-way dialogue, which strengthens and nurtures the personal relationship.

This one-to-one call also helps my prospective client to identify whether they would like to work one-to-one with me to implement what they are learning through the Academy modules. There are three choices: they can go with a "Do-It-Yourself" basic membership, add-on a "Done-With-You" individual mentoring package is a good fit for them – time, budget, skills, etc – or opt for a fast track experience by joining the 8-week intensive group programme. All paths can ultimately also lead into a high-end consulting partnership.

Increased competition in the marketplace is what led Nathalie Lussier to devise The Login Optin Strategy™, which uses a more substantial free course as the lead magnet and a membership site as the trap. Rather than a downloadable, which is a one-off done deal, offering a free course in daily doses and action steps means that your subscribers aren't overwhelmed, are active learners and importantly, they have to return and login into your membership site to get the goods.

The psychology behind this is that the more people keep re-engaging with you and taking action on your material, the more invested they become in your approach and what you have to offer. Your free course can just be a series of videos, audios, written content, exercises - or a multimedia mixture – i.e. structuring, repurposing and repackaging tried and tested material you already use in your everyday client work.

On the face of it, all this may seem like you're being forced to be way more generous than perhaps you're comfortable with. Yet, giving away your best material is fast becoming what's needed to entice people to join your email list. But there is a ray of hope: sharing high-quality educational content with your audience (of potential high-end clients) also provides a means to reap what you sow.

By requiring your subscribers to sign into your membership site and return to access the content, you're nurturing the relationship. Your autoresponder email series should entice and encourage continued re-engagement while your course delivers the education that leads to higher enrolments into your paid programmes and services.

Chances are you have more than one lead magnet and opt-in offer. With a membership site you can keep rewarding your subscribers for logging into your membership site by giving them access to more free stuff as well as offering them upsells to your paid products and services.

Online education membership sites provide a very natural digital upsell.

The method is fairly simple to implement. You'll need to use either an all-in-one online course platform with a membership feature or a membership and course delivery plugin for a hosted site that integrates with your CRM/email system.

(There's more detailed guidance about choosing your essential leverage tools in the *iSuccess Business Academy* members' area.)

BOOSTING YOUR CRITICAL LEVERS

Improving the critical dimensions of your business is crucial for growing and scaling. Whatever your business ambition – and whichever level you want to get to next in your business growth, I believe you should build your leveraged strategy from the inside out.

Let's hop back to the flywheel diagram that represents our leveraged system from chapter 1. You'll recall that first of all we placed YOU into the core, because at the heart of your expert business is "you" as an individual. This establishes the "inner eye" as a reference for everything else.

Next, we looked in depth at the principles of leveraging you, your marketing, sales and delivery - all completely inter-dependent across the *Engage-Educate-Enrol* process in the middle section. Now, let's insert the inner workings that drives your client acquisition engine.

In the original model, I left a gap (white space) in the inner ring - remember? The inner workings – I call the *7 Dimensions of Success* – provide critical levers to support all of our leveraged consulting strategies and allow you to build, market, grow and scale your business successfully.

Look at these seven dimensions as critical levers that drive the success of your leveraged marketing, sales and delivery strategies – as they line up across the flywheel. Together these moving parts are mutually reinforcing - the inner wheel drives the middle wheel to give you the leverage. Strengthen each part and you can move the needle in your growth strategy.

The *7 Dimensions of Success* also form the basis of the curriculum for my signature programme within the *iSuccess Business Academy*, which helps people achieve both clarity and leverage so you resolve those common frustrations we outlined in chapter 1 and your business becomes more dependable, workable and scalable.

From everything I've studied, seen and experienced with my own business and working with clients, I believe that improvements in these seven dimensions is what makes the biggest difference between those who are successful at growing their enterprise and those who struggle to win clients. We'll go through each one in a moment.

Let me emphasise: if you don't start with *clarity* in your marketing, sales process and service delivery model, you cannot create leverage. If you try to scale, you will end up growing existing problems into much bigger issues. Sources of inefficiency will have an even greater negative effect on performance. If you have bottlenecks in your business operations, then the issues they cause will be multiplied.

> ※
> "Automation applied to an inefficient operation will magnify the inefficiency." – Bill Gates

Sadly, business planning is seldom taught in a holistic and inside-out manner. In books, topics are nearly always taught separately, never looking at the dynamics of the full picture. Business courses too lean heavily towards the mechanics and skills side rather than looking at overarching strategic business models or the personal traits and attitudes of the business owner.

Most business education is quite linear; it covers the tangible, operational components but can fail to give you a feel or flair for business as a whole.

I've also found this with business improvement methodologies like Six Sigma or Kaizen, which are intended to help identify root causes of problems or inefficiencies and identify any unbeknown co-dependencies in a process, including both human and technical errors. It's very useful in a manufacturing process, but I've found it's quite hard to apply this directly to a service business, because the moving parts are very different.

As an independent consultancy, your business vision is totally yours to define – remember that with your goals, it's personal not just business. What you want to be known for, your mindset as CEO, what kind of work you want to do, and how you wish to operate are much softer factors in achieving success. As such, service businesses tend to require an additional set of impact indicators than manufacturing or retail business performance metrics.

Not appreciating how one part of your business affects another is without a doubt why many people struggle to identify the real causes of business problems. Let me illustrate this with three examples from client projects I've been involved in (which are all quite common).

- A business with low staff morale may not be about pay or working conditions but can result from a poor sense of the culture and brand.

- A problem that manifests as a sales performance issue may in fact be a consequence of a mismatch between a product and the brand or audience.

- Poor profits may be due to low sales, high operating costs or the wrong pricing strategy, which are very different problems to resolve.

Each one of the seven *iSuccess* dimensions offers a critical lever for improving your leverage and capacity for growth – and they're all mutually reinforcing like the cogs in a powerful machine. Putting effort into each cog will propel the whole flywheel and enable your business to reach new levels in ways that are effective, authentic and lucrative.

In the fuller viewpoint of the inner circle - the diagram here - you'll see each one is set against the *outcome* they help to achieve for the business. These provide broad indicators of success – some will be qualitative measures (how your business *feels* to you) and others are quantitative (e.g. the growth metrics outlined in chapter 2 Planning for Growth). I'll explain each dimension in the next section, then we'll go through a quick self-evaluation exercise – more in the downloadable workbook.

If you hadn't guessed it already, *iSuccess* is my expert system – (the little image at the centre is my consulting logo). It locates critical business design elements within a structured and pragmatic framework and forms the basis of my diagnostic review and improvement work with a client. It's proved itself as a reliable tool for resolving those typical business challenges and common frustrations my clients face that I outlined in chapter 2.

Starting with the aligning lever, each dimension either enables or strengthens the next – or indeed can limit or weaken the whole structure. The outer labels are our indicators of success – the intended outcomes that build leverage into the business in terms of marketing, sales and delivery.

What this means in practice in terms of creating leverage so you grow and scale the business is that the most critical parts of your operation need to work effectively and efficiently, individually and collectively.

A visual model like this provides clients with a clear view of the road ahead (and gives you an example of what an expert system actually looks like, in visual graphic design terms.) I've deliberately kept to simple SmartArt graphics to emphasise that anyone can easily create a visual like this for their own expert system. It doesn't have to be a flashy design, that's not the point.

While we can use process improvement methodologies to help get any problems ironed out in the machinery, we also need to be looking at whether the machine as a whole is doing what it's intended to do – that is, to support the digital roadmap for our leveraged strategy and business growth.

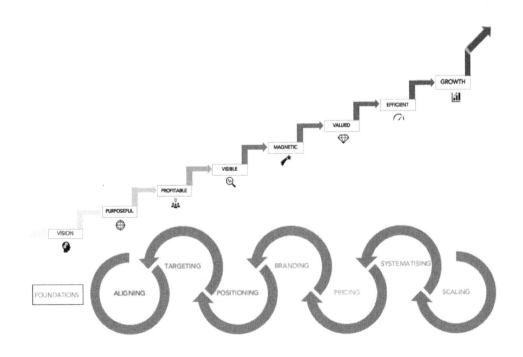

Believing a strategy can double or triple your income is not easy. Even though an approach may appear very feasible, most of us are intrinsically risk averse and our cynical brain may dismiss it entirely.

Yet, I've used this unique *iSuccess* framework for many years working with my clients and it's proven very effective. Let's go through each of the *7 Dimensions of Success* briefly in turn and then we'll break it down into a sub-set of elements that you can use in a practical way to self-evaluate your business. (Note: we cover all of them in much more detail in the *iSuccess Business Academy* courses.)

#1 – The ALIGNING lever

The aligning lever ensures your road is paved with purposeful intent and your business is a source of happiness not stress.

Building a business that achieves your vision of how you wish to serve people, and the impact you want to have, means aligning everything you do with your authentic self, as the foundation for your brand and behaviour in the marketplace.

If you started your own business with the idea of greater freedom and control in your life – what I call *leveraged living* – you need the right philosophies, strategies, tools and support to succeed, especially if you have a bigger vision for how you want your business to grow. Make sure your growth model is one that does not end up with your business running your life and taking up all of your time.

Your goal is to be working "on-purpose" and in integrity with who you want to be in making a difference in this world. Your business should be a source of joy.

#2 – The TARGETING lever

The targeting lever is used to identify a clear, relevant and profitable niche. Pinning down your best market – in other words, getting clear on your "ideal" audience and "unique value proposition" to them specifically - is by far one of the most important yet frustratingly difficult aspects of building a successful and viable business.

It's really worth spending time on this dimension. You want to get crystal clear on your "perfect people" by pinpointing a single persona or avatar who is totally right and primed for what you do. You need to ensure this group are hungry and willing to pay for what you deliver. Identifying the biggest beneficiaries of your expertise is a vital investment, because this will determine your profitability.

With a strong message-to-market match, you will attract a constant string of interest to you. When your messaging is generic, vague or fluffy and lacks the right "hooks", your marketing becomes a constant struggle: time-consuming, expensive and ineffective.

Your best target market is one where you can quickly position yourself as an expert and specialist. A top niche is only profitable if you can gain competitive advantage.

#3 – The POSITIONING lever

The positioning lever helps you to becoming a visible authority in your field of expertise. It's the front engine for your business that generates leads.

Simply put: no leads, no income, no business. When positioning is weak, lead generation tends to be patchy and inconsistent, which you see reflected in your client work and income.

When you're well-positioned in the marketplace, you don't have to work as hard to attract high quality prospects and win them over. It removes all the frustrations and anxieties that keep you stuck in panic and overwhelm.

When you have a unique niche and way of working, you can more easily identify with your target audience and peers, establish a credible reputation as an expert authority for what you do, which attracts business to you.

But you must be visible for clients to find you, have a "signature" communication style (and channel), professional client processes and build a "velvet rope" around your service community.

#4 – The BRANDING lever

These days, branding is an essential part of the success equation. The branding lever is all about creating an inspiring, irresistible and magnetic brand. And that includes your messaging, copy and content.

Before anyone will do business with you, it's highly likely they will "google" you to check you out. Any time you interact with people - online or off - your visibility will matter.

However, don't fall into the trap of doing this backwards - you need to test your messaging with your niche *before* you start creating brand logos and designs. This means engaging with your audience! Only once you're clear your core concept resonates with your ideal target market, and you've positioned yourself as the expert most uniquely and best placed to serve them, should you start creating your branded packaging.

#5 – The PRICING lever

Charging for the value, results and transformation you deliver is an essential dimension of a leveraged strategy. But figuring out what to charge for your services can be tricky. There are usually certain money blocks each of us has to overcome to do with belief, self-worth, selling, and many more.

The best way to charge what you're worth, rather than just the standard rate of others in your industry, is to consider the real *impact* your products and services have on your clients and how effectively and efficiently you can deliver a highly desired outcome for them.

Rather than always taking on new clients, you can also increase your revenue by earning more from existing clients without investing time and money to acquire new ones. This can be providing additional value to your core offer through up-sells, down-sells, cross-sells. People will pay more for the same information available in different formats too – like upselling the audio book when people buy your print or e-book.

People don't pay for consulting or your time, they pay for a project and results! Start with a product or service that delivers one small first step towards the result your client wants, and then build up to premium products, programmes and services that deliver bigger transformations.

#6 – The SYSTEMATISING lever

The systematising lever is about creating systems for efficiency and smarter working. A lack of clear and straightforward systems is one of the biggest things that keeps a service business from being able to grow.

Frankly, I'm shocked at how many business owners and consultants don't have a marketing system in place or even a game plan. Instead of having a robust workflow for their lead generation and business development, many service professionals are just flying by the seat of their pants.

There's little point aligning, targeting, positioning and branding if you don't also have an effective enrolment process and a delivery system working on your behalf 24/7. Creating structure and reducing labour intensity means you have less anxiety and more time to enjoy the fruits of your success winning new business.

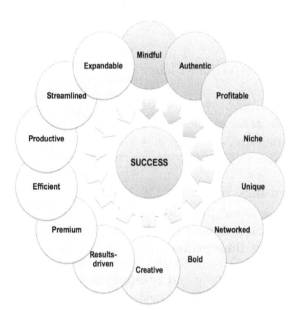

#7 – The SCALING lever

The scaling lever is about expanding your business in a way that helps you achieve both your business growth and personal lifestyle goals.

A successful business is expected to grow, even in economic uncertainty, and in so doing is able to serve more people and increase turnover. However, as a solo professional or group of associates, there are only so many hours of one-to-one you can provide. Even if you manage to hire other consultants who are as good as you as the expert, there's an income ceiling.

Scalability is the ability of your business (and business processes and people) to handle a growing amount of work in a capable manner or its ability to be expanded to accommodate that growth.

Hiring, outsourcing and putting a good operational team in place around you means you can leverage your high-level skills and earning potential rather than spend time doing admin, sorting tech and other time-drainers.

OPTIMISING THE KEY ELEMENTS

From my experience supporting business growth over the last decade, I've narrowed this down even further. Within each of these dimensions in fact lie two contributing elements, so 14 elements in total. I'll go through these briefly here by way of a self-evaluation diagnostic for your own business (or business plan).

The Companion Workbook provides a detailed explanation for each element plus further questions to reflect on. I'd definitely urge you to use it to delve more deeply into the self-evaluation, so that you arrive at well-thought through findings.

Because the *iSuccess* dimensions and elements map onto the entire leveraged consulting matrix, I call this diagnostic the *iSuccess "Leverage Test"* – it's something I use with my clients to evaluate weaknesses in their business that are holding back growth.

When looking at their own business, clients tell me they can't "see" the weaknesses. That's often because they're in a blind spot! Overcoming possible mindset, marketing and money blocks you may have can help you to cut to the heart of what's holding back momentum and growth in your business.

The *Leverage Test* helps shine some light on what's hiding in those blind spots. Imagine if you wanted to attract a consistent stream of clients to your business, but also increase how many clients you can serve beyond the constraints of trading time for money. What would need to be in place?

Use the table here to assign a quick "score" on where you are with each element right now.

	DIMENSION	ELEMENT	OBJECTIVE	SCORE (1 - 10)
1	ALIGNING	MINDFUL	Keep your eyes on the prize, aligned to your goals and the core purpose of your business.	
		How mindful are you about the driving force behind your business vision?		
		AUTHENTIC	Work in true integrity to the big idea of your business, your beliefs and values.	
		To what extent do you feel you're authentic in what you stand for?		
2	TARGETING	*PROFITABLE*	Identify your ideal client as having the hunger, urgency & willingness to invest in your help.	
		To what extent is your chosen target audience a profitable market?		
		NICHE SPECIFIC	Claim your sweet spot for how you help people and work in your genius zone.	
		How specific and well defined is your niche?		

3	POSITIONING	UNIQUE	Stand out with your ideas that meet the needs of the audience you most wish to help.	
		How strongly do you stand out as unique in your ideas, expertise & methodology?		
		NETWORKED	Associate with people who support you & raise your game.	
		To what extent do you participate in networking partnerships & groups?		
4	BRANDING	BOLD	Be confident and irresistible so your brand reflects the results that you uniquely deliver.	
		How bold, confident & irresistible are you in your brand & offer?		
		CREATIVE	Find novel ways to package & deliver your expertise.	
		How creative, innovative & flexible are your delivery methods?		
5	PRICING	RESULTS DRIVEN	Develop effective practices that deliver intended outcomes.	
		How results driven is your service, programme or product?		
		PREMIUM	Go beyond what your best competitors offer.	
		To what extent do you feel able to offer premium services?		

6	SYSTEMATISING	EFFICIENT	Develop multiple paths of engagement and qualify your audience.	
		How efficient do you see your business operating model?		
		PRODUCTIVE	Prioritise doing real work & planning forward.	
		How would you rate your overall productivity week on week and over 90-day cycles?		
7	SCALING	STREAMLINED	Create a model that increases your income over time.	
		How streamlined is your business development process?		
		EXPANDABLE	Move beyond typical growth plateaus.	
		How expandable do you believe your business potentially can be?		

DOWNLOAD THE WORKBOOK

For full explanations, a deeper set of questions, and to record your scores, use the digital companion workbook available free to download at: **jayallyson.com/leveragedconsulting/workbook**

The workbook also includes a quick guide on how you can plot your scores onto a spider chart to visualise the overall picture so you can analyse the strongest and weakest areas of your business architecture.

VISUAL ANALYSIS FROM THE LEVERAGE TEST

Once you're finished reviewing each element, plot your self-evaluation ratings on a spider chart like the one shown here, so that you can easily visualise the overall picture of your business architecture. There's a full-page one in the companion workbook, or you could make a copy from the book or just draw it out by hand.

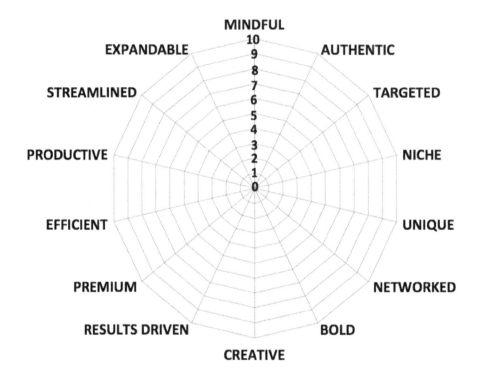

Go ahead and plot your scores 1-10 for each element. Use a pencil or crayon to shade in your score for each section to the right of the title. Those that you feel are strong, shade closer up to the outer ring; those that are weaker will have mostly only the inner area shaded.

Of course, there may be many more success criteria you could add; but being brutally honest, they most likely still fit within one or more of the seven dimensions. Furthermore, you might be tempted to want to take this as far as weighting the relative importance of each element, that really depends on the individual business and the operating environment. Let's say for our purposes here that they are all important because they are mutually reinforcing.

In the workbook, you'll find instructions on how you can use Microsoft Excel to produce the spider chart and the shading: an example is shown below. (I tell you this, as you may want to produce a similar evaluation or quiz yourself for your own expert system.)

Here's an example output and analysis.

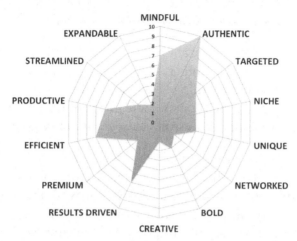

Here's the same data plotted using a clever series of formulas to lay out the scores, which as you can see produces a rather nice combined output across our 7 dimensions. It's a bit over-the-top, but I'm loving the *iSuccess* themed visual!

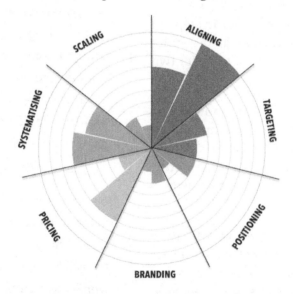

Once you have all 14 sections charted or shaded, what are the results for each element telling you about your current and desired situation?

Start with mindfulness and authenticity at the top and think about how clear you are about your end goals. Are you clear on what you wish to achieve personally and financially? What is the real benefit or impact you wish to achieve helping others?

Look at each dimension and its two elements in turn. What do your scores reveal that lead to you to think how you might improve things – e.g. your messaging, branded offers, pricing, operational and delivery processes.

In terms of the corresponding leverage areas, on the right or left quadrants, where is the shading heavier? Can you spot the problem areas that may be hampering your marketing offers, sales process and growth potential?

More shading in the top right quadrant indicates you've picked a purposeful and profitable niche; bottom right suggests you feel you have a distinctive and compelling message. If you're shading is heavier in the bottom left quadrant, this suggests you think you have an impactful and efficient way of delivering results; and top left denotes a workable and scalable operational system.

Analysing the example spider chart from the 14 elements, by way of an example (i.e. here's one I made earlier), the shading pattern for that business suggests there is clarity around their purpose, but that this is not well aligned to their target audience or being communicated effectively in their brand. It suggests that they are productive and get results, but are possibly charging too little and there is little leverage in terms of streamlined and expandable operational processes.

Being able to identify the general area of the barriers and bottlenecks in your business as well as the specific steps in your operating process is a super important skill to learn how to do for two reasons.

Firstly, these constraints can snowball on your overall revenue and capacity to grow, so you need to look at your business as a whole. And secondly, there's always a bottleneck in a business even if it's a small one.

Learn how to find and resolve the most constraining one first and keep your eyes on your key performance indicators that illuminate new ones as your business grows. As you expand the capacity of one aspects of your business, it can create a build-up of problems in another aspect.

> ※
>
> "As a business, as long as you're always looking to grow, there will always be another bottleneck. Your job is to identify it and to fix it, and realize that you will get incremental and even exponential gains in doing so, but it's never going to be infinite.
>
> Your strategy is all about focusing on the highest point of leverage, the one thing that you can change that will have a positive effect on everything else that you do. And when you fix it, you move on to the next one." – Danny Iny, Business Ignition Bootcamp

When you've gone through the exercise and evaluated where you see your strong points and the weaker elements, you'll have started to formulate your leveraged roadmap for implementing your most critical levers for digital transformation.

The table here will help you map it all together.

MAPPING ISUCCESS TO LEVERAGED STRATEGIES

DIMENSION	ELEMENT	LEVERAGING YOU	LEVERAGED MARKETING	LEVERAGED SALES	LEVERAGED DELIVERY
ALIGNING	Mindful Authentic	☑	☑		
TARGETING	Targeted Niche-specific	☑	☑		
POSITIONING	Unique Networked	☑	☑	☑	
BRANDING	Bold Creative		☑	☑	☑
PRICING	Results- driven Premium			☑	☑
SYSTEMATISING	Efficient Productive		☑	☑	☑
SCALING	Streamlined Expandable		☑	☑	☑

Once you can "see" the priority areas for your business, if you want support to implement your action plan, then do look to becoming a member of the *iSuccess Business Academy* and look at the fast track offer at the close of the book!

Bear in mind the co-dependencies here. Operational inefficiency may well be an area that's holding you back, because it causes inconsistency in your client acquisition process, reduces your productivity, limit ROI and so forth - and ultimately that's costing you money and creating headaches and stress. However, when you look at a deeper strategic level, it's often a limitation in the business model manifesting as an operational bottleneck.

When revenue is down or growth is slow, consider whether the problem is an operational one or a strategic one.

My business growth clients often tell me "we don't have enough turnover to hire new people or outsource" when actually it's that their revenue model is limited or their gross profit is insufficient or their working capital model limits cash flow month on month.

Now this strategic review skill is actually my superpower! When I first got started in my consulting practice, I built my business around my evaluation expertise where you look at aims and objectives of a project or programme of change, design an evaluation, gather data and analyse against the intended (and unintended) outcomes, benefits and impact that the programme and its constituents projects intended to deliver. The work taught me how to dive deeper to uncover the relationship between cause (what was done) and effect (what resulted).

Later, I was looking more at operational business and marketing processes, but again more often than not, the underlying problems were strategic in nature. So, what does this mean for you and your business?

1. First, remember there's no single fix or silver bullet as we've spoken about before. You have to look at your business holistically to gain new perspectives on the design, structure, co-dependencies, flow and key metrics of the business – as well as seeing change and innovation as a process of continuous improvement.

2. Finding and fixing critical levers in your business is a strategic way to review your business architecture and look at where the constraints exist in each dimension of your business.

3. Reviewing your business model on a deeper strategic level will mean better decision making on process improvements that identify the real root causes so you can open up your bottlenecks, let things flow faster and more consistently, in a way that support your desired goals for growth.

The secret to building a business that is not just surviving, but actually thriving and growing, is to move beyond only tweaking the day-to-day problems you see in front of you. It's also about building the capacity to shift tack as the market changes. In the uncertain world we live in today, this is a major success factor to staying in business.

When you take a step back and look at your business in the wider strategic sense, you can see more clearly the influence of both local and global shifts in your industry. Customer behaviours, needs and preferences are ultimately what should determine why, when and in what ways you need to let go of older business models.

This leads us to ways of leveraging the real big opportunities in the consulting industry in the digital age today and staying in front of the wave in the perfect storm.

GROWING IN AN UNCERTAIN WORLD

Let's return to the SCALE model that I introduced in chapter 2 when we looked at leveraged strategy. We're now going to look at some of the practicalities for implementing the approaches you choose to go with.

If you want your business to grow and scale exponentially, you need to transition from a freelance or traditional small firm model (at the S-C-A end) to a more transformational business model (at the L-E end).

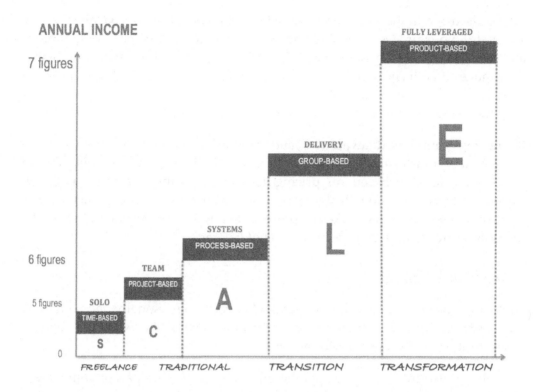

Depending on the way you like to work, you can choose to implement leverage in your marketing, sales and delivery within any level as you grow your business.

Take each step forward at your own pace. You can build any column upwards or you can build from left to right. But bear in mind that growth within each step (columns S-C-A-to-L) will have different limits., while growth in a fully leveraged business (E at the far right) brings almost limitless growth.

Let's see these steps in pragmatic terms.

1. Stay SOLO

At the S-level, depending on your income goals and pricing, with great strategies in place to leverage you and boost your expert status, you could achieve a degree of leverage just by increasing your fees. Bear in mind, fees should be in line with the specific kind of client you help and the specific kind of result you help them get.

It's likely you'll be able to demand higher fees doing work for corporate organisations than working with individuals or micro businesses. But it really depends on the business, their goals and turnover and the relationships you build up. Nonetheless, if you can acquire high-end clients consistently, and you're happy with the level of influence, impact and income you're achieving, there's no reason not to stick with a time-based solo model.

As we discussed in the pricing section, when your consulting or coaching work is successful, your processes evolve and with leveraged approaches to marketing and sales (along with client onboarding) can become more effective and efficient. That makes it both cheaper for you to deliver and gets your client a result faster, which is worth more to them. It makes perfect sense then to raise the price in line with the value and effectiveness of your programme or service.

By raising your brand awareness and reputation as someone who delivers significant or transformative results, you can demand higher fees. In this scenario, it's entirely feasible based on pricing to reach multiple 6-figures as a solo freelancer. However, you will at least need to outsource some routine activities or hire admin assistants, as it makes no sense to do low-level tasks yourself. And this moves you automatically to the next level of leverage.

2. Build TEAMS

At the C-level, you can choose to expand what you can personally deliver and/or your capacity through rigorous recruitment and selection of new people – a team-based strategy and project-based model.

As well as outsourcing routine operational activities, another part of your growth strategy might be to hire consultants "as-good-as-you" – i.e. people who have a similar level of expertise and can deliver projects to the same quality as you.

Either way, you'll need to create a good programme of induction to your working approaches, methodologies, systems, tools, customer care standards and so forth. (In this sense, any educational materials you create will provide valuable learning and development for new staff.)

Hiring people means your investment will be in the time and effort to transfer your knowledge and skills to others, training new associates, talent management and managing the division of roles according to specialisms.

3. Create SYSTEMS

Another way to scale what you already do is to move to the next level, A, which is where you will rationalise, standardise, streamline and automate certain aspects of your business – a process-based model that helps you build leveraged marketing and sales activities.

When you systematise your key processes, you augment both your solo work and the effectiveness of your team-based approach. Hiring individuals who can play a supporting role (such as in client management, preliminary fact-finding, administrative, marketing, IT and analytical work, customer follow-up, and sales / enrolment), will free up your high-end consultancy time to do the complex and specialist work.

The result can be an increase in quality and efficiency, because the day-to-day stuff runs like clockwork by people who are good at those tasks and can keep a firm eye on standards and quality assurance processes.

4. Work with GROUPS

Moving on up to the L-level means moving to a group-based business model, we're looking at shifting towards a leveraged delivery business model. Rather than delivering solely one-on-one services. A group programme increases your capacity to serve more clients at a time. You can still provide individual support, but most of the delivery is done in a group setting.

When you know your consulting or coaching process is effective and clients love it, you can leverage your success by turning your expert system into a group programme, building on the team-based and systems-based models to inject leverage into your marketing, sales and delivery processes.

5. Produce PRODUCTS

With a product-based model, you start providing some (or all) of your know-how and expertise in digital format. At this end of the SCALE model, you can leverage all of the above efficiency strategies and create additional streams of revenue. You're now at the top of the ladder – the E-level – and have a fully leveraged strategy.

BEST STEP FORWARD

From my experience helping people to develop and implement this leveraged business strategy, it's not enough to listen to a seminar or read about it in a book. Awareness and knowledge are all well and good; this gives you the direction of travel to where you want to be. And having a success mindset is vital, but you won't magically manifest any transformation without taking focused action.

Hopefully you've learned how using the leveraged consulting model for growth can help you to build a highly profitable and successful global service business. All the moving parts can appear rather daunting to some, so I trust the step-by-step guide through the principles and practices helps break it into manageable stages. You will inevitably have to step forward at times with imperfect action, which isn't easy for a perfectionist procrastinator, I can assure you!

What I know is this. You can do it! I know for sure, because I'm doing it. Certainly, along the way, I had my own limiting beliefs, self-doubts and mental blocks. But I've overcome these by identifying the right strategies for my business, putting in the work and getting the right kind of support.

What you should have gained as you worked through this book is the beginnings at least of a personalised strategy for your business, one that aligns purpose with profits and positioning with systematising. We covered how to brand yourself, promote your message, and package and price a compelling offer. We also looked at how to systematise your marketing so you can automate the engagement process as your prospect moves through your sales process. The result is a consistent flow of leads that convert gracefully and painlessly into paying clients.

Getting your brain in gear is equally important if you want to achieve your goals, which is why it's so hard going it alone. There's a time to float free and let your subconscious work for you; there's a time to actively review, analyse, plan, create and implement; and there's a time to get some help.

While a book can attempt to engender dialogue, or at best self-reflection, by providing ideas and insights, posing questions, providing exercises and urging you strongly to take action, actual results depend on whether a person has the mindset, skills and discipline to take the suggested steps forward.

Here's some practical next steps you can take using the companion workbook. It'll work best if you do these soon while this is all fresh in your head.

#1 - Look at where you are now in your business and identify exactly where you'd like to be in terms of your "success" (e.g. the level of influence, impact and income you're working at and want to work at).

#2 - Gather up your results from *The Leverage Test* (assuming you completed it already) to look where there is room to increase the leverage in your current business architecture.

#3 - Look at the spider diagram you produced from your leveraged scorecard. Which elements come out strongest and how can you build on these? Which come out weakest, and what are the opportunities to improve these?

#4 - Read and reflect on your action planning notes from reading the book and compare with where in the companion workbook you ranked yourself in the activity checklists from each of the 7 dimensions as critical levers for change.

#5 - Look at which dimensions you ranked yourself lowest – attention to these areas are likely to yield the biggest returns. Highlight anything that jumps out at you and look for common themes or ideas you will take forward.

#6 -   Fast track your success with training, mentoring and a supportive community - see next chapter for a special invitation for my book readers to join the *iSuccess Business Academy* for free ;-)

Let me emphasise, you can only improve your performance by making a change (in one or more aspects of your business). Obvious, I know - but you'd be surprised how many people self-sabotage their success and may abandon ship altogether, because they don't know what to do or don't believe it will help!

If you're already investing time and energy into growing your business, getting the right support at the right time gives you the best possible chance for success. So, stay with me – we're in this together now…

FAST TRACK YOUR SUCCESS

When you look at the state of marketing and sales today, not to mention education, technology has made things both easier and harder. It's easier because online systems enable effective planning and organisation, and efficient automation of your marketing and sales processes.

And yet, success seems harder because people get overwhelmed with so many choices of platforms, tools and tactics. Independent business owners often lack both a strategic roadmap and the skills to implement digital approaches; they need guidance and support.

Strategy, structure, feedback and accountability are powerful allies to your success and I'd like to offer you that personal support on your on-going journey - for free. Now, you might be wondering why I would help you for free. If so, let me explain…

Money isn't massively important to me – what really counts for me is *freedom*. Money is just a way to keep score. As Zig Ziglar famously stated: "You can get everything in life you want if you will just help enough other people get what they want."

In every business relationship, someone has to make the first move; someone has to make the first investment and take the risk. I wrote this book to build a relationship with the people I believe I can most help. It's been an investment and a risk – albeit a passion project too. I've invested an insanely huge amount of time and money to write it, pulling content together from work spanning many years: studying, applying lessons learned about what growing a business really involves. And the risk is that the whole endeavour could be a complete flop rather than an outright success.

You've already made your first move in our relationship by buying and reading *Leveraged Consulting in the Digital Age*. I hope you found lots of value in these pages and give it a 5-star review or at least a fair feedback. And because of your investment, and if this resonates with you, I want to keep things going and invest in you back, personally.

This isn't all selfless; it's good business. I know that the better "educated" you become, the better client you'd be should you choose to work with me in the future, and therefore the better and faster results you'll get. It makes perfect sense for me to invest more in you. If not, you'll get some great business education absolutely for free, we part company for now and I genuinely wish you all success.

The dilemma for both of us is that with just a book, it's impossible for me to guarantee your results because success relies on you taking action on what you've learned – and only you can commit to that. Most people do need help to bring about real actionable change, for all kinds of reasons, so it makes sense to both of us if I offer you further opportunities to work together.

> ※
> "Whenever I am asked what is the missing link between a promising business person and a successful one, mentoring comes to mind. If you are looking to make your way in business, find a mentor." – Sir Richard Branson

Research shows that the best education incorporates some kind of deep engagement and dialogue. We can attempt to mimic this in exercises, which is why I created the workbook and diagnostic - but what's missing and highly valuable is the two-way interaction and feedback you get from mentoring that keeps you moving forward.

This is exactly why if you had light bulb moments from reading the book and gained clarity on your next best steps, then you're super primed to get results fast working with me directly and masterminding with others on the same journey. I know that people who actively engage with me through my consulting, workshops and individual mentoring programmes perform significantly better in their business.

If you resonate with *Leveraged Consulting in the Digital Age*, I hope I've provided you with a success roadmap to implement new approaches that will help close the gap between where you are now and where you want to be.

When you're ready to take your journey further and want some support working with me directly to create and implement your leveraged action plan, here's your options.

#1 - Come join our community of practice in our private group on Facebook, *The Leveraged Living Club* – at **facebook.com/groups/TheLeveragedLivingClub**. It's free.

#2 – Find out about *iSuccess Business Academy* membership and mentoring at **isuccessbusinessacademy.com**.

Dedicated to your great success!

Jay Allyson

Any questions, don't hesitate to get in touch at <u>jayallyson.com/contactme</u> or in the open group at <u>facebook.com/groups/TheLeveragedLivingClub.</u>

P.S. If you want to learn more about any of the techie tools I've mentioned, there's a handy list within the *iSuccess Business Academy* resources area.

LET ME DO YOU A FAVOUR

Activate your FREE membership at:
isuccessbusinessacademy.com

Here's exactly what you need to do right now to grab your free membership.

1. Go to **isuccessbusinessacademy.com** & click "Become an iSuccess Member" to grab your *iSuccess* member spot. (If it's showing a *Wait List* notice, opt-in so you get an email alert when it open to new members.)

2. At the payment section, enter the promo code '<u>bookreader</u>' to get your first month's subscription covered as a thank you from me for taking the time to invest in and read this book.

3. Once subscribed, you'll need to confirm your email address to get your login details (so if you don't receive anything, please check your junk/spam folder).

4. Once logged in, you'll see the modules you have access to, including:

   ✓ **New Members Success Compass** - a guide to getting the most out of your membership. It picks up exactly where the book leaves off. Plus, I'll share with you the single most important factor in your business success.

   ✓ **Brand Clarity Project**: *Mindset, Marketing & Money Breakthroughs to Attracting Clients on Demand* webinar and worksheets.

This is one of my most popular courses. I've previously charged £397 for this training as a live half-day workshop (the title was slightly different) - that's about $500 at the time of writing. But for you it's free to download within the *iSuccess Business Academy* membership site, whether or not you decide to keep your membership subscription going.

Of course, I hope you'll love *iSuccess* and see the value in remaining a member as you continue your business journey. With free access to *The Leverage Test*, the knowledge from this book, plus a compass to guide you, I trust you will be primed and raring to go developing your leveraged consulting strategy.

Don't delay – hop on board right away at:

isuccessbusinessacademy.com

WOULD YOU DO ME A FAVOUR TOO?

If you enjoyed *Leveraged Consulting in the Digital Age*, would you mind taking a minute to write a review of Amazon? Even a short review helps, and it'd mean a great deal to me.

If someone you care about is struggling with any aspect of building and growing a service business – whether it's professional identity, brand clarity, marketing, sales, delivery models or implementing new approaches – please send them a copy of this book. You can send the link or gift it to them on Amazon.

If you'd like to order copies of this book for colleagues or students, please mention that there is also a free downloadable Companion Workbook as well as the online courses available in the *iSuccess Business Academy*.

Finally, if you'd like to receive further iSuccess bonus materials for readers of this book, you can sign up for updates at jayallyson.com. You can also follow me on social media, links on the website.

Transformation awaits you. Go leveraged, grow big!

INDEX OF QUOTES

INDEX OF FIGURES

INDEX OF TABLES

Made in the USA
Middletown, DE
10 September 2020